ISSUES IN SCIENCE AND THEOLOGY

ISSUES IN SCIENCE AND THEOLOGY

This series is published under the auspices of the European Society for the Study of Science and Theology (ESSSAT)

Creative Creatures

Values and Ethical Issues in Theology, Science and Technology

Creative Creatures

Values and Ethical Issues in Theology, Science and Technology

Editors

Ulf Görman
Willem B. Drees
Hubert Meisinger

T & T CLARK INTERNATIONAL
A Continuum imprint
LONDON • NEW YORK

Published by T&T Clark
A Continuum imprint
The Tower Building
11 York Road
London SE1 7NX

15 East 26th Street
Suite 1703
New York
NY 10010

www.tandtclark.com

British Library Cataloguing-in-Publication Data
A catalogue record for this book is available from the British Library.

Typeset by RefineCatch Limited, Bungay, Suffolk
Printed on acid-free paper in Great Britain by MPG Books Ltd, Cornwall

ISBN 0 567 03088 1 (hardback)
0 567 03089 X (paperback)

Contents

PART II: MORALITY, NATURE AND CULTURE

PART III: MORALITY IN A TECHNOLOGICAL SOCIETY

Preface and Acknowledgements

The city of Alexandria on the north coast of Africa was founded in the fourth century (332–31) BCE, by Alexander the Great. From the beginning of the third century BCE Alexandria became the intellectual centre of Hellenistic culture. Its library became the first known public scientific library, with 400,000–700,000 books, according to different sources. The importance of the city as an intellectual centre was successively degraded by warfare and conflicts from 48 BCE. As a part of its task as an intellectual centre, Alexandria was also a religious centre, with cults of a large number of different gods of Greek as well as oriental origin. Important among these was Serapis, a syncretistic Hellenistic god of partly Egyptian origin. A temple, Serapeion, was built for Serapis, with a library of its own. Serapeion was not closed until 389 CE, which is sometimes regarded as the end of the era of Alexandria.

A drawing has been found, illustrating interesting technological equipment planned for Serapeion. A hollow altar for burnt offerings was placed in front of a temple building. Piping, vessels, ropes and hinges connected the altar to a pair of temple doors. The idea was that the burnt offering should heat and expand the air within the hollow altar, with the effect that the temple doors opened.

We do not know whether this automatic temple door opener was ever built, but it is an interesting example from the antiquity of a conjunction of science, religion and technology. This early unity of religion and applied science is also an interesting piece of thought about the values and ideas allowing this synthesis. What kind of ideas allowed this technological vision to be united with religious belief?

In antiquity, the conviction that the newly discovered physical principles were of the same origin and revealed the same forces as religious wonders may well have been the inspiration for this engineering effort. In modern times the relation between the ethical aspects of the visions of science on the one hand, and religion and theology on the other, is a field of tension and contest. Not least, this complex relation is evident when it comes to the application of science in technology. In the interdisciplinary field of science-and-theology, however, these questions have so far received relatively little attention. This book is the result of an effort to fill that gap. The 14 contributions all explore different aspects of the relation between ethics, values, science, religion and technology.

This volume has its origins in the Ninth European Conference on Science and Theology, organized by ESSSAT, the European Society for the Study of Science and Theology. ESSSAT aspires to be a scholarly society which promotes the study of interactions of science and theology, thus creating opportunities for scholars from a wide variety of backgrounds, disciplinary, linguistic and confessional, to interact on such issues. At the conference there were five plenary lectures, financially supported by the John Templeton Foundation, given by René Munnik, Frans de Waal, Nancey Murphy, Ulf Görman and Margaret Boden. In addition, there were about 80 papers presented in various workshops, some of which have been revised and included here, while some others have been published in *Studies in Science and Theology* 9, the 'yearbook' of ESSSAT, which appears every other year. SSTh 9 and previous volumes can be ordered via our website, www.ESSSAT.org. We are grateful to T&T Clark, now part of Continuum, for the cooperation on this 'Issues in Science and Theology' series, of which previous volumes were titled *The Human Person in Science and Theology* (IST 1) and *Design and Disorder: Perspectives from Science and Theology* (IST 2).

With gratitude we acknowledge the support ESSSAT received for the conference in Nijmegen from the Royal Netherlands Academy of Arts and Sciences (KNAW), the Catholic University of Nijmegen (now Radboud University Nijmegen), its Heyendaal Institute and its Soeterbeeck Programme, the Radboud Foundation, the Sormani Foundation, the John Templeton Foundation, the Counterbalance Foundation, Erik & Gurli Hultengrens Foundation at Lund University, and the Royal Society of Letters in Lund. The support of these organizations and foundations does not imply that they endorse any or all of the opinions presented at the conference or in the publications emerging from these conferences. ESSSAT also greatly acknowledges the hospitality provided by the Radboud University Nijmegen, and especially the efforts invested in this conference work by its Heyendaal Institute and the director of its section on theology and science, Prof. Dr Palmyre Oomen, and the director of the Soeterbeeck programme of the Radboud University Nijmegen and professor on the Van Melsen chair, Prof. Dr Wil Derkse.

List of Contributors

Margaret A. Boden is research professor of cognitive science at the University of Sussex, UK. She is a member of the Academia Europaea, and a fellow of the British Academy and of the American Association for Artificial Intelligence. In 2002 she was awarded an OBE for services to cognitive science. Her writing has been translated into 18 foreign languages, and her book *Mind as a Machine: A History of Cognitive Science* will be published by Oxford University Press in 2006.

Christopher J. Corbally, SJ, is vice director of the Vatican Observatory. As such, he oversees the observatory's research group in Tucson, while maintaining contact and occasional visits to the headquarters at Castel Gandolfo, Italy. He is adjunct associate professor at the Department of Astronomy, University of Arizona. He is also past president of the Institute on Religion in an Age of Science, which has held meetings since 1954 on a 'small but beautiful' island off Portsmouth, New Hampshire.

Willem B. Drees is president of ESSSAT, the European Society for the Study of Science and Theology, and professor of philosophy of religion and ethics in the Department of Theology, Leiden University, the Netherlands. He has been executive director of ALLEA, the federation of academies of sciences and humanities in Europe. Drees is the author of *Creation: From Nothing until Now* (Routledge, 2002), *Religion, Science and Naturalism* (Cambridge, 1996), and *Beyond the Big Bang: Quantum Cosmologies and God* (Open Court, 1990).

Ulf Görman is professor of ethics at Lund University, Sweden. Görman is past president of ESSSAT, the European Society for the Study of Science and Theology. His research focuses on bioethics and on ethical issues in science and religion. He is currently heading a national research programme, where

Swedish ethicists investigate ethical aspects of postgenomic research. Current publications include articles on bioethics and the anthology *Etik och genteknik* (in Swedish, 2004).

Jan-Olav Henriksen is professor of systematic theology and philosophy of religion at the Norwegian Lutheran School of Theology, Oslo. He has published more than 20 books, especially on ethics, moral philosophy and philosophy of religion, as well as on theological anthropology. Presently he is working on theoretical and empirical elements relating to religion in a postmodern context. He also holds a chair as adjunct professor at Agder University College, Kristiansand, Norway.

Noreen Herzfeld is professor of theology and computer science and director of the Koch programme in Catholic thought and culture at St. John's University in Collegeville, Minnesota. Herzfeld is the author of *In Our Image: Artificial Intelligence and the Human Spirit* (Fortress, 2002). She has also published numerous articles on such diverse topics as cyberspace as a venue for spiritual experience, embodiment as a *sine qua non* for personhood, the religious implications of computer games, and the prospects for reconciliation among Christians and Muslims in Bosnia.

Otto Kroesen studied theology and presented a thesis on the philosophy of the French-Jewish philosopher Emmanuel Levinas. He worked as a minister and is now chaplain and lecturer on ethics and technology at the Delft University of Technology, the Netherlands. Most of his published work has been on Rosenstock-Huessy, sociologist and language philosopher of the twentieth century.

Zbigniew Liana is a Catholic priest and lecturer in philosophy of science and epistemology at the Pontifical Academy of Theology in Krakow, Poland, where he also holds a doctorate in philosophy. He is working on science-religion projects in the centre for interdisciplinary studies at the academy. Since 1998 he has been a member of the ESSSAT Council. He is co-author of *Science and Theology: Conflict and Coexistence* (in Polish, 2001).

René P. H. Munnik studied chemistry, theology and philosophy. He is Radboud professor at the University of Twente and associate professor in philosophical anthropology and philosophy of religion at Tilburg University, both in the Netherlands. He has published several articles on process philosophy and on the interrelations between religion, natural science and technology. Selected articles: 'Donna Haraway: Cyborgs for Earthly Survival?', in H. Achterhuis (ed.), *American Philosophy of Technology: The Empirical Turn* (Indiana University Press, 2001) and 'Whitehead's Hermeneutical Cosmology', in D. J. N. Middleton (ed.), *God, Literature and Process Thought* (Ashgate, 2002).

Nancey Murphy is professor of Christian philosophy at Fuller Theological Seminary, Pasadena, California. She holds a PhD in philosophy from the University of California, Berkeley, and a ThD from the Graduate Theological Union, Berkeley. Her publications include *Theology in the Age of Scientific Reasoning* (Cornell, 1990), *Bodies and Souls, or Spirited Bodies* (Cambridge, forthcoming), and *On the Moral Nature of the Universe*, with George Ellis (Fortress, 1996).

Lluís Oviedo studied theology at the Gregorian University, Rome. He is professor of theological anthropology in the Antonianum University and lecturer in faith, society and culture in the Gregorian University, both in Rome. He has published *La secularización como problema* (1990), *Altruismo y caridad* (1998), and *La fé cristiana ante los nuevos desafíos sociales: Tensiones y respuestas* (2002).

Angela Roothaan is assistant professor in ethics as well as in philosophy and spirituality at the Vrije Universiteit, Amsterdam. She published books on Spinoza, *Vroomheid, vrede, vrijheid* (1996) and on the meaning of experience of nature for ethics, *Terugkeer van de natuur* (2005). Her present research, titled *Identity, Experience, Transformation: An Intercultural Ethics of Moral and Spiritual Formation* focuses on the development of a new anthropology.

Taede A. Smedes studied theology at Groningen University and currently works as a postdoc at the Faculty of Theology of Leiden University, the Netherlands. In 2002 Smedes won an ESSSAT student award for an article on determinism and divine action. Since 2004 he has been the scientific programme officer of ESSSAT. He is the author of *Chaos, Complexity, and God: Divine Action and Scientism* (Peeters, 2004).

Frans B. M. de Waal is director at Living Links Center and C. H. Candler professor of primate behaviour at Emory University, Atlanta, Georgia. His research has involved studies on chimpanzees at Arnhem Zoo and Yerkes National Primate Research Center, and their close relatives, bonobos, at the San Diego Zoo. Apart from a large number of scientific papers, his work includes *Chimpanzee Politics* (Johns Hopkins, 1982), *Good Natured* (Harvard, 1996), *Bonobo: The Forgotten Ape* (University of California, 1997), and *The Ape and the Sushi Master: Cultural Reflections by a Primatologist* (Allen Lane, 2001).

1

Introduction: technological and moral creatures or creators?

Willem B. Drees

We as humans use our technology – hammers and nails, cars and computers, frozen food and microwave. We are the creators of our technology. But we are also created by our technology. Our dependence upon technology goes back as far as the control of fire, the making of tools from flint stone, and the domestication of animals and wheat. Without such technologies human culture would not have been what it has become. Modern science-based technology has become a prominent feature of our lives, reshaping human identities and relationships. Among the most prominent developments in our time are the new information and communication technologies (ICT, e.g. computers and the Internet) and biotechnology.

Whereas discussions on technology often concentrate on the question of what should be allowed or prohibited, we also need to explore and evaluate how these powerful technologies redefine, for better and for worse, human identity. Thus, what values shape our dealings with technology? And influence in the other direction: How does our technological culture reshape our values? Such questions were central to the Eighth European Conference on Science and Theology, which was held in Nijmegen, the Netherlands, March 19–24, 2002. The conference was titled 'Creating Techno S@piens? Values and Ethical Issues in Theology, Science, and Technology'. In this volume, you will find papers based on the plenary lectures and a selection from the papers presented in workshops.

The standard view of technology's place in 'religion and science' can be illustrated well with the titles of two books from Ian Barbour: *Religion in an Age of Science* and *Ethics in an Age of Technology*. This may seem an obvious pair of titles, but it is nonetheless a particular way of dividing the field, which brings some discussions into the open, while leaving other interactions out of view.[1] As the current volume shows, there is also a need to reflect upon 'Religion in an Age of Technology'. What does technology do to our worldview and values?

This includes issues of human identity and values. Human identity is central to the first part, four essays reflecting upon technology's impact upon our worldview, our identity and relationships, even with those who are absent or dead. Some essays in the third part of this volume will consider issues of morality in a technological culture pertaining to biotechnology and AI, value education, and more. As our technological powers change, the domain of moral responsibility increases as we have less justification to sit down and throw our hands in the air in powerlessness. However, we are not necessarily well prepared for new choices we have to face.

Other essays will explore the roots of morality and the nature of culture. Is morality a product of culture, coming into being with the emergence of humanity? A classic articulation of this view has been given by Thomas Huxley, a younger contemporary of Darwin, who argued that human morality had emerged out of the evolutionary process but was clearly distinct, even condemning the process that had brought it forth as an immoral struggle. Frans de Waal argues, on theoretical grounds and on the basis of his research with apes and other monkeys, that this opposition of immoral nature and culture as ambiance of morality and of technology is mistaken. Nancey Murphy argues so too, though on theological and philosophical grounds. Thus, the place of morality in our understanding of reality, whether natural or technological and cultural, will be considered here as well. Perhaps the opposition of the natural and the cultural breaks down, as we are by nature cultural, moral and technological.

In the remainder of this introduction to the volume, I will discuss the prominence of technology in our culture, which could well be called a technological culture. Thereafter, I will offer some personal reflections on theology and technology. In the third and final section, I'll offer a preview of the contributions in this book.[2]

Technology

Dimensions of technology

When speaking about technology, most people at first refer to *devices* such as the telephone, the car, and the refrigerator. We live in their midst. But these devices cannot function without *infrastructure*. Think of telephone lines, of receivers and transmitters, electricity, and gas stations, and behind those, more infrastructure: refineries, ships and pipe lines, oil wells. There the sequence ends, as the oil deep down in the ground is not itself a product of human technological activity.

'Devices' and 'infrastructure' are material manifestations of technology, but technology is a *social system*, both for the organization it requires and for the services it provides. And technology depends on *skills* (and thus on educational systems) as much as on hardware. Highly technical medical disciplines such as surgery are certainly also about the skills of the humans involved. Skills are also involved for ordinary people; driving a car is a technical skill. Technology is more than the devices of metal and plastics that may come to mind first. Technology has its material manifestations in devices and infrastructure, and a social and human dimension of organization and skills. We can also consider particular *attitudes* 'technological'. It refers to a way of life in which a problem, whether a leaking roof, illness, or miscommunication, is not treated as if it were to be accepted as fate, but rather seen as a problem to be addressed. An active attitude, sitting down to analyse a problem in order to solve it by practical means, is part of our lives. This is to us so much a self-evident part of our lives that we find it sometimes hard to really understand cultures in which a tragic or fatalistic attitude is more common.

'We live in *a technological culture*' could be an adequate summary of the pervasive presence of technological means and attitudes. Technology is not a separate segment of our lives, realized in devices and infrastructure, but characterizes the world in which we live. Antibiotics and sewage systems changed the sense of vulnerability (limiting enormously the number of parents who had to bury their own infants). The Pill changed relations between men and women, and hence between parents and their children. Thanks to the refrigerator and the microwave we can eat whenever it suits us, individually, and each according to his or her taste, and thus the common meal as a major characteristic of the day has lost significance. Central heating has made the common room with the fireplace less important; we can each spend our time in our own rooms in the way we like. Technology makes life easier and more attractive; music is available without effort on my side except switching on the stereo. Such developments were considered by the philosopher Albert Borgmann in his *Technology and the Character of Contemporary Life*. His concern is that, while consumption has become easier, some of the more demanding but meaningful and rich experiences are lost out of sight.

A brief history of technology and culture

That technology and culture are intertwined can be made clear by considering the history of technology as cultural history, and not just as a history of inventions (e.g. Diamond 1998; McNeil 1990). Technology has made us human, as tool-making and the ability to make, maintain and use fire intentionally is tied up with the emergence of our own species, including its social structures. In a more recent past, some 1500 BCE, the transition from copper to iron changed social structures, since copper was relatively rare and thereby created an elite, whereas iron was more widely available and thus more democratic, but at the same time more demanding as regards handling, thus strengthening the emerging division of labour (smiths). Interaction between cultures had to do with trade, and thus with technologies of transport, production and use. Agricultural technologies such as the domestication of animals, the improvement of wheat and other crops, and much later the introduction of farming tools such as the plough allowed again and again a greater production with fewer workers, thus creating the opportunity for the emergence of cities.

In more recent European history, accurate time-keeping and the invention of the printing press may have been major factors in the transition from the mediaeval to the modern period. It might be argued that the protestant Reformation was made possible by the printing press. In subsequent centuries new labour relations arose due to the introduction of machines. An example is the shift from home production of textiles to factories, and the further shift from waterpower, with locations spread out along the river, to coal as the source of energy. Factories were concentrated close to the coalfields. In the absence of affordable passenger transport, workers had to live nearby, in houses they had to rent from their masters. Thus, we see the rise of the major industrial cities, with social arrangements such as regular working hours and further standardization.

The steam machine, accompanied by 'railway mania', was followed by the freedom of internal combustion. What the car has done to social relations is enormous: separating for all those commuters the spheres of home and work, while diminishing the possibility for children to play safely outside. Controlling electrons in the late nineteenth century (telephone and electrical light) with subsequent developments in the twentieth century (radio and TV, computers and the Internet) added to the enormous cultural transformations of our time. As just one indication of how fast developments are going: the very first 'www'-type communication took place between just two computers at CERN, the European Research Centre for Particle Physics, in Geneva on Christmas Day of 1990 (Berners Lee 2000, 30).

Technology also influences our self-understanding: Who has never been 'under stress', feeling 'huge pressure'? Do you occasionally need 'to let off steam'? These are images from the steam age. We may consider ourselves as made in God's image, but we speak of ourselves as if we are in the image of machines. This is not exclusive for the steam age. The early radio receivers left their own traces in our language – we need 'to tune in' –, and computers and the Internet are modifying our vocabulary and self-understandings right now.

This brief tour of the history of technology and its multifaceted character shows that technology is intimately related to our identity and relationships, and thus to our beliefs and values. In the following section I'll offer some personal reflections on technology and religion.

Some religious reflections on technology

A god-of-the-gaps in our dealings with technology?

In daily life we do *not* put our trust in prayer and pious words. When something needs to be done, we want a competent professional. It is only when the doctor is unable to offer hope that many of us may be tempted to spend money on aura-reading, alternative medicine, or prayer healing. If the pilot of our plane suggests to us as passengers to pray, we may well be frightened as it appears that the technicians can't solve the problem. In conversations on religion and science, the expression 'god-of-the-gaps' refers to the temptation to focus on gaps in our knowledge, and to assume that that is where God is at work. Whenever we become blessed with greater understanding, such a god-of-the-gaps will be pushed back. A similar danger arises in the context of technology: to look for God when our human skills fall still short of what we wish we could. Introducing God when technology fails results in an instrumental type of religiosity: God is asked to help us when we need help, but to keep out of our way as long as we do well.

Against this tendency it seems preferable to me to appreciate the efforts of the professionals, and to appreciate these not only commercially, but also religiously. Looking to engineers for our salvation is not an anti-religious move, as we may appreciate their knowledge and skills as gifts of God, as possibilities to serve the neighbour 'with all your heart, and with all your soul, and with all your strength, and with all your mind' (Luke 10:27).

New words and images

To articulate our identity and values, we humans need songs and stories we can recognize. Of Psalm 139 there is a new version, somewhere in the wonderful world of the Internet.

> O Lord, You have searched me and You have accessed me
> You know my logging on and my logging off.
> You discern my outlook from afar.
> You mark when I surf and when I download,
> All my cache lies open for You.
> . . .
> If I take the links of AltaVista
> And dwell at the innermost ends of the Net

Even there your cookies would find me
Your mouse hand holds me fast.
. . .
O God that You would slay the viruses
Keep away from me hacking hands
With deceit they act against us
And set our hard drives at naught.
. . .
O scan me God, and know my directories
Defragment me and know my files
See that I enter not the wrong password
And highlight for me the paths of life eternal.

Such new articulations are welcome; some of us feel addressed more directly by images and words that relate the tradition creatively with our own situation. But is it only new words and images we need? Or does the content change as well? Is it not Microsoft or Intel who knows me better than I know myself? And for shelter, would we not go to Symantec, Norton and the other virus-scan programs? If the computer breaks down, on my desk or on board a plane, it is no good if the people of the helpdesk pray 'O God, that you would slay the viruses'. Our knowledge and power has increased, and thus our situation has become different.

Stories and images are the manifest forms of symbols that influence our moods and motivations, but they can only do so persistently if these stories are understood to reflect in relevant aspects the way the world is. At the same time, they should not be misunderstood by investing the embellishment with more significance than needed. The Harry Potter story carries us beyond divertissement only if we acknowledge its non-reality (and thus do not take all aspects too seriously). If we fail to see the story as fiction, we will miss its realism about human nature, friendship, and good and evil. A re-wording of the religious heritage needs the free play of imagination and consideration of our changing conceptions of reality, including our technological powers to modify reality. In a technological culture, religion needs new images and stories, but mere translation is not enough.

Technology in tension with natural theology

Interest in the technological and artificial fits ill with the European, and especially British, tradition of natural theology, of arguing from nature to its author. Brooke and Cantor quote the political radical Richard Carlile who wrote in 1829: 'With the doctrine of an intelligent deity it is presumption to attempt anything toward human improvement. Without the doctrine, it is not any presumption.' Brooke and Cantor add: 'It is as if arguments for divine wisdom require this to be the best of all possible worlds, with the corollary that attempts at improvement would both be sacrilegious and ineffective' (1998, 314). Traditionally, natural theologies have been based on sciences which observe and describe nature, such as astronomy, physics, and the study of insects. Chemistry as a transformative discipline is almost completely absent from this discourse. However, chemistry and its precursor, alchemy, was more than knowledge. It was about purification and thereby a return to an original state of perfection, about transformation towards a better state. Aside of introducing the theme of purification, in a material and a spiritual sense, chemistry also correlates often, as Brooke and Cantor observe, with 'a kind of process theology', not in the technical sense of today (based on Whitehead and Hartshorne) but as a view which saw in the world a collaboration of humans with God. Implicitly, any such theology seems to look towards the future for the realization of perfection, rather than to the past or the present. This way of looking fits ill with any argument from the existing order of nature towards a divine designer.

If we are ourselves creators, or at least co-creators, of technology, how may we articulate religiously this active human presence? In the Bible and the liturgy, images of the good are present in two varieties, as images of the past, to be remembered, and as images of a future to be hoped for, a City of God, a new heaven and a new earth, the Kingdom to come. Thus, there is a basis for looking back in time, to a good situation worth preserving and restoring, as well as for setting one's eyes on the future, on that which might come.

In relation to the use of human knowledge and power some of the stories regarding Jesus may be illuminating as well. In the synagogue Jesus meets someone with a withered hand. Will he do healings on the Sabbath? Then Jesus asks: 'Is it lawful on the Sabbath to do good or to do harm, to save life or to kill?' In this story of healing, from Mark 3, and in many other stories, a human is freed of the burdens of his past. A tax collector and a prostitute are accepted again as fellow human beings; deaf persons hear again, and those possessed by spirits are freed from their burdens. Those who have been less well off get new chances. Discipleship as serving the poor and needy has often been forgotten, but it has resurfaced again and again in the history of Christianity. In the one parable about stewardship (Matt. 25:14–30) a landlord entrusts his property to three servants. One received five talents, one two and the third only one talent, 'each according to his ability'. The one with five talents made another five; the one with two talents made another two, but the one with only one talent buried it and returned it to his master. In the end, the landlord commands to cast the worthless servant into the outer darkness; there men will weep and gnash their teeth.

Of this brief tour of biblical texts I would like to retain the following: in biblical language the good is not only to be found in the past but also in the future; humans, even when considered as stewards, can be active and even ought to be active although the initiative is with God, and this activity is normatively determined as care for the weak and needy. One might summarize this as 'We ought to play God'.

Playing God

Sometimes the concern is voiced that we go too far in our technological activities; we are 'playing God'. This metaphor has been used in debates on genetic modification and on cloning; less than a century ago similar images were used against those who put up lightning rods. Why would even non-believers find 'playing God' a useful metaphor in criticizing new technologies? The American philosopher Ronald Dworkin suggested in *Prospect Magazine* (May 1999) that this is because those new technologies create insecurity by undermining a distinction that is vital to ethics. Underlying our moral experience is a distinction between what has been given and what is our own responsibility. What is given is the stable background of our actions. Traditionally this has been referred to as fate, nature or creation: domains of the gods or of God. When new technologies expand the range of our abilities, we thereby move the boundary between what is given and what is open to our actions. Hence, we become insecure and concerned. It is especially in such circumstances that the phrase 'playing God' arises. There is a reference to 'God' when something that was experienced as a given becomes part of the domain of human considerations. The fear of 'playing God' is not the fear of doing what is wrong (which is an issue on our side of the boundary), but rather the fear of losing grip on reality through the dissolution of the boundary.

New technologies imply a different range of human powers, and thus a changing experience of fate, nature, creation or God. If God is associated with what which has been given (creation), our technological activity will be seen as pushing God back to the margin. However, why should we assume such a god-of-the-gaps? Is that religiously adequate?

If we do not accept this god-of-the-gaps, how to proceed? *Theism* with its root pair of metaphors of power (on the side of the transcendent God) and dependence (on our side) is challenged to rethink itself in the light of the powers we have acquired. *Naturalism* faces a different challenge. In operating on the basis of 'what is', any strictly naturalistic philosophy has difficulty in articulating normative ideals (Drees 2000, 851–2). In the present context, the concern is not about the derivability of norms from facts. That would be an 'epistemological' issue, of how we can have knowledge of, or legitimize, certain norms. This is often discussed as 'the naturalistic fallacy', pointing out the logical impossibility of deriving norms ('ought') from facts ('is') – a fallacy

Creation
Grace

that may arise in ethics and in epistemology. My concern is not of this epistemological kind. One may well reject the naturalistic fallacy (as a pattern of reasoning) and still appreciate this world as 'the best of all possible worlds', believing that this world is deep down good or sacred. However, when engaging in technology we seem to assume that the world can be improved. Those naturalists who acknowledge the reality of imperfections and evil, and have the desire to improve rather than merely to affirm 'nature', face the challenge of avoiding to treat the given as normative. If we shift the vocabulary again and draw upon the biblical, Christian heritage, we find as well that quite a variety of attitudes may be articulated. Stewardship may be interpreted as a call to conserve this world – appreciated as the best of all possible worlds, just as in the arguments of natural theology. However, in the biblical traditions God is also associated with a vision of a Kingdom of peace and justice, a city of light and glory, where death will be no more. Images of redemption and liberation are integral to the Christian understanding of God. In that light humans are not merely stewards who are to keep and preserve what has been given. Humans are also addressed as persons who should abandon their old ways, take the risk of living in a new way (Exodus, Pentecost); they are called to renew themselves and the world. In the Christian tradition there has been from its very beginning (as the first major heresy, that of Marcion, testifies) a tension between the focus on God as creator – and thus on the world as a God-given created order – and on God as the gracious, loving Father of Jesus Christ, who longs for the renewal of the world. Distrust of technology springs from emphasis on the given; in contrast, technology could be part of the Christian calling.

Preview

René Munnik gives in his paper 'ICT and the Character of Finitude' an illustration of the way technologies have changed our lives again and again. He concentrates on the way the past, and especially dear ones who are dead, may be present in ways mediated by information technologies. Whereas earlier forms of presence via texts – themselves already a remarkable form of technology with the invention of the alphabetical notation and the blank space – required interpretation, later forms such as photography and recording of voices represented the absent by reproducing aspects of their presence. The opposition of absence and presence itself has changed, due to technologies. *Zbigniew Liana* explores in another historical essay how our ideas about the nature of nature have changed, in relation to the rise of science and of technology. One major aspect of this development has been the disentanglement of the empirical sense of a law of nature from the moral and theological sense of nature's order. This moral dimension still needs our attention, however, not because it shows itself in scientific discoveries as a given law, but because aspects of the world which are valuable can easily be destroyed. *Noreen Herzfeld* considers a different vocabulary for speaking about our responsibility in relation to technology, by considering the understanding of humans as 'co-creators'. If it is emphasized that we are creators, human agency becomes central, whereas an emphasis on the 'co-' emphasizes the relational and corporate dimensions of our existence. She combines this with an analysis of the *imago Dei* concept from the theological tradition and of functional and relational approaches in Artificial Intelligence. *Otto Kroesen* emphasizes the relational nature of existence as well, by discussing information technology with insights drawn from the understanding of human dialogues as developed by Rosenstock-Huessy and Rosenzweig. Information technology provides means of mass communication in a global society, but information technology is itself the result of human communication. From this perspective the humanities and the sciences belong to one another. *Taede Smedes* takes his point of departure in understanding ourselves as cyborgs, as a whole of mind and body, of technology and biology, of culture and nature, which cannot be disentangled in two distinct components.

The second group of papers begins with a contribution by *Frans de Waal*, rooted in his extensive studies of primates as well as in his theoretical interest in understanding the evolution of moral culture, with conditions such as empathy, forgiveness and retribution. He argues that the origins of morality can be traced back far into the animal kingdom. Thus, nature and culture differ in degree, rather than in kind. They are certainly not opposed, as was the attitude of Thomas Huxley, Thomas Hobbes, and in our time Richard Dawkins. To argue his view, de Waal discussed the work of Edward Westermarck (early twentieth century), while reaching beyond him to Darwin and to Mencius, a Chinese sage of the fourth century BCE. *Nancey Murphy* uses de Waal's biological work to argue for two theological theses. One is expressed in the title of her contribution, the notion of 'the moral nature of nature', thus an ontological (and ultimately theological) basis for morality. The other theological thesis surfaces later in her article, when she comes to speak of 'an Anabaptist theology of nature', that is, a theology of nature which orients itself on the suffering of Christ, in understanding creation as travail, where suffering, as happens in evolutionary processes, 'is given meaning by seeing it as participation in the sufferings of Christ'. God identifies with the prey rather than with the predator. *Lluís Oviedo* discusses in his contribution whether it is suitable to discuss theological notions such as original sin in scientific terms. He considers various proposals, such as those by Ralph Burhoe, Philip Hefner and Patricia Williams, but concludes that a full identification (translation, assimilation) fails. Thus, theology has a contribution of its own to make.

The third group of papers turns towards moral issues that arise in a technological culture. *Margaret Boden* describes various examples of current developments in biotechnology and information processing, and distinguishes seven classes of ethical issues that are involved. *Ulf Görman* discusses in his paper how the three religions of the book, that is Judaism, Christianity and Islam, react to the possibilities opened by biotechnology, such as blood transfusion, organ transplantation, gene therapy and reproductive cloning. Reactions and arguments are more multi-faceted than we may expect. The paper illustrates and discusses how each tradition tries to deal with the complexity of being true to its tradition while dealing with opportunities unknown of in history. *Jan-Olav Henriksen* focuses on one particular development, cloning, and especially the cloning of human individuals for reproductive purposes. He offers theological and ethical arguments as to why we should not allow such cloning, even though we might accept cloning for therapeutic purposes. *Christopher Corbally* comes to quite a different example where opinions on technology have clashed, the construction of telescopes on a mountaintop in Arizona. Whereas the astronomers considered their work as bringing in the open the beauty of 'the heavens', others more oriented on 'earthly beauty' and the biological sciences were concerned about biodiversity or the 'violation' of pristine nature. Thus, various values related to science and technology clashed. Corbally, himself as astronomer involved in this process, suggests that reconciliation might have been achieved if the underlying fundamental values had been discussed in a timely manner, and if the common source for the seemingly opposed values had been acknowledged. *Angela Roothaan* writes on values education, precisely in such a situation of conflicting and implicit ideologies. She argues that courses need to fit the pragmatic, 'technological', attitude of young people, but also should stimulate reflection on the meaning of their interactions with the world. In her paper, she then explores an anthropological model of human development that clarifies the aims of such values education.

Notes

1 An observation I owe to Ron Cole-Turner, in a conversation years ago. It is not implied that Ian Barbour denies the relevance of the two alternative projects indicated in the text, but merely that the focus on these two widely read and deservedly appreciated titles may pass by other important issues, including the religious (rather than moral) impact of technology.

2 The first two sections are derived from (Drees 2002a, 2002b) and my unpublished presentation at the Ninth European Conference on Science and Theology.

References

Barbour, Ian G.

1990 *Religion in an Age of Science* (New York: Harper & Row).

1993 *Ethics in an Age of Technology* (New York: HarperCollins).

Berners Lee, Tim

2000 *Weaving the Web: The Original Design and Ultimate Destiny of the World Wide Web* (New York: HarperCollins).

Brooke, John, and Geoffrey Cantor

1998 *Reconstructing Nature: The Engagement of Science and Religion* (Edinburgh: T&T Clark).

Diamond, Jared

1998 *Guns, Germs and Steel* (London: Random House).

Drees, Willem B.

2000 'Thick Naturalism: Comments on *Zygon* 2000', *Zygon: Journal of Religion and Science* 35 (4 December): 849–60.

2002a 'Religion in an Age of Technology', *Zygon: Journal of Religion and Science* 37 (3 September): 597–604.

2002b ' "Playing God? Yes!" Religion in the Light of Technology', *Zygon: Journal of Religion and Science* 37 (3 September): 643–54.

McNeil, Ian, ed.

1990 *An Encyclopedia of the History of Technology* (London: Routledge).

PART I

TECHNOLOGY'S IMPACT ON OUR WORLDVIEW

2

ICT and the character of finitude

René P. H. Munnik

Introduction

Since an exposition about 'technology and human finitude' would fairly exceed a contribution of this humble size, I will restrict myself to a specific aspect of human finitude: *mortality*, namely, the kind of finitude we are aware of in the absence of the dead, and in our own consciousness of becoming absent some time in the future. Furthermore, it is not the *fact* that we are mortal that I will consider, but the *character* of that fact. The central question of this article is: *What did ICT do with the boundary between the presence of the living and the absence of the dead?*

I have to make a second restriction. I indicated my theme in the past tense – what *did* information and communications technology (ICT) do . . . As a matter of fact, the main part will be about the past. Of course, the notion of 'ICT' suggests the kind of technology we have experienced since the late twentieth century: computer technology, multimedia technologies, telematics, and so on. Many books have been written about the enormous societal and cultural impact of the information revolution. But be that as it may, the development of technologies in general, and the role they play in the making of history, is extraordinarily complex and quite unpredictable. I will try to be cautious, and make no predictions about the future of the information society. On the contrary, I will confine myself to the information and communication technologies of the *past* – the ones that already have become part of everyday life and are deeply embedded in society. It is from the lesson of history – from what these embedded technologies actually did – that I want to detect a kind of tendency concerning the impact of information and communications technology on the character of mortality.

Embedded technologies and technological mediation

The successful technologies of the past are those that have been integrated into everyday life. They got embedded in our life-world; they became a part of the presupposed material substratum of our culture – they became a kind of 'second nature'. But just in so far as these technologies became 'second nature', they lost their specific recognizability as technologies. Once you take the machinery of motor cars for granted, a car dealer doesn't primarily sell *machines*; he rather sells *services* such as mobility, comfort, facility, status, and so on. And hardly anyone who sees a statue of the apostle Peter carrying with him a key is reminded of an early outcome of information technology. But keys and locks are in fact ancient exponents of information processing; the key is an iron password, and it is processed by a lock that functions as an automated gate-keeper. Now, for a start, let me give you just two simple examples of embedded technological inventions, which – in my opinion – were of great significance.

Chirographical space – Why is it that some medical doctors in the fifth century recommended reading books as a therapy for respiratory diseases? And why was Augustine astonished when he saw Ambrose read, and noticed that Ambrose's '*voice and tongue were silent*' (*Confessions* VI, 3). These questions have a simple answer. In the fifth century texts weren't read in silence. They were performed by reciting or even singing them in a monotonous voice and in long phrases that take a lot of breath. Reading was *physical effort.* Reciting texts loudly – even if the reader was alone – was not just a peculiar habit of ancient readers. For most of them it was inevitable, because at the time of Augustine Greek and Latin texts had no typographical (or rather: 'chirographical') spaces between single words, but only between very long strings of characters constituting full sentences (see Fig. 1). For that reason it was very difficult to recognize a word in one glance. And unless you were as literate as Ambrose, you were forced to *recite* the text so that you were assisted by the sounds your mouth was producing. For a long time this practice has been forbidden in modern libraries. But at *that* time with *such* texts, someone who could read in silence was nearly as remarkable as a director who reads a musical score and is able to appreciate the music without the aid of a piano.

Now, the implementation of a space between written words may seem a technical innovation as simple as a paperclip. But actually it was a step toward the exclusion of orality and physical labour from the practice of reading. The typographical space confined reading to the interplay of the text and the eye – it gave rise to an exclusive *ocular* meaning of literacy and intellectuality, which

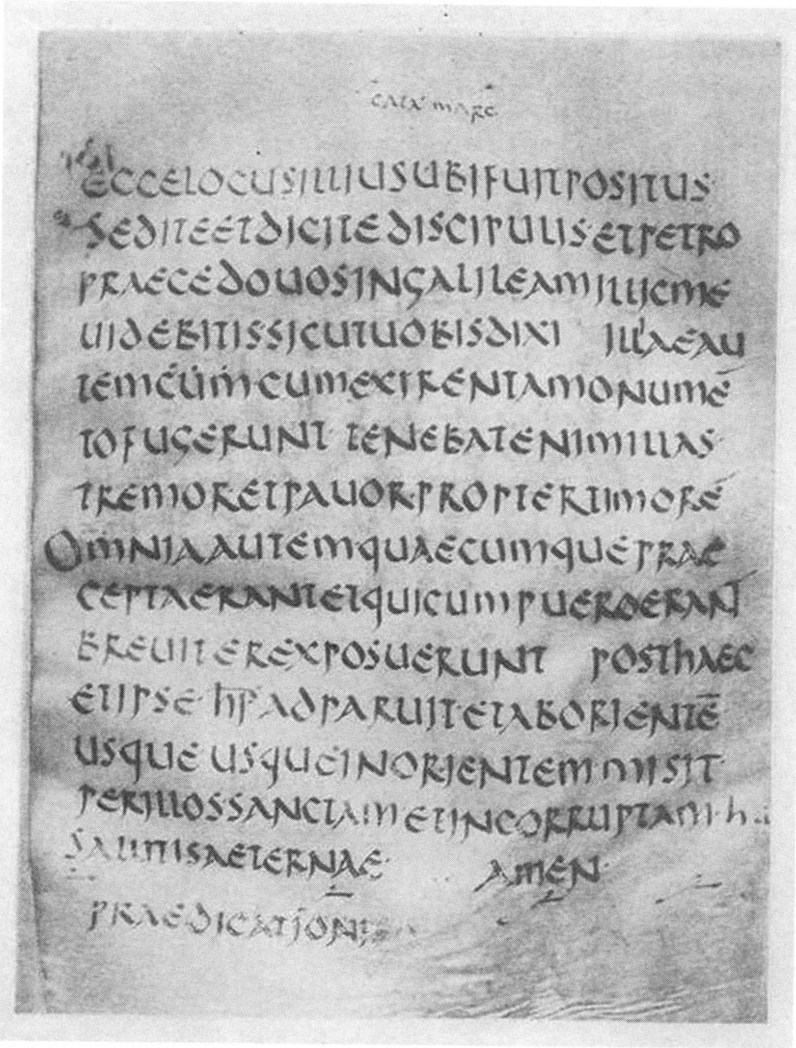

ECCELOCUSILLIUSUBIFUITPOSITUS
SEDITEETDICITEDISCIPULISETPETRO
PRAECEDOUOSINGALILEAMILLICME
UIDEBITISSICUTUOBISDIXI ILLAEAU
TEMCŪMCUMEXIRENTAMONUMĒ
TOFUGERUNT TENEBATENIMILLAS
TREMORETPAUORPROPTERTIMORĒ
OMNIAAUTEMQUAECUMQUEPRAE
CEPTAERANTETQUICUMPUEROERANT
BREUITEREXPOSUERUNT POSTHAEC
ETIPSE IHS ADPARUITETABORIENTĒ
USQUE USQUEINORIENTEMMISIT
PERILLOSSANCTAMETINCORRUPTAM
SALUTISAETERNAE AMEN
PRAEDICATIONIS

Figure 1. Facsimile of the final leaf of Mark's Gospel in Codex Bobbiensis, in *Portions of the Gospels according to St. Mark and St. Matthew from the Bobbio MS*, eds John Wordsworth, Henry J. White and William Sanday (Oxford: Clarendon Press, 1886).

we today presuppose as a matter of course, and which is tacitly assumed in the humanities and the *Geisteswissenschaften*.

Linear perspective – The architect and artist Filippo Brunelleschi, in the first half of the fifteenth century, drew a picture of the baptisterium of *San*

Giovanni when he constructed the dome of the Cathedral of Florence. It was the first picture in linear perspective. He invented it. Soon it became a widely applied technique. For most modern observers, drawings and paintings in perspective count as much more 'natural' or 'realistic' than non-perspectival works. Such a judgement tacitly presupposes that there is a primary meaning of a 'realistic image', and that the precursors of Brunelleschi were either unable or unwilling to produce 'realistic images'. But Greek architecture, Greek geometry and Greek sculpture hardly substantiate this point of view. In fact, it is much more probable that the invention of perspective wasn't just a discovery of a technique to produce 'realistic images' for the first time, but that it was an element in the production of *a new meaning of 'realism'*; a meaning which gradually became a natural, obvious presupposition in modernity.

This opinion is supported by the fact that initially drawing in perspective had to be exercised and learned, with the aid of *machines* invented by Albrecht Dürer (see Fig. 2). A contraption is placed between the observer and the observed. Now, the question is: How did such machines interfere in the relation of the observer and the observed? (1) Space was disclosed as a

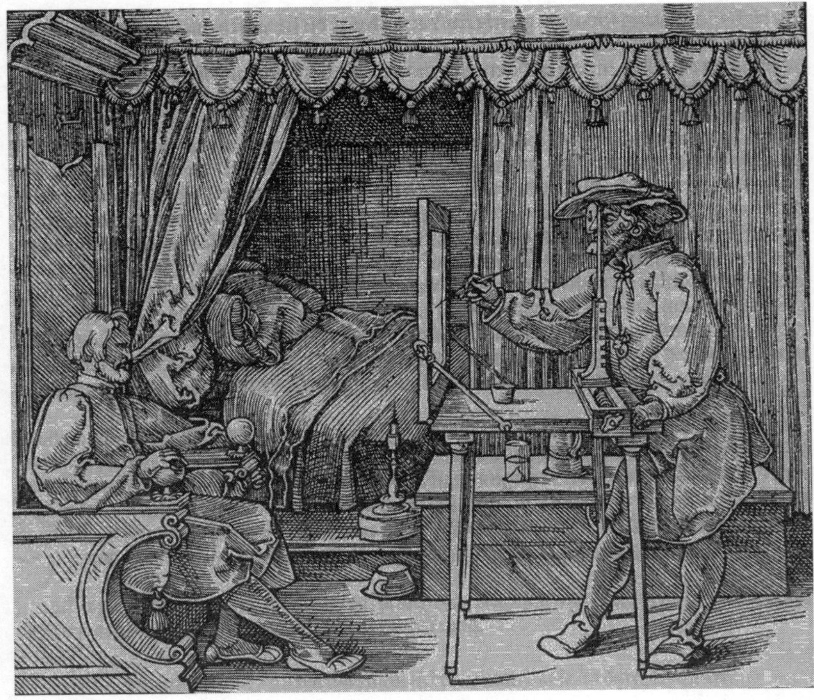

Figure 2. Unterweisung der Messung. Facsimile of a woodcut by Albrecht Dürer. Reproduced by permission of Bayerische Staatsbibliothek München.

Euclidian space; (2) the visible objects became part of a scene, structured from an exactly pinpointed monocular viewpoint; and (3) the spectator was drawn back behind the framework in the middle with its tracing-lines (the *velum*). The draftsman reproduced on paper what appeared through the *velum*, thereby creating a seemingly three-dimensional picture in just two dimensions. But *this* arrangement of the relation between the observer and the observed was not natural in an unqualified sense – it was literally *technologically mediated.* According to Erwin Panofsky (1991) and others, *this* relation of an uninvolved spectator experiencing a geometrical tableau and being unsure whether he is looking *through* a window or *to* a *trompe l'oeil*, was brought to philosophic formula by René Descartes.

My point as regards these two simple examples is that what counts as 'natural' or obvious – the propinquity of ocular literacy with *Geisteswissenschaft* and the realism of perspective – in fact have their technological conditions, and are *technologically mediated.* But they are so by a technology that became a matter of course – almost totally neglected as a technology, and thus seemingly 'natural'. This notion of technological mediation is very important and at the core of this article. It means that technological artefacts, devices, machines are not just neutral means for human action or self-realization, or that they are instruments we have to evaluate, but that they are *agents*; they actively redefine what human action means and they are involved in the ways we think about ourselves and about the world. Technological devices, techniques and so on, are not just a class of things we have to reflect upon, but they also regulate the way we reflect. Technology, according to Martin Heidegger (1962), is a mode of dis-closing, *entbergen*, *alètheia.* I do not follow him in his massive, transcendental elaboration of his insight. But I agree in so far as *specific* technologies have specific and complex consequences as to our understanding of ourselves and the world.

In the introduction I articulated my central question as: *What did information and communications technology do with the boundary between the presence of the living and the absence of the dead?* But now I can rephrase it as: *In what sense is the boundary between the presence of the living and the absence of the dead redefined by the mediations of information technology?* And again I will confine myself to a specific group of technologies – technologies for data storage or 'graphic technologies': chirography, phonography, photography and 'zoography'.

Chirography; the alphabet

In the past 5000 years a lot of writing systems or scripts have been developed: cuneiform scripts, rebus-scripts, hieroglyphs, ideographic, pictographic, syllabographic characters, and so on. But, according to Walter Ong, there was only one alphabet,[1] and it was developed quite late – in a time span between 1500 and 1000 BCE from early Semitic scripture. It was unique because it was entirely *phonographic*. Its phonographical character is probably the reason for its late development. It was extremely abstract: oral expressions had to be detached from their meanings and referents, and they had to be reduced to mere sounds – phonemes – in order to be alphabetically written down. But, since the phonemes of most spoken languages can be more or less represented by about two dozen characters, it needed only a small number of them – almost nothing, when compared with the 40,545 Chinese ideo- and pictographic characters in the K'anghsi dictionary. And so it was pretty easy for young children to learn, which, I presume, contributed to its great success.

The invention and the cultural implementation of alphabetic writing was not just an historical event of the first order. It was far more than that. Alphabetic writing *marked the beginning of history* as we know it. The alphabet was the necessary precondition for the origination of a culture that could acquire a cultural historical consciousness of itself; alphabetic writing marked our sense of the boundary between prehistory and history. We, modern literate people, can hardly imagine what it is like to live in an exclusively oral culture with its continuous story-telling and its never-ending imperative to memorize in order to rescue past things from total oblivion. Perhaps you read about Plato's rejection of the technology of writing.[2] Well, Plato's rejection of writing would never have reached us as an historical fact if it hadn't been a *written* rejection of writing.

Alphabetic writing conquered the world, and with it, the metaphor of the 'book'. Anything understandable was conceived as an 'open book', and anything incomprehensible was conceived as a 'sealed book'. Nature – a book. History – an archive. Even God had to learn to write; before the beginning of all time the Father brought forth the Son as the Word – a spoken word (Ong 2002, 179). And in the beginning of all time God created the world, again with a spoken word. But, by the time God revealed godself to Israel, he had learnt to write with his own hand[3] – for the law was a text from which 'not one jot or one tittle shall in any wise pass' (Matt. 5:18). Finally, for Christians, God's word, the Bible, is a book. And much later, the second birth of a human being into a *humanist* consisted in the initiation in the circle of readers of the canon of great texts that constituted the foundation of Western culture (Sloterdijk 1999). It is very hard to imagine what our legal system would be, what Christian theology would look like, or even what the great monotheistic religions would be, if they couldn't look back at the invention of the alphabet. In a sense Judaism, Christianity and Islam are *technologically mediated* religions, because their perspective on divinity, was (and is) the perspective of an alphabetic, literate mind. And in that sense, Christian wisdom has been *techno-sapientia* from the beginning.

But let us turn to the (extremely embedded) technological side of the alphabet. What did it do? It transformed a passing *event* into the structure of a durable *thing*. More precisely, it transformed a spoken word into a written word, and in doing so it de-temporalized the word. It conserved the word. A spoken word is extremely ephemeral; it lasts just as long as it sounds. But a written word is durable and spatial. It can be located somewhere on a page; it has some functional position in the grammatical structure of a full sentence. Writings, conceived as things, are durable; you can keep them in a library, just like pickles in a jar. But a text – the structural 'whatness' of many individual writings – is as non-temporal as an Aristotelian form. By transforming a temporal, spoken word into a spatial, written word, the alphabet *immortalized* the word. First, it immortalized the stories that were lucky enough to get written down and to be preserved and copied. And later, when the cultural figure of the author arose – the one who is entitled to a certain property-right of the text – the author could enjoy the impression of achieving a kind of immortality, because he or she was able to bequeath articulated messages to the yet unborn, without the necessity of the life-thread of an oral tradition. This kind of technologically mediated immortality of authors, and of those who were written about, marks the difference between historical figures such as Plato, Caesar and Napoleon and prehistorical figures which have no name at all, or – if we have access to their name – remain faintly in their pre-alphabetic 'realm of ghosts' behind the river of forgetfulness. *This difference between pre-historical anonymi and historical figures is a difference of their absence. Plato is dead and so is any anonymous sage or story-teller of the pre-alphabetic era. Both are absent. But Plato lives as his texts, mediated by the technology of the alphabet.*

Paradoxically, this kind of 'objective immortality' was accomplished by the 'dead letter'; writings were often conceived as a sort of epitaph – in fact they could be compared with mummified verbal expressions, awaiting to be resurrected into a living meaning by a reader. The threefold notion of Dilthey's hermeneutics – life, expression, understanding[4] – resembles an alphabetical resurrection-story: mortal life, expressing itself in an immortal dead letter, waiting to be awoken again into a living but transitory meaning in the understanding of someone in the future. Of course, there was nothing historical in writings as durable things. Philologists practising their *constitutio textus* emphasized that texts weren't *meant* to be historical. But it was the business of interpreters and hermeneutical philosophers to discover the historicity of their *interpretations*. And so, this non-historical thing served as a means to gain a consciousness of historicity. For, in a purely oral culture, life was so radically and immediately historical that its historicity could not enter in its own consciousness; it lacked the distance that writings provided for, by reflecting it.

But let us keep ourselves to the main point: the technology of the alphabet introduced a novel kind of immortality of verbal expressions. *It gave birth to historical figures, which possess a different kind of absence than that of pre-historical anonymi.* Of course, the invention of book-printing had an enormous effect on intellectual history, Humanism and Reformation. It popularized the book; it had a tremendous effect on the pervasion of books in society, and on the general literacy of the peoples. But it could only have this effect within a culture that had already embraced alphabetical texts as its foundations. As a *technological* innovation, book-printing wasn't the invention of the text, but of its mass production.

To summarize: (1) the alphabet *is* a technology. (2) This technology had immense consequences; it marked the beginning of history and was a pre-condition of Christian religion, not only because Christianity 'happens' to base itself on texts, but mainly because it moulded the sense of history that is presupposed in Christian religion and theology. (3) This technology implied a mediation that redefined the boundary between the absence of the dead and the presence of the living: *some* expressions of the dead gained a place among the living, *some* texts became immortal and *some* dead could become 'historical figures'.

Phonography

In December 1877 Thomas Alva Edison invented the tinfoil phonograph. The phonograph was a reading-writing device. It wrote and read *sounds*. The new possibilities given with this machine were founded on what it left out: the writer, the reader and the alphabet. You just spoke into the horn and a needle inscribed a groove in a cylinder – a kind of script no human cryptologist could decipher and no human interpreter could understand. But that wasn't necessary, because the machine did the job itself. You only had to put the cylinder back into the machine, the needle began to 'read' it and the horn reproduced the double of the original voice. Edison's phonograph, and its more sophisticated technological inheritors, marked the beginning of the massive production of sound-materials. That was its economic significance. But the historical meaning, which I want to draw your attention to, was that it had tamed the goddess Echo. From a technological point of view, there was nothing mysterious about the phonograph. On the contrary, it was a beautiful, transparent machine – easy to understand by anyone who has the slightest notion of the physical concept of sound. But what it realized was a miraculous thing: *it gave the past a voice.* History preceding the invention of the phonograph was a history of irrevocably lost voices. It was silent as a grave. But after the invention of the phonograph, the past began to make itself known by sound.

'Mary had a little lamb . . .', spoken with Edison's own voice, was the first sentence that achieved immortality. Admittedly, it is a humble message from the past, but from that time the voices of Enrico Caruso, Maria Callas, Frank Sinatra, Elvis Presley, Martin Luther King and countless others were saved from total oblivion. From that time, *the voices of the dead could affect the souls of the living, from beyond their graves.* We know that a certain Giulio Caccini (1545–1618) must have been a marvellous singer, but we only know that from texts that testify that he was, because he died 250 years before the invention of the phonograph. The voice of Enrico Caruso, however, is still able to touch us. And again, the mysterious thing is not the phonographic machine; it is the fact that it enables an ephemeral voice to affect us at this very moment, though its owner died more than 80 years ago.

Let us for a moment take a little excursus in order to become aware of the consequences of this ordinary and yet extraordinary technological mediation between the dead and the living. Let us look at the realm where sound belongs to the essence of things: *to music* – especially to the performance of the works of dead composers.

In the first half of the eleventh century the Benedictine monk Guido d'Arezzo invented musical notation as we know it. In the time before Guido's invention, musical scores consisted of *neuma. Neuma* were signs written above the text and indicated a rise and a fall in pitch. But this notation was very inexact, and it served only as a mnemonic aid to remind singers of music they had already memorized by practising it. But when Guido d'Arezzo had invented his musical notation, songbooks began to look like modern scores. From that time melodies did not need a life-thread of singing and playing practices in order to survive. They could be conserved on paper or parchment, they could be forgotten and they could be rediscovered to sound again. And what the invention of the alphabet had done for intellectual and cultural history, Guido's notation did for the history of music: *it marked its beginning.* Certainly, there has been music in the times of Plato and in the early ages of Western culture, but it faded out irrevocably. For the modern mind, the history of music preceding Guido's invention is *pre-history.* Composers and compositions simply had to wait for Guido's invention in order that they could become the *great* composers and the *immortal works* that constitute the history of Western music.

Now, to possess the musical score of a piece is one thing – but performing it is quite another matter. The performance demands an applicative hermeneutical endeavour in order to revitalize the dead notes into an appealing interpretation of them. Musical scores, just like any text, are poly-interpretable. That is why it makes a lot of difference if the same masterpiece is performed by different musicians. The question of which of these performances is appropriate and authentic is a difficult one. At this point the relevance of the phonograph comes in – namely, when we arrive at the question of what an 'authentic' performance of the work of a dead composer implies.

Take, for an example, two dead composers: Johann Sebastian Bach and Igor Stravinsky. Both left a legacy of masterworks in the form of scriptures or scores. Bach died 125 years before the invention of the phonograph, but Stravinsky could dispose of the technology and he used it; he left an extensive discography, which makes him immediately another kind of dead composer to perform. Bach and Stravinsky both left poly-interpretable manuscripts, but Stravinsky additionally left samples of his own exemplary interpretations. Thereby the technology of phonography changed something in the relationship between dead composers and the living performers of their compositions.[5]

If, on the one hand, the performer intends to produce an 'authentic' interpretation, consisting of a *re*construction of the original sound the composer intended at the time, Stravinsky solved his problem beforehand, while Bach makes a lot of trouble. *If*, on the other hand, the performer claims to be an *artist* of his or her own kind and not just an artisanal sound-restorer, he or she has to make decisions concerning the independence of the work from its creator and concerning the normative status of the creator's own interpretation of his or her work. The difference between Bach and Stravinsky is that such decisions concerning the work of Bach remain fairly indefinite because you have only very indirect knowledge of his own interpretations. Concerning Stravinsky's work, however, such decisions are very definite: you can know exactly where you follow the creator's interpretation and where you differ. From the perspective of the performer, the difference between the two dead composers comes to this: Bach rests in his grave silently, and he does not interfere with musicians playing his heritage. Stravinsky rests in his grave, but his own phonographical echos are still around. And a performer who claims to be an artist has to decide which echos are to be exorcised back into the past and which echos have the privilege of remaining. As a dead composer Stravinsky is closer to the skin of a living performer. Audible history in the main became closer to the skin of the living.

Photography

While the technology of phonography was an invention in one piece – suddenly it was there – the invention of photography gradually evolved as a combination of different techniques, inventions and discoveries: drawing with the camera obscura, silhouette-drawing, the chemisty of photo-sensitive chemicals, and so on. In fact photography was invented by Nicephore Niépce about half a century earlier than the phonograph. Niépce's business partner,

Louis-Jacques-Mandé Daguerre, developed the *daguerréotype* – and it was exceptionally successful. It produced perfect images, and it aroused a veritable 'daguerréotypomania' in Europe and the United States.

Before his research work on photography, Louis Daguerre, like a lot of other early photographers, was a painter. And as a painter he considered photography to be *painting without a painter*. And that was exactly the opinion of others, for example Samuel B. Morse, another great inventor and artist. He praised Daguerre because he had introduced Nature to us in the character of a painter. Until the invention of photography, painting, drawing and other artistic techniques were the only means of immortalizing images of landscapes, still-lifes and portraits. This technology did the same thing: *it immortalized passing images*, but without the mediation of a human eye, a human hand, a human skill and a human taste. It created images 'not-made-by-a-human-hand', somewhat like the *eikoon acheiropoiètos* in Eastern Orthodox spirituality. This elimination of human interference and subjective interpretation was the reason why positivists of the late nineteenth century apprehended the photographic plate as the 'retina of the scientist' (Didi-Huberman 1998, 71). Of course, they could only do so because *their* interpretation of the eye was already technologically mediated: they conceived the eye as a sort of *camera obscura*, and if you are convinced beforehand that the human eye is a *camera obscura*, then the assertion that the photographic plate is its retina is quite tautological.

But it would be wrong to think of photography as producing unprejudiced 'objective' representations of 'reality' in an unqualified sense. Just as scientific observations are theory-loaden observations, photographic images are technologically mediated images. Photography has its own semiotic dynamics, and its own means of generating meanings. Moreover, photographers have a whole range of darkroom techniques at their disposal in order to modify, convert and remodel the picture. Photography has, among other things, become an art form *sui generis*, with its own means of expression. And, of course, photography has also become a means of false suggestions and deliberate deceit in commercials and propaganda. But it can only do so *effectively*, because it suggested truthfulness in the first place.

Although photographic images are technologically mediated and can become a means of artistic expression in their own right, and even though they can be deceitful, there still is some truth in the opinion of early photographers: that photography is 'painting without a painter', and that photographic images for that reason bring you closer to the 'real thing'. This is what we habitually presuppose when we accept a photograph of a traffic offence as 'proof', while a watercolour painting of that same offence counts for almost nothing. In court-rooms photographers generally aren't allowed for reasons of privacy, but draftsmen making their sketches usually are.

Photography carries with it a directness that painting or sketching can hardly achieve.

Painting without a painter . . . Orthodox spirituality cherishes the *Mandilion of Christ*, that is, the image of Christ himself, not painted by a human hand, as a most precious relic. This picture is conceived as a 'window', giving the eye access to 'the real thing' no eye can see. Modern Western theology claimed to be much more rational than Orthodoxy. From the time of Hermann Samuel Reimarus onwards it had its own *scientific* conception of getting to the 'real thing', and of taking a short cut through the tradition of human interference and story-telling: the *Leben Jesu Forschung*. And in 1898, in the last days of the *Leben Jesu Forschung*, coincidental or not, Secondo Pia discovered the modern technologically mediated relic on the shroud of Turin: something that might be interpreted as a photograph of the image of Christ. According to Paul Claudel it *was* a photograph of the body of the Lord (Didi-Huberman 1998, 75). It is probably not the thing Claudel thought it was and perhaps it is a practical joke of the master of Italian renaissance art: Leonardo da Vinci. But that does not contradict my main point: *if* the shroud contains a sort of photograph of the historical Jesus *then* it brings you closer to the visible image of the man worshipped as the incarnation of God.

The phonograph of Edison and all its more sophisticated technological successors immortalized sounds and voices, and made them reproducible. The photographic camera of Niépce, Daguerre, Fox Talbot and other inventors did the same thing with *passing images*: it immortalized them and made them reproducible. By doing so they changed the kind of absence of past events and of persons passed away. And, later, the technology of motion pictures developed: silent films from Edisons *mutoscope* onwards. He named his film-producing company the *Biographical Company*: it was meant to 'write life'. The abstract but real shadows of past events became immortal. And when this technology was combined with phonographic technologies, it gave some events the opportunity to generate their own monumenta; they could time and again touch our minds – events like the Hindenburg exploding in Lakehurst 1938, the assassination of J. F. Kennedy, and the two airliners crashing into the World Trade Center towers.

Let me summarize.

- The invention of the *alphabet* immortalized verbal expressions and eliminated the necessity for a human oral mediation in order to survive; it gave rise to the text, and it marked the beginning of history. The difference between an historical figure like Augustine and prehistorical anonymi is a difference of their absence, due to the invention of the alphabet.

- The phonograph immortalized *sounds*. It eliminated the necessity for human mediation by writers, the alphabet and readers. It simply reproduced sounds. It did *not* mark the beginning of history, but it marked a change in the character of the past; it made itself known by sound. From that time, audible history wasn't as absent as it was previously. And a singer like Caruso is a different kind of absent singer from Caccini. In general terms, Caruso is closer to our ears than Caccini.
- Photography, cinematography and sound movies immortalized *images* and shadows of events. They eliminated the necessity for human mediation by painters. From that time visible history wasn't as absent as it was previously. Phonography and photography bring you back to the past real thing. Or, stated the other way around, past things can be represented in the present. Adolf Hitler is a different kind of historical figure from Nero or Attila or Napoleon, not only because of the uniqueness of his cruelty, but also because of all the video and audio materials we possess of Hitler and nothing of the kind of Napoleon, Attila or Nero.

'Zoography'

At this point I arrive at contemporary technology. I will extrapolate the trend that we found in chirographic, phonographic and photographic technologies: to immortalize something passing and gradually bring it closer to the skin of the living. Now, what you can actually do with words, sounds and images, you might be able to do with *life forms*, provided that these life forms disclose themselves as somehow adaptable to reading and writing technologies. The result is what I call zoography. I might have called it 'biography', not as a literary genre but in the sense of Edison's 'Biographical Company'. It is the endeavour to make life forms immortal or resurrectable, just like stories, sounds and images.

The dream of immortal life, of the salvage of things from total oblivion, of the retrieval of things gone by, up to the resurrection of the dead, was never very far from the daydreams of science. In 1886, the French astronomer and Darwinist, Camille Flammarion, wrote his popular book *Le monde avant la création de l'homme*. It contained illustrations like Figure 3, expressing the author's opinion concerning the eschatological meaning of paleontology. At the bottom of the picture you see different nineteenth-century reconstructions of extinct species. Above them, sitting on a rock, is Charles Darwin with some simians at his feet. Next to him: the angel with the trumpet from the book of Revelation. The text accompanying this picture says: 'The trumpet of science has sounded, they are risen from the dead.' For Flammarion the promises of science and of religion flow together in one

Figure 3. Camille Flammarion's (1842–1925) *Le monde avant la création de l'homme* (Marpon, Paris, 1886).

evolutionary salvation history, ending with a superman of science who, with the aid of his science, retroactively saves all that has been lost in time.

Today's readers will find his optimistic prophecies rather naïve and overstressed. Nevertheless, Flammarion simply extrapolated the tendency I detected in the graphic technologies and its mediations. As for Flammarion, nature already was a *book* and natural (pre-)history had disclosed itself as a geological *archive*. You only needed a *key* to open this sealed book in order to understand it and be able to read it again. And Darwin provided the key.

For Flammarion this reconstruction of lost life forms was an important but purely *theoretical* matter. It was the business of paleontologists to reconstruct these extinct life forms; and it was the business of museums of natural history to erect their memorials from their fossilized bones. This was all in the service of their commemoration, but above all it was in the service of the self-awareness of humankind: of the recognition of its animal origin and of the obligation for continual development. And this, for most modern people, isn't fictional at all. Flammarion in a sense was a realist. He knew how far to go . . . he never thought of a *real resurrection* of dinosaurs, trilobites, pterodactyli.

You need another kind of concept or paradigm of life, organisms and bodies, in order to achieve a real outlook at the possibility of a real re-presentation of these extinct, absent life forms. The conception of the body in modern times is closely related to technological developments. In the time of the introduction of machine technology, the body was disclosed as a machine. It was a metaphor. But it was a good, strong and very effective one. It worked in a lot of instances – it brought us modern medical science, and it suggested the possibility of an endless repairability of the body.

Today, in the age of *information technology*, the body is disclosed not so much as a *machine*, but rather in terms of information processing. At the beginning of the third millennium the secret of life is thought of as inscribed in a kind of text, which it is the aim of the Human Genome Project to decipher and store in a database. Again, it is a strong, effective metaphor. Life is conceived as a vast process of reading and writing, with ribosomes as the transcribers in their scriptorium/cell. Meanwhile, the life sciences have become a form of textual reading practice and cryptology; the technology of genetic recombination is an instance of quoting one passage of a DNA-text in another; genetic mutations can be conceived as a form of textual corruption, and so on. Biologists tell me that it is not as simple as it sounds; that DNA isn't simply a codebook containing recipes in the form of a one-to-one relation of a gene and an enzyme, a polypeptide or an 'expression' in the organism. But such remarks do not mean that life isn't conceived under the metaphor of a text; it only means that the text is very complex, and that other kinds of texts and contexts have to be taken into account. Just like any other kind of text that isn't simply a codebook.

Once life, in the biological sense of the word, is disclosed as 'text', it can be saved from oblivion just like stories, sounds and images. *Jurassic Park* was a nice family film. My children were fond of it. It was fiction, but it was intelligent fiction, just like Mary Shelley's *Frankenstein*. It played with the theoretical possibility that you can revive extinct life forms if you can find the right documents in the geological archives, just as you can revive a forgotten musical piece of Monteverdi if you find a lost manuscript in an old library. *Jurassic Park* was a technologically mediated *Auferstehungsgeschichte* of the kind Camille Flammarion could not dream of.

But how fictional is it? Dolly the sheep exists, and so does CopyCat.[6] In 1999 the Hunt family lost their little son when he was ten months old. They loved him and couldn't cope with his death . . . his irrevocable absence. His father decided to collect the proper cells from his body and he got in touch with Dr Brigitte Boisselier in order to clone him.[7] How close can the dead come to the skin of the living, if a child that will perhaps be born is conceived by his father as a relic or even a 'second chance' of a dead child?[8]

Presence and absence

At this point we seem to arrive at the situation the feminist theorist Donna Haraway describes in her cyborg-manifest (Haraway 1991, 149–81). According to Haraway, modern technology produces several boundary breakdowns: between human beings and animals, between living bodies and cybernetic machines, between body and mind. From a technologically mediated perspective, these fundamental differences appear to fade away. And, as a consequence, modern technology is able to confuse and contaminate them. It creates cyborgs; contaminated beings – bastardizations of nature and technology. In this article I have been considering a similar type of boundary breakdown I didn't find in Haraway's writings: that of the presence of the living and the absence of the dead.

All the technologies I have been considering do the same thing: they transform a passing event into the structure of a thing. The thing is *durable*, the structure is *timeless*. Be it alphabetical characters on a page, be it wave-like grooves on a tinfoil cylinder, be it dots of colloidal silver on a photographic plate, be it pixels on a screen, or bytes on a hard disk. By doing so they 'immortalize' the passing event by making it reproducible; be it a story in its interpretation, a voice in its playback, an image in your album, an event on a screen, a cat in a CopyCat and perhaps one day a dead child in a living one.

My question was: *In what sense is the boundary between the absence of the dead and the presence of the living redefined by the mediations of information technology?* Here is my answer. In the pre-alphabetic era, time did not disclose itself as *history* in our sense of the word, because the past was simply too absent. The technology of the *alphabet* gave us history, for the text introduced a specific balance of presence and absence of the past – a balance that defined our sense of history, with its specific spaces for tradition, interpretation and development. As an implicit technological mediation, this balance of presence and absence was at the base of philosophical hermeneutics (and hermeneutical philosophy). For these disciplines affirm that the past is present as a text. But they also acknowledge that the only way to disclose it is in the interpretation, which is never simply a representation, but also a novel production of meaning.

Modern technologies, however, seem to destabilize this 'textual' balance, for they approach a *total reproduction*, *re*-present-ation or reiteration of human (bodily) expressions. By doing so, they interfere in the 'alphabetical' sense of history. For they gradually succeed in treating any reality as an a-historical structure. The mediation of modern technologies comprises an ontology of structure, in which 'reality' discloses itself as convertible with 'structure' in the scholastic sense of 'convertible' (as meant in the well-known mediaeval dictum *ens et unum/verum/bonum convertuntur*, or 'being and unity/truth/goodness are mutually convertible'). Now, in the vocabulary of such an ontology of structure some words simply do not occur: words like 'substantiality' or 'individuality', and especially 'natality' ('coming from absence into presence') and 'mortality' ('falling from presence into absence'). For it conceives 'being qua being' in terms of matterless and timeless form: *in-form-ation*. The gradual technological implementation of this idea brought us the immortality of Plato's works, it brought us the sound of the voice of Caruso in our ears, and perhaps it may bring the presence of a body of a dead child into the body of a living one.

If you are 'modern' you may say that this is a triumph of a 'metaphysics of presence' you hold on to. And in a sense you are right. If you are 'post-modern' you may argue that the gradual evaporation of reality into nothing but 'structure' confirms the 'metaphysics of absence' you hold on to.[9] And in a sense you are equally right. But both possibilities seem to be due to the fact that the *opposition* of 'presence' and 'absence' is becoming uncannily indecisive. I am not in a position to offer any solutions here. But I hope to have shown the crucial role of technological mediations for our awareness of history and our self-awareness as historical beings. The alphabet gave us history, and perhaps modern information technology will take it from us again.

Notes

1 See Walter Ong's *Orality and Literacy* (2002). An other illuminating introduction into the cultural significance of the alphabet is Eric Havelock's *The Muse Learns to Write* (1986).

2 *Phaedrus*, 274c–275e.

3 *Exod.* 24:12; 31:18; 32:16; 34:28 and *Deut.* 5:22.

4 *Leben, Ausdruck, Verstehen*. See Dilthey 1968, 86–8.

5 For an interesting account of the influence of the phonograph on the history of music, see Day 2000.

6 In December 2001 a cloned kitten, named CC (for 'carbon copy') was produced at the laboratories of Texas A&M University. It was nicknamed 'CopyCat', although the kitten proved to be not an exact reproduction of its genetic mother.

7 The child was never born, and Hunt terminated his cooperation with Boisselier.

8 *If* he is conceived like that! I'm not making any ontological claims about the real possibility (or contradictory notion) of the reproduction of a unique and singular individual. I only point at the perplexity of the technologically mediated viewpoint. Once you conceive the individual as an instance of a genetic structure, and once you conceive its personality and behaviour in terms of algorithms etc., the individual is released from its temporality and contextuality. It becomes reproducible and 'resurrectable'.

9 Isn't this a dominant theme in the works of authors like Jacques Derrida and Jean Baudrillard?

References

Day, T.
2000 *A Century of Recorded Music: Listening to Musical History* (New Haven/ London: Yale University Press).

Didi-Huberman, G.
1998 'La photographie scientifique et pseudo-scientifique' in J.-C. Lemagny and A. Rouillé (eds.), *Histoire de la photographie* (Paris: Larousse-Bordas).

Dilthey, W.
1968 'Der Aufbau der geschichtlichen Welt in den Geisteswissenschaften', in *Wilhelm Dilthey: Gesammelte Schriften*, vol. VII, (Leipzig/Göttingen: Teubner/Vandenhoeck & Ruprecht).

Flammarion, C.
1886 *Le monde avant la création de l'homme* (Paris: Marpon).

Haraway, D.
1991 *Simians, Cyborgs, and Women: The Reinvention of Nature* (London/New York: Free Association Books/Routledge).

Havelock, E.

1986 *The Muse Learns to Write: Reflections on Orality and Literacy from Antiquity to the Present* (New Haven: Yale University Press).

Heidegger, M.

1962 *Die Technik und die Kehre* (Pfüllingen: Neske).

Ong, W.

2002 *Orality and Literacy: The Technologizing of the Word* (London/New York: Routledge).

Panofsky, E.

1991 *Perspective as Symbolic Form* (New York: Zone Books).

Sloterdijk, E.

1999 *Regeln für den Menschenpark: Ein Antwortschreiben zum Brief über den Humanismus* (Frankfurt am Main: Suhrkamp).

3

Technology and the changing notion of nature

Zbigniew Liana

The notions of techno sapiens or techno s@piens, technology, Creator and co-creator are mutually related. It is my intention in this paper to discuss the mutual relationship of these notions in order to try to unveil their proper meaning. However, the key notion, which should enable us to perform this analysis, will be the notion of nature. All these notions are in fact intimately related to the concept of nature. Man's attitude toward nature is crucial for our understanding of Creator, creation, technology, and man itself. Another important reason for our interest in the notion of nature comes from the theological discussion of human technological capabilities. Usually theologians enter this discussion equipped with the notion of nature, which serves them to make critical assessments. Very often the results of this evaluation raise many controversies.

My analysis will be done a historical perspective. All our notions have historical roots and knowing them makes it easier to understand their meanings today. The notion of nature has without doubt ancient roots, but for our purposes it is more important to look at the mediaeval and the modern understanding of nature and man's attitude toward nature. The conceptual developments in the Middle Ages and in the early Modern period remain a direct background for today's discussions and controversies. Commonly a sharp distinction is made, and it is believed that a kind of conceptual revolution occurred during the passage from the former to the latter period, thanks to scientific and technological progress. I will try to show that this is only partially true and I will advocate a different, evolutionary approach. The core of the idea of nature remains unchanged, but many additional characteristics were rejected or changed. Moreover, another conceptual process took place, namely the process of individuating many different meanings attributed confusedly to the term 'nature'. This confusion still seems to play an important role in the misunderstandings between theologians and scientists.

Contemplating and obeying nature

Contemplation and obedience – these two words seem best to express humankind's proper attitude toward nature as seen by mediaeval authors. The notion of nature entered Christian thought in a very specific intellectual situation during the twelfth century. It was overtaken, without doubt, from the ancient philosophy; nevertheless it received in this time a strong Christian meaning. Together with the renaissance of the ancient natural philosophy during the eleventh and twelfth centuries and the introduction of the translations of some Arabic and Byzantine naturalistic texts to the Western European schools, the question arose as to how to explain the dynamical properties of material beings, and how to harmonize the answer with the Christian idea of Creation and of Divine Providence. According to Platonic and Aristotelian philosophy the primary matter is completely passive, lacking any inner force or energy. The only operating force in the world beside the divine could have been demonic. Whatever happened in the physical and human world was seen as an effect of the direct will of God or of that of the Devil. Until that time it was commonly accepted among the European Middle Age writers to look upon the world as a speculum, a mirror of God's direct creative and providential action. The material world was treated as a convenient receptacle of symbols and metaphors of a deeper and spiritual divine reality. As Tullio Gregory (1984, 442) puts it, the world was lacking any proper substantial consistency. Nobody was interested in investigating it for itself. This kind of activity could have been but a sinful curiosity infringing on God's omnipotence and wisdom.

An increased interest in natural texts led some writers such as Abelard and William of Conches to accept a very controversial thesis (at least on the language level) that the force operating in plants, animals and other animated beings (like planets) also called Anima Mundi was identical with the Holy Spirit. This kind of crypto pantheism gave rise, through long investigations, discussions and condemnations, to the new idea of nature as an instrument of God's action in the world. The leading proponents of this solution can be found in the twelfth-century School of Chartres (Gregory 1955, 132–54; Liana 1996, 199–232). A late twelfth-century theologian, deeply influenced by the intellectual movements of Chartres, Alanus ab Insulis, or Alan of Lille, was the scholar who best expressed these new ideas. In his *De planctu naturae* Nature is presented as a Lady or Queen whose garments represent the structure of the whole material world: heaven and earth. Her main task is to generate new things in the world (*genitrix rerum*) and to guard constantly the harmony and the order of this world. She is called by the very suggestive names: *vinculum mundi stabilisque nexus, pax, amor, ordo, lex, finis, via, dux, regula mundi.* She fulfils her task of guarding the order of the things by giving each its own nature according to the forms or ideas present in God's Mind. In this duty she is called *vicaria Dei*, God's assistant or instrument. She is totally dependent on God, being created by Him and being called His child: *Dei proles*. Humans are supposed to obey the laws and order of nature in the same manner other things do, paying that way tribute to God, giving Him glory. However, this is not the case. Nature is weeping because of human disobedience and sin (Alan of Lille 1978, 831–3).

This picture heavily influenced later theology, where the notion of nature became pivotal, especially in the field of moral theology. First of all nature was presented there as a notion unifying all creation under the universal law which maintains order and harmony according to God's will and Providence. Mediaeval man did not sharply distinguish the law of nature from natural law, deterministic and physical rules governing the material world from moral rules governing human beings capable of free will.[1] Secondly, for these people the law of nature had a deep moral dimension. This was a teleological law leading everything to its perfection and completion according to God's design. Man, being free and imperfect, can reject it, but this also means his rejection of God's will, viz. a sin. Nature was God-given and had to be obeyed and accepted by human beings in a kind of humble religious act. Lacking any deeper operative knowledge of nature, humans could only use the forces of nature in a very restricted way. The contemplative and humble attitude was dominating the whole culture of that time, at least in the theological and philosophical texts.[2]

One more fact concerning the medieval notion of nature should be stressed here. The confusion of two aspects of the law of nature, cosmological and moral, was due to another confusion, of the physical or cosmological and the metaphysical orders. When we talk of nature governing bodies, we speak about physical or biological rules that can be discovered by empirical investigation. However, when we talk about the nature of man, we enter a metaphysical dimension of the world, which completely escapes the modern empirical methods of science. Medieval man did not know the physical, i.e. empirical laws, and the mathematical laws. His view of the order of the world was shaped by the unifying metaphysical and theological notion of nature. Whatever constant behaviour was observed in the material world it was attributed to the nature of things. We can still find this notion present in the scientific investigations of Francis Bacon in the seventeenth century (the nature of heat) and even in the writings of John Herschel in the nineteenth century (Bacon 1889; Herschel 1830).

By this time scientists started to abandon the search for the nature of things and forces, this objective being too difficult to reach. According to the new positivistic methodology, they limited their inquiry to empirical and mathematical laws, albeit still hoping to be able to arrive at the end of the long inquiry to grasp something of the nature of things. However, the notion of the laws of physics as hypotheses about reality were gradually distinguished from the notion of the laws of nature and introduced into the scientific vocabulary, leaving the latter notion to the philosophers and theologians. Scientific language and enquiry became methodologically detached from the metaphysical and theological debates about hidden reality and nature. Because of this fact science and theology began to speak different languages, which made mutual understanding very difficult. Today, when scientists and theologians speak of nature, they speak of two different realities. Scientists mean only an object of empirical investigation, whereas theologians mean some kind of deeper and normative God-given reality. Moreover, many strong ontological positivists and proponents of scientism of the nineteenth and twentieth centuries have banned completely the philosophical and theological notion of nature and the notion of the laws of nature, not only from the language of science but also from the philosophical domain, claiming that they are meaningless. Unfortunately for the science and theology dialogue, the idea of scientism, that the empirical language of science is the only language meaningfully describing the whole reality, became very popular.

Cooperation and mastering nature

The contemplative mediaeval approach to nature started to change radically at the turn of the Middle Ages. A new idea of cooperation with and mastering nature was making its way through the Renaissance period, due to the divulgation of the magical worldview and technological achievements, finally to become a distinguishing mark of modern mentality. The major contribution to this change was made by the Renaissance magical worldview.[3] The new philosophy was created at the end of the fifteenth century accentuating the 'evolutionary', perfection-oriented idea of nature itself. The Magus was given a special role in this process of perfecting the nature of things and of the world. Thanks to his knowledge of the mysteries of nature he was thought to be able to help and to accelerate the process of perfecting things (for example, changing metals into gold, which was believed to be a perfect, natural end of the evolution of every metal) and the whole world. Very often this kind of activity was given a theological interpretation, being considered a kind of redemption of the material world from its fall, related to the original sin of man. We have many examples of such thinking in Ficino, Pico, Paracelse and many others. From the contemplation of nature, man (at least the Magus) shifted to the cooperation with nature. Whatever was the official position of the Churches to this kind of thought, it is true that the alchemical vocabulary entered deeply into the theological language of the sixteenth and seventeenth centuries.[4]

The Renaissance also saw another development, which was going to influence our notion of nature in a most decisive way. It was technological development. Geographic discoveries due to the improved knowledge of navigation, new mechanical devices, new medicine and new science led Bacon and Descartes to this famous ascertainment that man became 'as it were master and possessor of nature'. Thanks to the new knowledge, new possibilities in using nature were open to humanity. New devices enabled humans to 'enjoy without pain the fruits of the earth', especially to maintain health, as Descartes (1993, 35) puts it. This early modern idea received more and more empirical support during the past four centuries. Modern humans gained a much more active relationship with nature. Thanks to the technological capacities they became able to control and to take advantage of the natural forces in order to reach their own purposes. From being a humble subject of nature they seem to have become a co-creator of nature, changing the usual, 'natural' way of things. Today's technological achievements in the field of genetic engineering, using atomic and subatomic forces, constructing more powerful computers and other achievements, are only enlargements of the human possibilities to enjoy nature's fruits.

Without doubts, this idea of mastering nature enunciated *expressis verbis* must have had important consequences for the philosophical debate on morality. Nature lost (at least partially) its dominant role for the benefit of man and became stripped of its normative character. Thanks to the advancement of learning and to the technological improvements, humans could hope to liberate themselves from nature's grip. By analogy, for many, nature could not any more impose restrictions on moral behaviour. Morality turned into the domain of human autonomy, and the idea of the natural, moral law was abandoned. Again, historically, the evolution of science and technology led in many cases to the philosophical positions contrary to traditional theological views, making mutual dialogue still more difficult. The situation was only worsened by a strong conservative, from the philosophical point of view, and suspicious attitude from many theologians, who were unable to follow the new developments in science and technology in a critical as well as open-minded way.

Evolution not revolution

However, the radical opposition between mediaeval and modern, between contemplative and mastering approach, seems too easy. It wouldn't be true to say that Descartes and the whole of modern science rejected completely the contemplative approach to nature to the advantage of a more active and controlling attitude. It would be equally misleading to see only purely passive and humble relationship with nature in mediaeval society. It is much more accurate to see these two characteristics as two aspects present in both periods, but with different proportions and emphases. The contemplative attitude expresses the idea of nature as a gift. Nature is given to us, and Christians believe that it is given to us by God. Descartes, Bacon, Galileo, Kepler and Newton believed this to the same extent as Alan of Lille and other mediaeval authors did.[5]

An idea of determination and unsurpassable limit is intimately related to the idea of nature. The magic writers of the Renaissance, who stressed an infinite internal freedom of nature, the freedom from any constraint, constituted the only exception to this understanding. No deterministic laws were allowed to exist in the magical worldview. For nature everything was possible, even the most improbable and 'unnatural' results (Koyré 1971, 83). In this perspective the modern notion of nature is much more similar to that advocated by the mediaeval Christian writers and some Renaissance astrologers, such as Pomponazzi. The latter preached under Arabic influence the absolute determination of world processes and human events. They all are written by God in stars and signs as an inexorable law of nature. No one could escape it (Stabile 1984, 461). This way of understanding nature would become damaging for the future free development of modern science. For a long time ecclesiastical hierarchy and theologians became extremely suspicious when hearing scientists speaking about the deterministic laws of nature. However, the distinction made in modern philosophy between the deterministic laws of nature and the free moral natural law permitted the consensus.

Today we can use nature on a much larger scale than centuries ago, but we still have to accept the laws of nature as the limit of our operating in the world. We can overcome the gravitation on earth but we cannot annul the law of gravitation. We can change and manipulate human genes, but we are still bound by physical and chemical laws. We can use technology at large but we cannot avoid some laws governing the environmental equilibrium, unless we accept the destruction of our 'natural' environment. Many scientists speak of reality being a hard 'partner' in the scientific 'dialogue' with nature.

Scientists must be humble in approaching the universe. They are not creating, but discovering. Technology as an act of creation is only a metaphor with a very restricted meaning. Mastering the laws of nature means only knowing them, more or less, in order to use them for our own, human, purposes. We can create many things, which do not exist in the 'natural' world, but only by following the laws of nature. From this point of view, technology is only taking advantage of the many possibilities given to us by nature and discovered by science. The magic ideal of man being able to create anything is nothing but a pure fantasy. Speaking of genetic manipulations as creation activity and man being a 'creator' playing God is equally only a metaphor. It is true that for centuries everyone believed that God created the natural genera and they had to be respected as they are. Today we know that natural genera were not created directly by God but they are the result, quite fortuitous, of the evolutionary processes. Contemporary humans can use the laws governing these processes, the laws of nature, to reach their own purposes in the same way as they can use the law of gravitation or the law of electricity. The only difference is that the amount of ignorance about future effects is much higher, and this seems to open some very fearful perspectives for humans.

If it is true that the contemplative attitude is something essential in our approach to nature, it is also true that the technological, operative attitude is also essential to this approach. When we speak of the Middle Ages we should not forget the technological achievements, very important for the improvement of human life, that were made at that time. As Bertrand Gille (1963, 173) puts it: 'It was certainly in the sphere of mechanization, however primitive, that the inventive spirit of the Middle Ages found an outlet. The water mill offers the most striking example of this.' Other examples are the windmill, the screw jack and other hoisting devices, the first clockwork mechanisms and many military machines. Looking back at human history we can say, without doubt, that human culture since its very beginning is an attempt to master and use nature for our human purposes. What is really changing over the epochs is only the level of this mastery and of human capabilities. In this sense technology makes humans a kind of co-creator. Humans, thanks to their knowledge of nature, can interact and cooperate with it to produce new devices and effects, otherwise non-existent and remaining only a pure possibility. In this sense humans are also co-creators of themselves, of this part of themselves, which belongs to nature. Techno sapiens are a product of evolution and not of the revolution of human capabilities and resources.

Conclusion: technology and science need philosophy

One problem remains. With the conference question title 'Creating techno s@piens?' the organizers had only expressed the fears that are commonly experienced in today's world. These fears are about the possible and unknown effects of the use and abuse of our technical capabilities. Are there any moral limits of using technology? Should everything we can do be permitted? The ecological protests and movements and anti-nuclear demonstrations show that many humans would like to impose limits on technological developments in order to defend in the world something transcending or going beyond its purely empirical dimension. This something can be called value or nature of human life, of the person and of the world itself. Again, as in the Middle Ages, nature and human nature hold for us a moral dimension. However, the reason for this fact is different. We are aware today that these values can easily be destroyed. If we are to preserve them, because we think that they are an important good, we have to become responsible in using our technological resources.

This discourse, however, goes beyond the scientific discourse. We are back to the metaphysical and moral notion of the nature of things and the notion of good. This is a philosophical debate, which should not be avoided. This is the only way for human beings to reach a consensus. Probably questions and problems like these were present in the history of humanity since humans started to interact with nature and create culture and technology. Technology, being part of 'human nature', challenges our self-understanding and our responsibility at all times. As such it is an important starting point for philosophizing about the core values related to human identity or nature. Theology has an important part in this discussion. I do not want to enter the contemporary discussion about the understanding of the natural law in moral theology. That topic is too large and too complicated for this paper. However, theology should not forget that the technological cooperation with nature is an inherent feature of human beings and it should take into account the changing self-understanding of man itself. Maybe the language of natural law is not good enough to enter a dialogue with modern humans. Science and technology on their part cannot be performed outside this fundamental philosophical perspective, as in a value-free vacuum, and must also be able to enter this discussion if they want to remain human science and human technology.

Notes

1 The notion of the 'law of nature' as describing the empirically determined regularity was introduced only later in the seventeenth century (Milton 1981, 182), but the idea of the God-given law or rule ordaining the world was quite familiar even to the twelfth-century writers: William of Conches, Thierry of Chartres. For example, Thierry is writing of God's Logos as a 'lex and existendi eterna regula (law and eternal rule of existence [of things])' (1971, 574 n. 45) in which Anima Mundi and all forms and natures of things partake. William of Conches, in his *Glossae in Boethium* (1938, 128), speaks of nature as an instrument of God to produce order in

the world: 'ea dicuntur opera nature que a Deo fiunt natura subserviente (these are told to be the work of nature which are created by God by means of the subservient nature)'. Thomas Aquinas mentions only the natural law as a rational participation of man in the eternal law of God. However, he says, the whole world and all irrational things in it partake somewhat in the eternal law, although only by way of similitude: 'it is evident that all things partake somewhat in the eternal law insofar as, namely, from its being imprinted on them, they derive their respective inclinations to their proper acts and ends', these inclinations being natural: 'under divine lawgiver, various creatures have various natural inclinations' (Aquinas 1988, 20.27.41: ST I–II, q. 90, aa. 2 and 6; q. 93, a. 5).

2 Thomas Aquinas (1988, 11–55) discusses at length the relationship between God's eternal law and the nature of things in terms of impression and participation. According to him 'law denotes a kind of plan directing acts toward an end'. By means of the eternal law or Providence, God is governing the whole world toward its end. The irrational beings are simply obeying it, but in human beings the natural inclination to virtue is corrupted by vicious habits, and the natural knowledge of good is darkened by passions and habits of sin (1998, 37, 43).

3 On this topic see: Stabile 1984; Koyré 1971; Liana 2001.

4 John Brooke (1991, 67) quotes a text of Martin Luther praising the science of alchemy 'for the sake of the allegory and secret signification, which is exceedingly fine, touching the resurrection of the dead at the last day'.

5 For example, Johannes Kepler wrote to Herwart in one of his letters (April 9–10, 1599): 'To God there are, in the whole material world, material laws, figures and relations of special excellency . . . Those laws are within the grasp of the human mind; God wanted us to recognize them by creating us after his own image so that we could share in his own thoughts' (Baumgart 1952, 50); see also Descartes (1993, 36.92–3); Bacon (1889, CXXIV); Zilsel (1942, 260–9).

References

Alan of Lille

1978 *De planctu naturae*, in N. M. Häring (ed.), *Studi Medievali* 19, f. 2, 796–879.

Aquinas, Thomas, Saint

1988 *On Law, Morality, and Politics* (ed. R. J. Regan and W. P. Baumgarth; Indianapolis: Hackett Publishing Co.).

Bacon, Francis.

1889 *Bacon's Novum Organum* (ed. Th. Fowler; Oxford: Clarendon Press, 2nd edn).

Baumgardt, Carola

1952 *Johannes Kepler: Life and Letters* (London: V. Gollancz).

Brooke, John H.

1991 *Science and Religion: Some Historical Perspectives* (Cambridge: Cambridge University Press).

Descartes, René

1993 *Discourse on Method; and Meditations on First Philosophy* (trans. D. A. Cress; Indianapolis: Hackett Publishing Co. 3rd edn).

Gille, Bertrand

1963 'Technological Developments in Europe: 1100 to 1400', in G. S. Métraux and F. Crouzet (eds.), *The Evolution of Science: Readings from the History of Mankind* (New American Library; New York: Mentor Books), 168–219.

Gregory, Tullio

1955 *Anima mundi. La filosofia di Guglielmo di Conches e la scuola di Chartres* (Pubblicazioni dell'Istituto di Filosofia dell'Università di Roma, 3: Firenze: G. C. Sansoni Editore).

1984 'Natur II. Frühes Mittelalter', in *Historisches Wörterbuch der Philosophischen Begriffen*, vol. VI (Basel and Stuttgart: Schwabe & Co. Verlag), 441–7.

Herschel, John F. W.

1830 *A Preliminary Discourse on the Study of Natural Philosophy* (London: Longman).

Koyré, Alexandre

1971 'Paracelse', in A. Koyré, *Mystiques, spirituels, alchimistes du XVIe siècle allemand* (Paris: Gallimard, 1971), 75–129.

Liana, Zbigniew

1996 *Koncepcja Logosu i natury w szkole w Chartres* [The Notion of Logos and Nature in the School of Chartres] (Kraków: BMR).

2001 'Okultyzm a nauka w okresie przedoswieceniowym' [The Occult and Sciences in the Pre-Enlightenment Period], in M. Heller, Z. Liana, J. Maczka and W. Skoczny (eds.), *Nauki przyrodnicze a teologia: konflikt i wspólistnienie* [Science and Theology: Conflict and Coexistence] (Kraków and Tarnów: OBI-Biblos), 169–298.

Milton, John R.

1981 'The Origin and Development of the Concept of the "Laws of Nature" ', *Archives Européennes de Sociologie* 22.2: 173–95.

Stabile, Giorgio

1984 'Natur. Humanismus und Renaissance', in *Historisches Wörterbuch der Philosophischen Begriffen*, vol. VI (Basel and Stuttgart: Schwabe & Co. Verlag), 455–68.

Thierry of Chartres

1971 *Tractatus de sex dierum operibus*, in N. M. Häring (ed.), *Commentaries on Boethius by Thierry of Chartres and his School* (Studies and Texts, 20; Toronto: Pontifical Institute of Mediaeval Studies), 553–75.

William of Conches

1938 *Les Glosses de Guillaume de Conches sur la Consolation de Boèce*, in

J. M. Parent (ed.), *La doctrine de la Création dans l'école de Chartres* (Paris: Institut d'Etudes Medievales; Ottawa: Vrin), 124–36.

Zilsel, Edgar

1942 'The Genesis of the Concept of Physical Law', *Philosophical Review* 51.3 (303): 245–79.

4

Co-*creator* or *co*-creator?

The problem with artificial intelligence

Noreen Herzfeld

There are two very different projections current in our society regarding the possible future of artificial intelligence. Bill Joy, chief scientist at Sun Microsystems, warns that self-replicating robots could result, as soon as 2030, in the demise of the human species (2000). Hans Moravec, of the artificial intelligence (AI) lab at Carnegie Mellon, Pennsylvania, states that, 'by performing better and cheaper, the robots will displace humans from essential roles. Rather quickly, they could displace us from existence' (1998, 3). On the other hand, Manuela Veloso, also of Carnegie Mellon, envisions household robots that could provide companionship as well as service, and designs teams of robots that she hopes will soon face human teams on the soccer field. In science fiction we see similar scenarios. The *Terminator* series envisions computers that seek to replace humanity while the *Star Wars* series depicted lovable robots working in harmony with us. While the fulfilment of either of these visions lies in a future likely far more distant than 2030, which is more compelling?[1] Will intelligent machines replace us or coexist with us? Should we treat them as equals or as tools? Is AI all about doing work or about robots who can be our friends?

Philip Hefner describes human beings as 'created co-creators' with God. Hefner emphasizes the creator aspect of co-creator, viewing human beings in terms of agency, as actors who bring about the will of God in the realm of the natural world. Hefner writes: 'Human beings are God's created co-creators whose purpose is to be the agency, acting in freedom, to birth the future that is most wholesome for the nature that has birthed us' (1993, 27). Humans are not God's equals, but work with and for God in the world. The relationship between human beings and any artificial intelligence we might create can be viewed, analogously, as a relationship of creator and created co-creator, with each possessing agency in the material world to various degrees. What, then, if anything, distinguishes the computerized co-creator from the human? If computers come to possess the ability to execute most tasks as well or better than human beings, why should they not replace us as God's agents in the material realm; in other words, why should not they become God's co-creators, allowing the process to skip the human middlemen? Are Moravec and Joy right in suggesting that the future might have no role for human beings? I propose that we might find reason to be less fearful of replacement if we put the emphasis on the 'co' of co-creator, rather than on the agency implied by 'creator'. Human beings are relational creatures, living always in a context that is both material and social. A focus on the relationality of our human nature allows for the possibility of sharing the task of agency in this world, both with God and with our own creation, the computer, while retaining our unique position as human beings.

Two models of the *imago Dei* and AI

The goal of artificial intelligence is to create an 'other' in our own image. The part of our image we wish to duplicate we label as intelligence, thus we must determine just what it is in ourselves that computers must possess or demonstrate to be considered intelligent. That a being wholly other to human beings might share some important aspect with humanity is not a question new to the computer age, however. This question is central to the theological concept of the *imago Dei*, or image of God, in which, according to Genesis 1, human beings were created. Interpretations of the *imago Dei* have varied, yet most can be categorized in one of three ways: substantive interpretations view the image as an individually held property that is a part of our nature, most often associated with reason; functional interpretations find the image of God in agency, specifically our exercise of dominion over the earth; relational interpretations locate God's image within the relationships we establish and maintain.[2] Approaches to developing an artificial intelligence have followed similar lines, looking first for intelligence as the property of an isolated machine, but more recently moving toward intelligence as demonstrated in either action or relationship. This similarity is not a surprise. It is the human that stands in the centre looking out toward both God and computer; the questions of what we share with God and what we might share with an artificial intelligence are both rooted in an examination of our own human nature. Two approaches toward understanding the *imago Dei* are currently in the ascendancy, the functional and the relational. I will examine which of these might provide the best model for understanding ourselves as co-creators, both with God and with an artificial intelligence.

Function: emphasizing the creator in co-creator

Early understandings of the *imago Dei* were generally substantive. Such interpretations had the drawback of being both dualistic and static. A more promising approach was introduced by Johannes Hehn, who suggests that the image of God be understood as a royal title or designation rather than an attribute of human nature (1915, 36–52). Old Testament scholar Gerhard von Rad was one of several who extended Hehn's work into a dynamic, functional approach to the *imago Dei*, one that locates the image not in a quality we possess, but in our agency or activity. In his commentary on Genesis, von Rad argues for our creation 'as the image of God' rather than the usual 'in the image of God' (1961, 56). Von Rad writes: 'Just as powerful earthly kings, to indicate their claim to dominion, erect an image of themselves in the provinces of their empire where they do not personally appear, so man is placed upon earth in God's image, as God's sovereign emblem. He is really only God's representative, summoned to maintain and enforce God's claim to dominion over the earth' (1961, 58). This approach has come to dominate the field of biblical exegesis and fits well with Hefner's understanding of human beings as created co-creators whose purpose is to exercise agency in the natural world. We are God's hands, effecting the transformation of the material world – co-creators, with emphasis on creator.

A similar shift from a substantive to a functional definition occurred in the field of AI in the 1980s. The attempt to capture and mimic human intelligence through symbolic programming methods, though producing some early results in easily modelled fields such as game-playing, failed to produce anything like a general intelligence. However, if we view the computer in functional terms – in its capacity for carrying out tasks previously accomplished by humans – there has been quite a bit of success. Rather than trying to replicate the human process of reasoning, functional AI builds on the strengths inherent in computer technology, exploiting the speed and storage capabilities of the computer while ignoring those parts of human thought that are not understood or easily modelled. A good example of a successful functional program is the chess-playing program, Deep Blue, which defeated the then world champion Gary Kasparov in 1997.[3]

We have functional computers, exercising agency for us in many realms. Moravec's and Joy's fears that computers will displace human beings reflect the negative side of this functional view. Computers have already displaced humans from many roles. There is a much lower demand for factory workers, and office workers have had many of their tasks automated. Computers now assist doctors in diagnosis, play a pretty good hand of bridge, and gather and analyse information on the surface of Mars. However, we tend not to think of these roles as 'essential' once a machine can accomplish them. And here we have a problem. What functions are crucial to intelligence? A definition that includes as artificial intelligence any program that accomplishes some task human beings normally do would encompass virtually all computer applications – indeed, it would include almost all human tools – but it would be ludicrous to consider all tools or all computers to be intelligent. Thus, although a functional definition fits most current programs in AI, it leaves us with the uneasy feeling that something is missing, that intelligence or an image of the human will not be captured in this way. We seem to be more than the sum of our actions. On the other hand, functional AI does give us machines that do many of our daily tasks for us. While these machines may not exhibit total human-like intelligence, they do act in our stead, in places where human beings are not personally present, such as the surface of Mars, and in places where human beings used to be present, such as the factory floor.

Relationship as image: emphasizing the co in co-creator

Another approach is to consider being in relationship as that which we share with God and hope to share with intelligent computers. Here we place the emphasis on the co of co-creator, perceiving that our agency is effective only in partnership with God.[4] One of the most influential proponents of a relational interpretation of the *imago Dei* is Karl Barth. According to Barth, the image of God is identified with the fact that the human being is a counterpart to God (1958, 184–5).[5] Like the functionalists, Barth roots his argument in textual exegesis, focusing, however, on two very different portions of the Genesis text: 'Let us make man in our image' (Gen. 1:26) and 'male and female he created them' (1:27). Barth interprets the plural in 'Let us make man' as referring, not to a heavenly court, but to the Triune nature of God, one who contains both an 'I' that can issue a call and a 'Thou' capable of response (1958, 182). For Barth, this I–Thou confrontation, as a part of God's nature, forms the ground of human creation, rooting human nature in relationship as well. The image is in relationship itself, not the capacity for relationship. Thus the image of God can only be evidenced corporately. It exists first in our relationship to God and secondarily in our relationships with each other. Barth finds further evidence for this interpretation in the person of Jesus, in whom he sees human nature as it was intended to be (1958, 88–9). What Barth sees as significant about Jesus is his relationship with God and with other humans. Barth notes: 'If we see Him alone, we do not see Him at all. If we see him, we see with and around Him in ever widening circles His disciples, the people, His enemies, and the countless multitudes who never have heard His name. We see Him as theirs, determined by them and for them, belonging to each and every one of them' (1958, 216).

Barth suggests that it matters not so much what a human does, but that we exist in a web of relationship.

A relational approach has been posited for AI as well. The difficulty of defining what functions are crucial to intelligence was recognized by the British mathematician Alan Turing, shortly after the advent of the digital computer, in his landmark paper 'Computing Machinery and Intelligence', first published in 1950. Turing addresses this question with a proposal for a test in which an interrogator is connected by terminal to two subjects, one a human, the other a machine. If the interrogator fails as often as she succeeds in determining which was the human, and which the machine, the machine could be considered as having intelligence (1997, 29–32).[6] The Turing Test remains the most widely accepted way of describing how we might recognize an intelligent computer. It defines intelligence, not on the completion of any particular task, but on the machine's ability to relate to a human being in conversation.

Hefner points out the importance of culture as the locus of human learning and conditioning (1993, chs 9–12). Relationship is probably also the most expedient way for computers to acquire knowledge. Turing estimates that the programming of background knowledge needed for a restricted form of the game would take a minimum of 300 person-years to complete, assuming that we could identify the appropriate knowledge set at the outset. Rather than trying to imitate an adult mind, it might be easier to construct a mind like that of a child, a mind that is able to learn and develop (Turing 1997, 51–2). The Social Interaction Group in the AI lab at MIT is moving in this direction. The lab has constructed the much-publicized robots Cog and Kismet. These robots represent a new direction in AI in both their design and in the emphasis on social interaction with a team of researchers as a mode of programming. This project is much too new to assess at this point and may well prove no more successful than any previous work in AI in producing a machine able to interact with humans on the level of the Turing Test. Other research groups, such as the robotics lab at Carnegie Mellon, are working on communication among teams of robots, hoping to instil a level of relationality that would allow robots to work effectively in groups. The field of artificial intelligence, while showing only limited success thus far in the relational arena, is definitely moving toward the exploration of Turing's opinion that intelligence is both socially acquired and demonstrated. Any success in these projects would show that the 'co' is a necessary part of 'created co-creator'. If intelligence is relational no entity can function alone, but always needs others from which to learn and with which to act.

Agency or relationship?

Functional AI is a success; relational AI is speculative, a new movement in the field. So should the emphasis, for understanding either humans or AI, be on 'co' or on 'creator'? Contemporary Western society strongly supports a functional approach, in which both our tools and our very selves are defined by what we do or are capable of doing.[7] Within this approach we already have successful AI in machines and programs that do some task. Such functionality is easy to measure and produces results that contribute to our quality of life. However, emphasis on agency works best in the abstract. No particular program has been hailed as possessing intelligence.

Function is also a very risky category when applied to particular persons. The lens of agency, a definition of human beings as 'God's created co-creators whose purpose is to be the agency, acting in freedom, to birth the future', makes it all too easy to denigrate members of the human family who lack either the abilities or the power to use their abilities to effect change in the world (Hefner 1993, 27). My father suffers from Parkinson's disease. His capacity for agency is entirely diminished. Did he image God in the past but ceases to do so now? Is the homeless woman on the street less a person in God's image because she does not contribute to the creation of either material wealth or the meanings of culture? Is the third-world refugee less of a co-creator with God because she lacks the means to effect change in the world? Is the helpless infant only potentially in the image of God? Instinctively, we answer these questions with a resounding 'No!'

We also find the roots of our fears of being replaced by machines in a functional paradigm that emphasizes agency. If dominion on earth, as measured by the completion of tasks, is the centre of our being, Joy and Moravec may be right to warn us of the future. Machines will do much of our work for us. That they can, however, is not saying that they should. Ultimately, how we deal with the rest of the created world is our responsibility, in cooperation with God, and we must not deny that responsibility by passing it on to our own non-human creation. This becomes more difficult as we rely on technology that is increasingly complex. How many of us have not been told that an error in our credit card or bank transactions was 'made by the computer', or found an airline agent or shop clerk totally helpless because 'the computer is down'? As we depend more and more on technology, we risk losing the skills that allow us to make decisions without that technology. We are well reminded that it is a created *co*-creator we seek in the computer, not a created creator.

Computer technology may never move beyond functionality. Indeed, we may decide we do not wish it to move beyond functionality, because a relational computer that does all we ask of it carries overtones of slavery and dominion. On the other hand, just as functionality is an unsatisfying definition of the human person in the image of God, it is an equally unsatisfying definition of artificial intelligence as being in the image of humanity. Until computers move beyond the functional, we will not consider them as intelligent, as a complete image of ourselves, nor as a true co-creator. However, a relational understanding of our creation, while more satisfactory, has its own pitfalls. Just as Barth reminds us of the complete otherness of God, in whose image we are, we must always be aware of the complete otherness of any artificial intelligence. Just as God's ways are not our ways, we must be prepared for difference in the thinking, action and, ultimately, values of an artificial intelligence that does not share in the biological aspects of humanity, in our aging, death and decay. Computers may some day be relational enough to be considered our co-creators. But we must also resist the temptation to replace relationship with God or with other humans by relationship with our own creation. Such relationships might be less demanding but it is precisely in the demands we place on one another, in the difficult parts of human relationships, that we are called to grow.

Notes

1 AI has never lived up to the optimistic visions of either scientists or science-fiction writers.

2 Some have looked for the *imago Dei* in a quality of the human being, such as our physical form (Gunkel), the ability to stand upright (Koehler), our rationality or intellect (Aquinas), our personality (Procksch), or our capacity for self-transcendence (Niebuhr). Others have thought of God's image as dynamic, rooted in human actions such as our dominion over the animals (Caspari, von Rad). A third approach defines the image as emergent in the interrelationship of two beings (Barth, Brunner). See Westermann (1984, 147–8) for a summary.

3 Deep Blue does not attempt to mimic the thought of a human chess player but capitalizes on the strengths of the computer by examining more than 200 million moves per second, giving it the ability to look 14 moves ahead. Deep Blue does not use intuition, and to know anything of its opponent's style it must be reprogrammed for each opponent.

4 Indeed, Genesis 4–10 shows how disastrous it can be for humans to try to go it alone.

5 Barth lists and denies the variety of substantive and functional interpretations in vogue at his time: 'The fact that I am born and die; that I act and drink and sleep; that I develop and maintain myself; that beyond this I assert myself in the face of others, and even physically propagate my sperm; that I enjoy and work and play and fashion and possess; that I acquire and have and exercise powers; that I take part in all the work of the race; and that in it all I fulfill my aptitudes as an understanding and thinking, willing and feeling being – all this is not my humanity' (1958, 249).

6 Turing predicted that computers would pass this test by the year 2000. This, like most predictions in AI, was overly optimistic. No computer has yet come close to passing the Turing Test.

7 How often the first question asked on meeting someone is 'What do you do?'

References

Barth, Karl

1958 *Church Dogmatics*, vol. III, part 2 (ed. G. W. Bromiley and T. F. Torrance; trans. J. W. Edwards, O. Bussey, Harold Knight; Edinburgh: T&T Clark).

Hefner, Philip

1993 *The Human Factor: Evolution, Culture, and Religion* (Minneapolis, MN: Fortress).

Hehn, Johannes

1915 'Zum Terminus "Bild Gottes" ', in Gotthold Weil, *Festschrift Eduard Sachau zum siebzigsten Geburtstag* (Berlin: G. Reimer), 36–52.

Joy, Bill

2000 'Why the Future Doesn't Need Us', *Wired* (April), www.wired.com

Moravec, Hans

1998 *Robot: Mere Machine to Transcendent Mind* (Oxford: Oxford University Press).

Turing, Alan

1997 [1950] 'Computing Machinery and Intelligence', in John Haugeland (ed.), *Mind Design II: Philosophy, Psychology, Artificial Intelligence* (Cambridge: MIT Press), 29–56.

Von Rad, Gerhard

1961 *Genesis: A Commentary* (trans. John H. Marks; Old Testament Library; Philadelphia: Westminster Press).

Westermann, Claus

1984 *Genesis 1–11: A Commentary* (trans. John Scullion, Minneapolis; Augsburg Press).

5

From thou to IT: information technology from the perspective of the language philosophy of Rosenzweig and Rosenstock-Huessy

Otto Kroesen

Information technology and living speech

Information technology is conquering the world. Internet, communication by email and all kinds of data traffic constitute not only a climax of technological development, they also constitute the backbone of the global economy. By means of the zeroes and ones of computer language, IT is making all the different cultural groups, professional groups, classes and castes, tribes and consumer societies compatible with one another. The question, however, is whether the exchange of information can produce more than superficial communication. Can it also bring the representatives of different human cultures and religions into each other's moral neighbourhood?

This contribution contends that information technology in itself does not lead to mutual understanding. Rather, it is mutual understanding, the correlation of people facing one another, that leads to new technology. Information technology is therefore to be considered as the result of human communication. To summarize this contention: communication leads to information.

The development of technology thus goes through the full cycle of speech that is described by the 'grammatical method'.

The grammatical method

If indeed communication leads to information and thus to technology, then our present world needs the challenge of and dialogue between the representatives of the different cultures and religions of this planet. That same need was felt by two Jewish friends in the crisis at the beginning of the twentieth century. When, during and after World War I, the two friends Rosenstock-Huessy and Rosenzweig discovered for the first time the meaning of living speech, they developed what Rosenstock-Huessy later called the 'grammatical method'. It is significant that this new method, which describes the living process of human speech, was not discovered behind the desk of individual scientists but in the process of living speech itself.[1] This might be paradigmatic for the type of planetary communication that religions and cultures have to embark on.

Traditional philosophy still operates with a set of oppositions: subject as opposed to object, symbol opposed to number, means to goals, meaningful existence to anonymous systems. Thanks to this set of binary oppositions it becomes impossible to bridge the gaps. It is here – remarkable as it may seem – that the language philosophy of Rosenzweig and Rosenstock-Huessy proves helpful, because here for the first time the philosophy of human speech offers a thorough alternative for the binary oppositions that both philosophy and theology inherited from Descartes (Rosenstock-Huessy 1970, 1–19). Both Rosenzweig and Rosenstock-Huessy perceive the world and human society as constantly renewed by the dialogue between challenge and response, need and solution, God and man. The historical process of human speech dynamizes the static opposition between subject and object. In the tension between past and future time, again a new language is created, which serves to articulate common experience in response to the challenges of the future. The universe does not consist only of the two poles of subject and object, but also of the two other poles of past and future, and thereby the unity of the human subject is restored.

Both Rosenstock-Huessy and Rosenzweig drew upon a specific tradition of speech in formulating their conception of language. Central to Rosenzweig is his experience of being part of the Jewish community, which as it were realizes salvation in its internal community life, in its feasts and in its moral awareness. Central to Rosenstock-Huessy is his being part of the history of the Church in which time and again the Christian soul conquers new terrain, creates new institutions and new types of man. In other words, where Rosenzweig concentrates on the central event of language, which is the revelation of love, Rosenstock-Huessy concentrates on ever-new modulations of human speech and human existence as an act of faith, the confidence to enter upon a new and unknown future.

Their philosophies of language are in dialectical opposition to one another, as expressed by the titles of their main works: *Star of Redemption* and *Cross of Reality*.[2] For both friends, however, more important than their differences was their common opposition to the German idealist philosophy of the nineteenth century, which they considered to be a form of 'pagan' philosophy. In *The Star of Redemption* Rosenzweig expresses a conception of paganism as the human attempt to come to grips with the surrounding universe exclusively by means of thought and logic. In such a universe, thought can construct reality in any imaginable way. There is no fixed point of reference, no authority, no orientation (Rosenzweig 1976 [1921], 91–9). Everything may as well be true and untrue.

A similar thing happens in the creation and construction of technology. Just as the construction of meaning in language, the construction of technology is like swimming in an ocean. One research group may invent a new type of asphalt; another group may invent a machine to cut onions into pieces; yet another group may develop a new television screen. It is not only the interpretation of language that seems to be affected by postmodernism; technological development makes a postmodern impression as well. There is no common language to provide orientation. When no common terms are established, the only thing that remains is the ability to speak to one another, to try to create a common interpretation of reality by facing one another. This is the process the 'grammatical method' tries to describe.

In what kinds of situations does living speech originate? When do we really need to speak? Apparently this is always the case in situations of crisis and conflict (Rosenstock-Huessy 1981, 9).[3] When disaster comes upon human beings and when war is waged, then human beings need to speak. But at that very moment first we cannot speak. A new problem puts stress upon us, and no solution, and therefore no words, no names can serve as yet to reach a common understanding. In such a situation the first priority is to find the right name, the new name, which may articulate the present predicament. The articulation of a new name, which functions as a new imperative, is therefore the starting point of living speech. The answer is not yet found, but the item is on the agenda. It is named.

Since the meaning of the new name still has to be found, different answers are tried. In this second phase of speech there is opposition as well as dialogue between the different parties and participants. The word 'party' expresses exactly what is happening: everybody is capturing part of the truth. Everybody tries and wishes for a solution. The present, therefore, is not the present of the indicative, it is the present of the subjunctive.[4] The indicative 'indicates' states of affairs, but the subjunctive contains a longing. In the imperative the 'more than human' is bearing upon us; in the subjunctive it is the human being who speaks. People who give their different answers are confronting one another and opening up towards one another; they expose themselves to one another and at the same time they are striving for a new peace, a new community. Every existing community once came into being thanks to this process of answering to a common call. No community is just 'natural'.

When an issue is settled, when the different parties find 'speaking terms', a solution is found. Now the process of opposition and dialogue is more or less coming to an end. We know how the problem, the imperative that started the whole process, should be handled. 'We!' The parties belonging to this 'we' may still bear the scars of their conflicts, but in the end they have found new practices, a new code of existence that from now on is their common heritage. Let us, for example, look at the French Revolution and the way it tried among other things to instil a more rational way of measuring (Rosenstock-Huessy 1993 [1938], 201). The inch, foot and yard – measurement standards derived from the human body – were in need of replacement with more rational standards. The centimetre, metre and all the other features of the decimal system derived from the globe of the earth. It was primarily England, proud of its traditions, that showed intense resistance to this new method. But even England could not escape the necessity of standardizing measurement yardsticks that imposed itself thanks to the progress and the progressive application of science and technology.

The grammatical form of the imperative is an articulation of the future that imposes itself as urgent on the present. The subjunctive articulates the present, in which new solutions are tried. And the form of the verb, which articulates the past in which a common solution has been found, is the participle. When the issue is 'settled', when new terms are 'speaking', the huge problem that started the whole process of language is reduced to a technical question, a 'technicality'. Settling the issue by creating a common past is the third phase of speech.

Once we know how to handle the issue, what remains is implementation. Even on this level many problems need to be solved. But these are no longer problems between man and man, but between man and nature. At this stage in the language process we are confronted with problems related to the world outside. We need to create institutions; we need to create the material infrastructure for the whole fabric of human intercourse in order to make nature serve man. At this stage 'dead' matter is renewed and again made part of living processes (Rosenstock-Huessy 1963, 178).[5] This metaphor provides us with a nice definition of technology.

In this fourth phase the indicative is the predominant grammatical form of speech. The indicative indicates states of affairs, facts in the world outside. The world outside entails a whole set of institutions, practices, regulations, social agreements and human qualities, so it is quite appropriate to talk about technological regimes, which represent the prevailing paradigms of the relationship between human beings and the surrounding material and institutional world (van de Poel 1998, 12). Since technology is more effective if applied on a large scale, it is evident that effective technology cannot do without human agreement, common understanding and procedures. The ecological problems of our present world as well as the poverty that still plagues one-third of the world population are not primarily technological problems. Basically what is lacking is the establishment of human agreement on the way to handle the problems. The people involved have not gone through the full cycle of speech. There is too much application with lack of orientation.[6]

Information technology

Information technology has become the most influential technology of the twentieth century. Is that only coincidence? A matter of fortune and contingency? No, it isn't. It is the end result of a long historical development in which large parts of humanity, foremost in Europe and America, increasingly found a form of agreement and common understanding, in which technology in general and information technology as a climax could find its way and flourish.

Information technology is the result of a deep conviction that Rosenstock-Huessy dates back even to the cloister of Cluny and the days in which the feast of all souls was installed (Rosenstock-Huessy 1989 [1931], 122). The feast of All Souls, the day after the feast of All Saints, marks a new view on reality. It says that salvation is no longer a matter of heaven only, but it is also about changing our earthly existence. From now on redeemed man should partake in salvation by establishing and ordering justice in this world. This imperative lasted a thousand years. Its inspiration runs through all Western history, from the moment the Church formulated civil law thanks to the law book of Gratian in the Middle Ages, via the aspiration of natural scientists to discover the laws of nature (Toulmin 1993, 69) until the Russian Revolution with its aim to have technology satisfy all the needs of mass society.

The famous theologian and philosopher Pascal tried to invent a calculation machine. On the one hand he emphasized the grace of God over against human selfishness. On the other hand if God then showed himself to be merciful, human beings should be served, helped and sustained in their concrete material existence. The need for information automation was felt in those areas where a massive amount of data had to be processed. Accounts of computer history emphasize that the need for this calculation device was felt both in military industry and in those institutions that had to coordinate and fulfil the needs of mass society (Mowshowitz 1989 [1976], 40, 43).

The participation of every human being on the globe in the emerging world society and the introduction and the development of information technology are bound together. In a sense, the computerization of society has become the concrete form of Christian universality. When every person counts, no person can refuse also to be counted with. The original inspiration for exchange of information via telephone lines, and so on, from which the Internet originated consisted of the aspiration for scientific progress and its acceleration. The drive to serve mankind is the original inspiration behind the scientific development of the Western world. In antiquity, people would not share their inventions but keep them secret. The longing to serve humankind pushes the self-interest of the scientists involved to the background.

The 'we' of trial and temptation

Rosenzweig starts where Rosenstock-Huessy ends. He begins with the minimum of knowledge about language that philosophy had agreed upon, and he takes care to corroborate every point of his discourse before taking the next step. This means that he starts with the 'indicative', the language of mathematics and logic and also the language of philosophy. His first question is 'What can a logical mind know about God, world and man?' After a long discussion, his conclusion is that the only thing the human mind can do is make an intellectual construction of these three realities, whatever they are. Yet the human mind can do one more important little thing: it establishes the insight that these constructions of God, world and man are only constructions of the mind, so far. They lack reality. 'Reality' is like an infinite small number, approaching zero, but never reached (Rosenzweig 1976 [1921], 23, 96). From where does the human mind have this knowledge?

The human mind does know it, because being human is more than thinking. We were always already there. This 'always already there' represents a life that is already more than thought. There is already some order, some rightness, some kindness, some goodness, even in natural existence. This self-sufficiency and feeling all right and living straightforward is what we could call the 'pagan phase' of human life, that is, the phase of tradition, of repetition (Rosenstock-Huessy 1993 [1938], 219–29).

But this phase is only a preliminary to the second phase, in which a human being receives a calling and destination. When a person receives a calling, is chosen and assigned with a necessary task, then that person is singled out, is loved. Being loved and receiving a commandment is one and the same experience (Rosenzweig 1976 [1921], 197).[7] It is what Rosenstock-

Huessy called the state of receiving an imperative (Rosenstock-Huessy 1963, 759).[8]

A new imperative establishes a new community. Rosenzweig of course stresses the importance of Jewish community life as the decisive human answer to the imperative of the love of God. But he nonetheless leaves room for the Christian answer to this same call, which does not consist of the Jewish answer of 'eternalization', the marginal perpetuation of Jewish community life. Rather, the Christian answer encompasses the conquering of the world part after part, realizing time and again new partial attempts at an answer and recreating the world accordingly (Rosenzweig 1976 [1921], 378–80). The Jewish and the Christian answers represent a dialogue to be continued throughout history.

Now of main importance for us, keeping in mind the debate on information technology and technology in general, is the translation of the imperative heard in the answer given. In other words, the challenge put before us by history, or by God in history, is translated into a new community life, into a new 'we'. Here the word 'trial' is key. In German, Rosenzweig uses the word 'versuchen', which could also be translated as 'temptation', as is used in the prayer: Do not lead us into temptation . . . (Rosenzweig 1976 [1921], 296). The idea behind the use of this word is that every human answer consists of an attempt, a trial and a temptation as well.

Human beings are obliged and challenged to answer the imperative and yet their answer may be wrong. It is wrong if it is not right on time, when it is too early for this answer or when this answer is already out of date. One cannot establish the Kingdom of God all at once. One can only take the next step required. Many victims fall when untimely answers are put into practice, too early or too late. The answer is given too early or too late when people stop listening and speaking with one another. Then an old language, one that does not fit the present situation, is spoken too long and new aspirations are ignored, or a new language is established by revolution too early, without recognizing the heritage of the past (Rosenstock-Huessy 1963, 471–9). The challenge of the moment (1), the answer given (2), the human community that agrees on this solution (3) and the state of affairs in history (4) must come together at the right time to give effectiveness to this one answer.

The (un)timeliness of technology and of IT

It looks as if information technology did come right on time. It was the answer of technology to the emerging mass society of the twentieth and twenty-first centuries. It seems appropriate to call the twentieth century the technological century. In a sense, the somewhat cynical aspiration of the Russian Revolution has become the only language common to all mankind –

the mere fulfilment of human needs with the help of technology and organization or 'electrification and Soviets', as Lenin called it; quoted in Rosenstock-Huessy 1993 [1938], 170.

The language of technology, figures and numbers has become the one and only language that all people of this earth came to agree upon. And since large-scale technology depends on human understanding and agreement for its effectiveness, this agreement has proven to be a tremendous power in changing the face of the earth. The emerging global economy is the result of it. Correctly stated, it is the result not only of technological hardware as such, but even more of the technological mentality of humanity. Whatever country or civilization is involved, whatever critical attitude people may express towards Western affluent nations, the great ambition of every nation and civilization is to have its turn to enter the era of technology and to share in its fruits.

Information technology came right on time because here is a technology that creates the capacity for the organization of mass society. But from another perspective the reverse seems the case. Are we not rushing too quickly into a future that in fact overlooks the one next step that should be taken now? This rush into the future in fact victimizes large numbers of people all over the world, who do not have the power, whether it be production power or purchasing power, to cope with this global field of forces and who become marginalized more and more.

It appears that information technology shares the ambivalence of the entire technological era. The emerging global society cannot do without it and at the same time it has great problems with it. It – IT – is the fulfilment of the European utopia, the European ambition to reorder the world with the help of judiciary and natural laws. A worldwide economy of money and information is realized, but what is lacking is a worldwide economy of human qualities from different times and layers of history (Kroesen 2001, 143–59). Therefore in fact only half of Europe's ambition is fulfilled. Europe has always consisted of a plurality of cultural forms, which came into existence in a series of revolutionary efforts taking place in different countries and at different times. This plurality implies more than coordination alone.

Every European nation has gone through a learning process in which it had to receive and inherit qualities of cultures that it initially did not like, and maybe will not like in the future. Even Italy needs to inherit the qualities of the German civil servant; even England must make room for French individualism and genius and for France's appetite for the new; even Russia has to make room for England's parliamentarism. The fast communication of information technology cannot make redundant the slow communication process involved in the inheritance of different peoples and cultures. In this sense, information technology is not only a fulfilment of the European

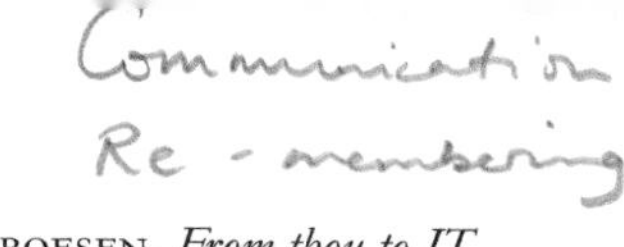

utopia, but also a temptation. Europe cannot escape the need to turn the technological neighbourhood of the global village into a moral neighbourhood as well.

Humanities and technology

Theology as well as philosophy has a long tradition of criticizing technology. The time has come to give technology its due honour for having established a living standard like never before for masses of people, for enabling a global economy that no people on this earth can do without. But it is also clear that the exchange of information cannot replace face-to-face communication between living people in opposition and dialogue, wherein people who start by being different end up finding common terms for their existence. Even in Europe the monetary unity is not sufficient to bring real unity. The European Parliament is the weakest part of the European Community because the peoples of Europe have not yet conceived something like a European citizenship together with a charter of political rights conferred in belonging to it (Ullman 1998, 89–90).

Speech, exchange of meaning, is needed to establish more than economic relationships. The humanities should no longer be proud that they are of no economical use, as if they were some luxurious nonsense. Instead they should emphasize their necessity, even their economical necessity. The 'grammatical method' of Rosenzweig and Rosenstock-Huessy shows that the humanities and the sciences do not constitute two separate spheres of existence in opposition to one another, but that they need one another and are part of the one process of human speech. They together and in their opposition constitute the recreation process in which the word of God (in secular language, the challenge society faces at this moment) echoes in the dialogue of human beings, in commonly accepted solutions and in the speechless (Rosenstock-Huessy 1963, 226) functioning of technology.

Notes

1 At the end of their correspondence during World War I, Rosenzweig asked Rosenstock-Huessy about his views on language. Rosenstock-Huessy answered with a long letter entitled 'Angewandte Seelenkunde', which was later published in *Die Sprache des Menschengeschlechts*. Thereupon Rosenzweig wrote his famous book *Star of Redemption*, which presented his version of the 'grammatical method'. His approach largely drew on the letter from Rosenstock-Huessy. Many years later Rosenstock-Huessy gave final form to his teachings on language in different works of which *Soziologie* and *Die Sprache des Menschengeschlechts* are the most important.

2 Rosenstock-Huessy published the first part of his *Soziologie* in 1956 and the second part in 1958 at Kohlhammer, Stuttgart. The title *Soziologie*, however, was forced

upon him by the publisher, who considered as unacceptable the original title, which read: *Im Kreuz der Wirklichkeit – Eine Nachgoethische Soziologie* (Translation: *The Cross of Reality – A Post-Goethean Sociology*).

3 Rosenstock-Huessy: 'In plunging into the darkness in which man cannot yet speak or no longer does speak to his brother man today, we shall prepare ourselves best for the answer to the questions: what is speech?, how does it originate?, why do we speak?, which of course, are one and the same question in its diverse aspects.' When speech is approached in this way, it suddenly appears that it cannot have originated, for example, as a communication device in hunting. Rosenstock-Huessy suggests that the first layer of language consisted of names used to keep the spirits of the dead alive.

4 The grammatical method of Rosenstock-Huessy and Rosenzweig gives us reason to stop the theological habit of talking about the love of God and God's mercy in terms of the 'indicative'. God's mercy is not a fact in outward reality, and there is no justification for talking about mercy in objectifying terms. Love is a vocative. Being loved is being called upon. God's love and mercy are an imperative by which we are awakened, challenged and authorized.

5 Rosenstock-Huessy: 'Technik ist Abfallverwertung: rückgliedert die Abfälle, die Werkstoffe zurück ins Leben' (Translation: 'Technology is recycling of waste: bringing the wastes, the materials back into life').

6 The large-scale 'Flood Action Plan' in the nineties of the last century in Bangladesh is a case in point. The plan did not fit with the local situation, and newly built dykes were even damaged because farmers needed the rising water to feed the soil.

7 Rosenzweig: 'Aber das Imperativische Gebot, das unmittelbare, augenblicksentsprungene und im Augenblick seines Entspringen auch schon lautwerdende – denn Lautwerden und Entspringen ist beim Imperativ eins –, das "Liebe mich" des Liebenden, das ist ganz vollkommener Ausdruck, ganze reine Sprache der Liebe' (Translation: 'But the commanding imperative, the immediate, momentous and momentously resounding – the resounding and originating of an imperative is the same process – the "Love me!" of the loving, that is complete and perfect expression, pure speech of love').

8 Rosenstock-Huessy: 'Liebe verwandelt. Sie beschwört und befiehlt. So wird das Du geradezu in der Liebesverwandlung des Imperativs erst entdeckt' (Translation: 'Love transforms. It conjures and orders. Thereby the thou is originally discovered in the transformation by a loving imperative').

References

Kroesen, Otto

2001 'The Empowerment of Floating Identities', in Anton Vedder (ed.), *Ethics and the Internet* (Antwerp: Intersentia).

Mowshowitz, Abbe

1989 [1976] *The Conquest of Will* (Delft: Eburon).

Poel, Ibo van de

1998 *Changing Technologies* (Twente: University Press).

Rosenstock-Huessy, Eugen
1963 *Die Sprache des Menschengeschlechts* (Heidelberg: Verlag Lambert Schneider).
1970 'Farewell to Descartes', in *I Am an Impure Thinker* (Norwich, VT: Argo Books).
1981 *The Origin of Speech* (Norwich, VT: Argo Books).
1989 [1931] *Die Europäischen Revolutionen und der Charakter der Nationen* (Moers: Brendow Verlag).
1993 [1938] *Out of Revolution: Autobiography of Western Man* (Norwich, VT: Argo Books).

Rosenzweig, Franz
1976 [1921] *Der Stern der Erlösung* (Den Haag: Nijhoff).

Toulmin, Stephan
1993 [1990] *Kosmopolis* (Kampen: Kok Agora).

Ullman, Wolfgang
1998 *Geduld liebe Dimut!* (Leipzig: Forum Verlag).

6

Being cyborgs: on creating humanity in a created world of technology

Taede Smedes

Introduction

The word 'cyborg' is a contraction of 'cybernetic organism'. Usually cyborgs are considered as beings that are partly human and partly machine, but it is not always clear how these two parts are exactly related. Often some connotations from science fiction are attached to the concept of 'cyborg'. In this paper I distance myself slightly from these connotations. I use 'cyborg' to denote *the whole that is formed by the human person and the technological extension of that person in whatever form.* This implies, thus, a broader notion of 'cyborg'. It is my point in this paper to argue that cyborgs are not creatures that inhabit the imaginary space of science fiction, but that we are in a sense all cyborgs. Being cyborgs is what makes us human. This has, of course, philosophical and theological implications.

The structure of the paper is as follows. First I will give a short historico-philosophical description of how the modernist paradigm came to be and what it entails for thinking about the relation between mind and nature. I argue that the modernist paradigm gave rise to a severe 'digitalization' of our worldview, and especially of the relation between humans and (the rest of) nature. Thereafter I indicate how 'postmodern' philosophy and neuroscience are challenging the modernist paradigm. Finally, there are some philosophical and theological reflections on the consequences of the emerging new paradigm. One small note: I do not have the intention of developing a full-blown theory, but I merely give some pointers for further reflection. I do not believe such a full-fledged theory is possible yet, because of the character of the novel approaches in philosophy and neuroscience.

Digitalization of the human person: the modernist paradigm

Roughly speaking, until the late Middle Ages Aristotelian thinking constituted the predominant worldview. In this worldview there was a radical difference between the sub-lunar or terrestrial region, where things are subordinate to incessant change, and the super-lunar or celestial region, the realm of the incorruptible and changeless (cf. Grant 1996, 54–69, 86–126). But besides this difference, the Aristotelian worldview can be characterized as an 'ontotheological synthesis' in which the cosmos was considered intrinsically meaningful. Humanity participated in this meaningfulness (cf. Dupré 1993). As one can read from Dante's *Divine Comedy*, the cosmos also was seen as having a hierarchical structure: a continuum ranging from the realm of change to the realm of the divine and changeless, where the border stones were placed at the lunar sphere. God was transcendent to the world, and as such not part of the physical universe, he was nonetheless part of the cosmos. The word 'cosmos' thus had a different meaning from ours: it denoted more than merely the physical universe, for God transcended the physical universe but was included in the cosmos (Dupré 1993, 17f.). How was the human person considered in this worldview, particularly in relation to the cosmos? The difference between humans and the world was considered one of degree, not of quality. Initially, humans were considered to occupy one level in the continuous hierarchy of the cosmos, but due to the influence of Christian creation theology, in particular due to the idea that humans were created in the 'image of God' (*imago Dei*), the status of humanity became increasingly important. Both the continuity between humans and cosmos as well as the particular status of humanity amidst the rest of creation are expressed in the image of humans as a 'microcosmos' (Dupré 1993, 53, 96f.).

The radical differentiation of humanity from the rest of the cosmos and a connected 'digitalization' of our worldview can be seen to have at least roots in nominalist thinking: under the influence of nominalism some dichotomies in thinking about nature arose, which led, in due time, to a rift between scientific modes of thinking and religious modes. Also, until the rise of nominalism human existence had been seen as an integral and inseparable part of nature, but now humans were seen as distinct subjects, able to scrutinize nature in a detached, neutral or objective way, as 'from the outside' through the faculties of reason. The relation between humanity and nature thus became one of polarization: there was the pole of nature and the pole of humans considered as 'rational animals', and this situation gave rise to questions considering the relation between the two.

The digitalization of nominalism culminated first of all in Descartes' thinking, as he presented the first representational theory of mind: the ideas in our minds are representations of things in the world given through the senses. With Descartes the digitalization continued with a dualism between mind and body, but also of mind and world. This latter dualism was adopted by Immanuel Kant, though he altered its content. For Kant we do not have clear ideas or representations of what the world is like, but the world conforms itself to our perceptions of it, instead of showing how it is in itself. Hence, due to Kant's 'Copernican revolution' another digital dualism was introduced between the Thing-in-itself and the Thing-as-appearance. We humans can only perceive the things as they appear to us, filtered through the cognitive apparatus in our heads. How things are in themselves remains unknowable to us. The upshot of this digitalizing development from Descartes through Kant until present-day philosophy of mind is that it led to the notion that humans are part of the world, in terms of, for example, their physiology and biology, but they are also located conceptually somewhere 'outside' of the world with regard to their cognitive faculties. But now, in the beginning of the twenty-first century, the cognitive sciences slowly start to alter this image of what it is to be human. Somehow we are coming full circle, abandoning the image of the detached, objective observer, and adopting a holistic view of humanity and world.

New possibilities for a 'leaky' mind

Consider a blind person using a long stick to find her way around in the world. How are the person and the stick related? This example[1] can be found in the works of two different though related thinkers. Michael Polanyi uses the example to elucidate the difference between focal awareness and subsidiary awareness. The blind person is only subsidiarily aware of the stick, as her focal awareness is on what the stick touches upon: the stick is used as a tool or a probe (Polanyi 1962, 55f., 58f.). And this 'subsidiary awareness of tools and probes can be regarded now as the act of making them form a part of our own body . . . While we rely on a tool or a probe, these are not handled as external objects . . . We pour ourselves out into them and assimilate them as parts of our own existence. We accept them existentially by dwelling in them' (ibid., 59). Similarly, Maurice Merleau-Ponty writes: 'The blind man's stick has ceased to be an object for him, and is no longer perceived for itself; its point has become an area of sensitivity, extending the scope and active radius of touch, and providing a parallel to sight. In the exploration of things, the length of the stick does not enter expressly as a middle term: the blind man is rather aware of it through the position of objects than of the position of objects through it' (Merleau-Ponty 1962, 143). He concludes then by saying that '[t]o get used to a hat, a car or a stick is to be transplanted into them, or conversely, to incorporate them into the bulk of our own body' (ibid.). Both Polanyi and Merleau-Ponty illustrate what Heidegger called the 'readiness-to-hand' of equipment, which is a characteristic of our everyday life (Heidegger 1962, 102ff.). The point is that even though physically there may still be a demarcation between body and the tool, in using the tool that demarcation does no longer exist: the tool at hand becomes an extension and hence part of the body. This already points us to the possibility that the boundaries between our bodies and the world are fluid, that we are cyborgs-in-principle.

The philosopher Andy Clark has recently pointed to the fascinating though perhaps more speculative possibility of viewing our cognitive apparatus as extended into the world. He writes that '[p]ortions of the external world . . . often function as a kind of extraneural memory store' (Clark 2001a, 141). Examples are cameras to take pictures or record something on film, or the hard disk of a computer to store written articles or pictures. All these devices serve to enhance our own memory which, as we all know by experience, is fallible and highly limited. If we are willing to broaden this perspective, we could say that many technological devices have the task of extending our sensory capabilities, as becomes especially clear when looking at scientific instruments. Take, for instance, the telescope and the microscope: both are able to extend our visual senses. Looking through a telescope or a microscope is using them as an extension of our eye to see what, without them, could not be seen by the naked eye. Often we are even unconscious of this process, as can be illustrated most explicitly by someone looking for his or her glasses while wearing them.

Clark emphasizes that it is not the case that these technologies replace the human cognitive apparatus. It is perhaps more appropriate 'to understand the cognitive role of many of our self-created cognitive technologies . . . as affording *complementary* operations to those that come naturally to biological brains' (Clark 2001a, 142; italics in original). In the process of extending our bodies and minds into the world by using physical objects, the role of language may prove crucial.

> For as soon as we formulate a thought in words (or on paper), it becomes an object for both ourselves and for others. As an object, it is the kind of thing we can have thoughts about. In creating the object, we need have no thoughts about thoughts – but once it is there, the opportunity immediately exists to attend to it as an object in its own right. The process of linguistic formulation thus creates the stable structure to which subsequent thinkings attach . . . The emergence of such second-order cognitive dynamics is plausibly seen as one root of the veritable explosion of varieties of external technologies scaffolding in human cultural evolution. It is because we can think about our own thinking that we can actively structure our world in ways designed to promote, support, and extend our own cognitive achievements (Clark 2001a, 147).

Thus, by using language we are able to think about our thinking and acting, and hence, to refine the instruments and tools used to cope with our world.

As such, by constructing, using and refining instruments which enhance our own bodily abilities, our cognitive apparatus or our mind 'is a leaky organ, forever escaping its "natural" confines and mingling shamelessly with body and with world' (Clark 1997, 53; cf. also Clark 2001b).

It is at this point that the interesting questions start. Where does our body stop and the world begin? One could say it all depends on which aspect one focuses upon. Looking at the brain as a physical organ, it is confined to our skull. However, looking at our cognitive apparatus, it is not so easy anymore to draw clear lines. Our cognitive apparatus is capable of transcending the boundaries of the skull and even our bodies by creating technology that extends the capabilities of our bodies. The boundaries between mind, body and world are fluid. Because we as humans are part of the world, in a sense here we have a case of the universe discovering itself (Barrow 2000). It is clear that this perspective differs significantly from that of the nominalists, Descartes and Kant. Here the digitalization of our worldview vaporizes. And as our technological abilities increase, new vistas of possibility open up. The cyberspace of the Internet might become an increasingly important memory bank. Email already enhances our communicative capabilities. And Artificial Intelligence and robotics might enhance our bodily abilities, especially in their medical applications. As such, it is no longer science fiction but science fact to speak about humans as cyborgs: 'For us humans there is nothing quite so natural as to be bio-technical hybrids: cyborgs of an unassumed stripe. For we benefit from extended cognitive architectures comprising biological and non-biological elements, delicately intertwined' (Clark 2001b, 142).

Philosophical and theological reflections

Philosophical reflections

What are the philosophical consequences of this view of human persons as cyborgs for our worldview? *First of all*, this view suggests some kind of holistic worldview, as mind, body and world are intermingled and cannot easily be detached. *Secondly*, this view also suggests the irreducibility of mind. The relationship of the mind to the brain might be seen, as many neuroscientists confirm, as the mind being an emergent property of the brain, while the mind can also influence the brain in a top-down manner. This relationship of mind and brain already testifies to the interconnectedness of mind, body and world.

Thirdly, such a holism may have serious consequences for the way we assess our actions. Chaos theory and the sciences of self-organizing systems have taught us that small causes may have big, unpredictable consequences. If it is true that the links between mind, body and world are interconnected, then what happens to one element may have critical repercussions for the other elements. Here we may also touch on some of the ethical consequences of such a worldview, for our actions towards the world and other persons within that world may have unforeseen effects. This holds not only for the human species as a whole, but also for individuals. For chaos and complexity support the encouraging as well as threatening view that the actions of individuals might have more effect than is often believed (cf. Zeyer 1997). Thus we need to take the sciences of chaos and self-organizing complex systems very seriously, as they study the interplay between individual elements and the whole of which the elements are a part.

Fourthly, this view of the interconnectedness of mind, body and world has repercussions for epistemological issues such as realism, perspectivism and the like. Traditionally, realism has always been strongly influenced by some kind of representationalism, which as we saw supports the digital dualism between mind and world. In realism the objectivity of the world is strongly emphasized. The other extreme, idealism, denies this objectivism, at least in the Berkeleyan sense. Both realism and idealism in a sense presuppose the digital paradigm of modernism and are themselves products of it. For without the digital paradigm both realism and idealism cannot emerge. But if this dualism no longer is valid, this has repercussions for epistemology. And indeed, both realism and idealism are, I believe, incompatible with the new paradigm of the interconnectedness of mind, body and world, as outlined above. More promising are Wittgenstein's notions of 'seeing as', aspect seeing, and perspectivism, though I am not able to explore these areas further at this point.[2]

Theological reflections

A question that is on the verge of philosophy and theology concerns matters of self and identity: if mind, body and world are not closed compartments, where does our notion of self and personal identity reside? Normally, we consider the self and our identity as closely connected to our bodily boundaries, but if the boundaries between body and world are fluid, where does the self end and the world begin? Theologically, this is closely connected to the idea of the image of God, the *imago Dei*. In the history of Western Christian theology, the notion of *imago Dei* has often been used to emphasize humanity's special place in and apart from the rest of creation. And too often this special place was connected to humanity's cognitive abilities. But if it is true that we are in a sense cyborgs, linking mind, body and world tightly together, then it is no longer possible to see humanity as being apart from the rest of creation. Indeed, as Polanyi stated, we pour ourselves out into the world, we dwell in it. On the other hand, it may be that our cognitive abilities to use and refine objects as tools is something that sets us apart from other closely related animals (cf. Tattersall 2000 [1998], 30–77).[3] But note that this stretches the meaning of 'cognitive'. 'Cognitive' no longer deals solely with our abilities to reason, but becomes a broader notion connected to all our actions. This is a long way from the anthropocentric or even logocentric meanings of the *imago Dei* – though it may yield valuable resources for reinterpretation.

It also works the other way around. Not only does this new view of what it means to be human have repercussions for the doctrine of the *imago Dei*, but also for our image of God. Even though we concede that we talk metaphorically, we talk about God as being personal (at least in the Christian tradition). God's personhood is then closely connected to our view of what it means to be a person. The classical theistic and logocentric notion of a transcendent God is compatible to the older paradigm that humans are somehow set apart from the rest of creation due to their rational abilities. The new paradigm of humanity's extendedness into the world might call for a reinterpretation of the image of God, and prove more compatible with, for example, a panentheistic or trinitarian image of God. And it might be that reinterpreting our image of God might have huge ramifications for the rest of theology. As such, it might be a renewing stimulus for doing theology in an interdisciplinary manner.

Notes

1 Other examples illustrating similar points are easily multiplied: typing, playing an instrument, hammering a nail into a piece of wood, wearing a hat, driving a car, painting, sculpting, and so on.
2 See Mulhall 1990 and Lynch 1998.
3 I do believe the distinction is only relative, for it is known that there are animals that use elements of the natural world as tools. The active improvement of tools, however, may be something that is particularly human, and given with the presence of self-consciousness.

References

Barrow, J. D.
2000 *The Universe that Discovered Itself* (Oxford: Oxford University Press).
Clark, A.
1997 *Being There: Putting Brain, Body, and World Together Again* (Cambridge, MA: The MIT Press).
2001a *Mindware: An Introduction to the Philosophy of Cognitive Science* (New York/Oxford: Oxford University Press).
——

2001b 'Reasons, Robots and the Extended Mind', *Mind and Language* 16: 121–45.

Dupré, L.

1993 *Passage to Modernity: An Essay in the Hermeneutics of Nature and Culture* (New Haven/London: Yale University Press).

Grant, E.

1996 *The Foundations of Modern Science in the Middle Ages: Their Religious, Institutional, and Intellectual Contexts* (Cambridge: Cambridge University Press).

Heidegger, M.

1962 *Being and Time* (Oxford: Blackwell).

Lynch, M. P.

1998 *Truth in Context: An Essay on Pluralism and Objectivity* (Cambridge, MA: The MIT Press).

Merleau-Ponty, M.

1962 *Phenomenology of Perception* (London: Routledge).

Mulhall, S.

1990 *On Being in the World: Wittgenstein and Heidegger on Seeing Aspects* (London/New York: Routledge).

Polanyi, M.

1962 *Personal Knowledge: Towards a Post-Critical Philosophy* (Chicago: The University of Chicago Press).

Tattersall, I.

2000 [1998] *Becoming Human: Evolution and Human Uniqueness* (New York/Oxford: Oxford University Press).

Zeyer, A.

1997 *Die Kühnheit trotzdem ja zu sagen: Warum der Einzelne mehr Macht hat, als wir glauben* (Darmstadt: Wissenschaftliche Buchgesellschaft).

PART II

MORALITY, NATURE AND CULTURE

7

The perennial debate about human goodness: the primate evidence

Frans B. M. de Waal

> We approve and we disapprove because we cannot do otherwise. Can we help feeling pain when the fire burns us? Can we help sympathizing with our friends? Are these phenomena less necessary or less powerful in their consequences, because they fall within the subjective sphere of experience?
>
> Edward Westermarck (1912, 19)

Are we naturally good? And if not, whence does human goodness come? Is it one of our many marvellous inventions – like the wheel and toilet-training – or is it a mere illusion? Perhaps we are naturally bad, and just pretend to be good?

Each of the above positions has been advocated by one school of thought or another. Here I will contrast the views of some contemporary biologists – from whom an admission of human virtue is about as hard to extract as a rotten tooth – with the belief of many philosophers and scientists, including Charles Darwin, that our species moderates its selfishness with a healthy dose of fellow-feeling and kindness. Anyone who explores this debate will notice it is old – including explicit Chinese sources, such as Mencius, from before the Western calendar – so that we can justifiably speak of a perennial controversy.

Edward Westermarck deserves a central position in this debate since he was the first scholar to promote an integrated view of morality that included both humans and animals, and both culture and evolution. That his ideas were underappreciated at the time is understandable as they flew in the face of the Western dualistic tradition that pits body against mind, and culture against instinct. What is less understandable is why these dualisms persist today. Westermarck was in many ways more Darwinian than recent authors, who have addressed the evolution of ethics from an evolutionary perspective.

Some are more accurately described as Huxleyan, that is, as followers of Thomas Henry Huxley (1894), who tried to drive a wedge between evolution and ethics.

Westermarck's books are a curious blend of dry theorizing, detailed anthropology and second-hand animal stories. The author was eager to connect human and animal behaviour, but his own work focused entirely on people. Since in his days little systematic research on animal behaviour existed, he had to rely on anecdotes, such as the one of a vengeful camel that had been excessively beaten on multiple occasions by a 14-year-old boy for loitering or turning the wrong way. The camel passively took the punishment, but a few days later, while finding itself unladen alone on the road with the same conductor 'seized the unlucky boy's head in its monstrous mouth, and lifting him up in the air flung him down again on the earth with the upper part of the skull completely torn off, and his brains scattered on the ground' (Westermarck 1912, 38).

We shouldn't discard such an unverified report out of hand: stories of delayed retaliation abound in the zoo world, especially about apes and elephants. We now have systematic data on how chimpanzees punish negative actions with other negative actions, called a 'revenge system' by de Waal and Luttrell (1988), and how a macaque attacked by a dominant member of its troop will often turn around to redirect aggression against a vulnerable, younger relative of its attacker (Aureli *et al.* 1992). These reactions fall under Westermarck's *retributive emotions*, but for him the term 'retributive' went beyond its usual connotation of getting even. It also covered positive emotions, such as gratitude and the repayment of services. Depicting the retributive emotions as the cornerstone of morality, Westermarck weighed in on the question of its origin while antedating modern discussions of evolutionary ethics, such as *The Biology of Moral Systems* by Richard Alexander (1987), which take the related concept of reciprocal altruism as their starting point.

That Westermarck goes unmentioned in this and most other treatises of evolutionary ethics, or serves only as an historic footnote, is not because he paid attention to the wrong phenomena or held untenable views about ethics, but because his writing conveyed a belief in human goodness, and a confidence that morality comes naturally to people. Contemporary biologists have managed to banish this view to the scientific fringes under the influence of the two terrible Toms – Thomas Hobbes and Thomas Huxley – who both preached that the natural state of humankind, and of nature in general, is one in which purely selfish goals are pursued with bloody teeth and claws.

Here I will first treat this school of thought, which has been considerably more forceful in rejecting human kindness than in explaining morality, and then return to the more integrated views of Westermarck, Darwin and Mencius.

Bulldog bites master

In 1893, for a large audience in Oxford, England, Thomas Henry Huxley publicly tried to reconcile his dim view of the nasty natural world with the kindness occasionally encountered in human society. Huxley realized that the laws of the physical world are unalterable. He felt, however, that their impact on human existence could be softened and modified if people kept nature under control. He compared us with a gardener who has a hard time keeping weeds out of his garden. Thus, he proposed ethics as a human cultural victory over the evolutionary process in the same way as the gardener conquers the weeds in his garden (Huxley 1989 [1894]). This was an astounding position for two reasons. First, it deliberately curbed the explanatory power of evolution. Since many consider morality the essence of our species, Huxley was in effect saying that what makes us human could not be handled by the evolutionary framework. This was an inexplicable retreat by someone who had gained a reputation as 'Darwin's Bulldog' owing to his fierce advocacy of evolutionary theory. His solution was quintessentially Hobbesian in that it stated that people are fit for society only by education, not nature (Hobbes 1991 [1651]).

Second, Huxley gave no hint whatsoever where humanity might have unearthed the will and strength to go against its own nature. If we are indeed born competitors who don't care one bit about the feelings of others, how in the world did we decide to transform ourselves into model citizens? Can people for generations maintain behaviour that is out of character, like a shoal of piranhas which decide to become vegetarians? How deep does such a change go? Are we the proverbial wolves in sheep's clothing: nice on the outside, nasty on the inside?

It was the only time Huxley visibly broke with Darwin. As Huxley's biographer, Desmond (1994, 599), put it: 'Huxley was forcing his ethical Ark against the Darwinian current which had brought him so far.' Two decades earlier, in *The Descent of Man*, Darwin 1981 ([1871]) had unequivocally stated the continuity between human nature and morality. The reason for Huxley's departure has been sought in his suffering at the cruel hand of nature, which had taken the life of his beloved daughter, as well as his need to make the ruthlessness of the Darwinian cosmos palatable to the general public. He could do so only, he felt, by dislodging human ethics, declaring it a cultural innovation (Desmond 1994).

This curious dualism was to get an enormous respectability lift from Sigmund Freud's writings, which throve on contrasts between the conscious and subconscious, the ego and super-ego, love and death, and so on. As with Huxley's gardener and garden, Freud was not just dividing the world into symmetrical halves: he saw struggle everywhere. He explained the incest taboo and other moral restrictions as the result of a violent break with the free-wheeling sexual life of the primal horde, culminating in the collective slaughter of an overbearing father by his sons (Freud 1913). And he let civilization arise out of a renunciation of instinct, the gaining of control over the forces of nature, and the building of a cultural super-ego. Not only did he keep animals at a distance, his view also excluded women. It was the men who reached the highest peaks of civilization, carrying out tortuous sublimations that women are not capable of (Freud 1930).

Man's heroic combat against forces that try to drag him down remains a dominant theme within biology today, which – because of its obvious continuity with the doctrine of original sin – I have characterized as 'Calvinist sociobiology' (de Waal 1996). Let me offer some illustrative quotes from today's two most outspoken Huxleyans.

Declaring ethics a radical break with biology, George Williams has written extensively about the wretchedness of nature culminating in the claim that human morality is an inexplicable accident of the evolutionary process: 'I account for morality as an accidental capability produced, in its boundless stupidity, by a biological process that is normally opposed to the expression of such a capability' (Williams 1988, 438).

Richard Dawkins (1996) believes that we are 'nicer than is good for our selfish genes', and that 'we are never allowed to forget the narrow tightrope on which we balance above the Darwinian abyss'. In a recent interview, Dawkins explicitly endorsed Huxley: 'What I am saying, along with many other people, among them T. H. Huxley, is that in our political and social life we are entitled to throw out Darwinism, to say we don't want to live in a Darwinian world' (Roes 1997, 3).

Darwin must be turning in his grave, because the Darwinian world implied here is not at all what he himself envisioned (see below). What is lacking in these statements is an indication of how we can possibly negate our genes, which the same authors at other times don't hesitate to depict as all-powerful. Thus, first Dawkins (1976) tells us that our genes know what is best for us, that they control our lives, programming every little wheel in the human 'survival machine'. But then the same author lets us know that we have the option to rebel. The obvious implication is that we should take his earlier position with a grain of salt.

Like Huxley, these authors want to have it both ways: human behaviour is an evolutionary product except when it is hard to explain. And like Hobbes and Freud, they think in dichotomies: we are part nature, part culture, rather than a well-integrated whole. The same position has been echoed by popularizers, such as Robert Wright (1994) and Matt Ridley (1996), who have gone so far as to claim that virtue is absent from people's hearts and souls. They bluntly state that our species is potentially but not naturally moral. But what about the many people who occasionally experience in themselves and others a degree of sympathy, goodness and generosity? Wright's answer is that the 'moral animal' is basically a hypocrite:

> [T]he pretense of selflessness is about as much part of human nature as is its frequent absence. We dress ourselves up in tony moral language, denying base motives and stressing our at least minimal consideration for the greater good; and we fiercely and self-righteously decry selfishness in others (Wright 1994, 344).

To explain how we manage to live with ourselves despite this travesty, theorists have called upon self-deception and denial. If people think they are at times unselfish, so the argument goes, they must be hiding the selfish motives from themselves. Thus, all of us follow two separate agendas: one hidden in the recesses of our minds, and one that we try to sell to ourselves and others (e.g. Badcock 1986). The first is base, the second noble. In the ultimate twist of irony, anyone who doesn't believe that we are fooling ourselves, and feels that we may be genuinely kind, is called a wishful thinker, hence accused of fooling himself. Some scientists have objected to this accusation:

> [W]e feel we should address a criticism that is often leveled at advocates of altruism in psychology and group selection in biology. It is frequently said that people endorse such hypotheses because they *want* the world to be a friendly and hospitable place. The defenders of egoism and individualism who advance this criticism thereby pay themselves a compliment; they pat themselves on the back for staring reality squarely in the face. Egoists and individualists are objective, they suggest, whereas proponents of altruism and group selection are trapped by a comforting illusion (Sober and Wilson 1998, 8–9).

The idea of a double-agenda of public and private motives in the pursuit of self-interest is another Freudian scheme. And as with most, it is unverifiable: hidden motives are indistinguishable from absent ones. All of these efforts to reconcile observable human kindness with dominant theory about the absence thereof is the unfortunate legacy of Huxley, about whom evolutionary biologist Ernst Mayr did not mince any words:

> Huxley, who believed in final causes, rejected natural selection and did not represent genuine Darwinian thought in any way . . . It is unfortunate, considering how confused Huxley was, that his essay is often referred to even today as if it were authoritative (Mayr 1997, 250).

Already in Huxley's time, there existed strong opposition to his ideas (Desmond 1994), some of which came from Russian biologists, such as Petr Kropotkin. It has been noted that given the harsh climate of Siberia, Russian scientists have traditionally been far more impressed by the battle of animals against the elements than against each other, resulting in an emphasis on cooperation and solidarity that conflicted directly with Huxley's dog-eat-dog perspective (Todes 1989). Kropotkin's (1902) *Mutual Aid* was a direct attack on Huxley, but written with great deference for Darwin, whom Kropotkin, rightly, considered as more thoughtful and balanced. Although Kropotkin never formulated his theory with the precision and evolutionary logic available to Robert Trivers (1971) in his seminal paper on reciprocal altruism, both pondered the origins of a cooperative, and ultimately moral, society without invoking false pretense, Freudian denial schemes or cultural indoctrination.

Instead, the origins were sought in how evolution shapes behaviour. Evolution favours animals that assist each other if by doing so they achieve long-term, collective benefits of greater value than the short-term benefits derived from straightforward competition. Unlike simultaneous cooperation (known as mutualism), reciprocity involves exchanged acts that, while beneficial to the recipient, are costly to the performer. This cost, which is generated because there is a time lag between giving and receiving, is eliminated as soon as a favour of equal value is returned to the performer (for modern treatments of this issue see, apart from Trivers 1971, Axelrod and Hamilton 1981; Rothstein and Pierotti 1988; Taylor and McGuire 1988). It is in these theories that we find the germ of an evolutionary explanation that escaped Huxley.

Moral emotions

Westermarck is part of a long tradition, going back to Aristotle and Thomas Aquinas, which firmly anchors morality in the natural inclinations and desires of our species (Arnhart 1998). Emotions occupy a central role in that it is well-known that emotions, rather than being the antithesis of rationality, greatly aid thinking. People can reason and deliberate as much as they want – neuroscientists have found that if there are no emotions attached to the various options in front of them, they will never reach a decision or conviction (Damasio 1994). This is critical for moral choice because, if anything, morality involves strong convictions. These don't – or rather can't – come about through a cool Kantian rationality: they require caring about others and powerful 'gut feelings' about what is right or wrong (Haidt 2001).

Westermarck (1912 [1906]; 1917 [1908]) discusses, one by one, a whole range of what philosophers before him, most notably David Hume (1078 [1739]) and Adam Smith (1937 [1759]), called the 'moral sentiments'. He classified the retributive emotions into those derived from resentment and anger, which seek revenge and punishment, and those that are more positive and prosocial. Whereas in his time there were few good animal examples of the moral emotions – hence his reliance on Moroccan camel stories – we know now that there are many parallels in primate behaviour. My own work gives me ample reason to support Westermarck's list of basic human impulses underlying moral decision-making.

Westermarck discusses 'forgiveness', and how the turning of the other cheek is a universally appreciated gesture. There is a rapidly growing literature on how chimpanzees kiss and embrace after fights, how monkeys groom each other, and how bonobos have sex to eliminate social tensions. The evidence is overwhelming that these so-called 'reconciliations' serve to maintain valuable relationships and to preserve peace within the community. Reconciliation is not the same as forgiveness, but the two are related in human social life. There is evidence for similar behaviour in non-primates, so that we can speak of a widespread tendency in social animals to overcome conflict and make up with opponents (e.g. de Waal 1989a; Aureli and de Waal 2000).

Westermarck also sees protection of others against aggression as resulting from what he calls 'sympathetic resentment', thus implying that this behaviour rests on identification and empathy with the other. Protection against aggression is common in monkeys and apes, and in many other animals, who stick up for their kin and friends. The primate literature offers a well-investigated picture of coalitions and alliances, which some consider the hallmark of primate social life and the main reason that primates have evolved such complex, cognitively demanding societies (e.g. de Waal 1998 [1982]; Harcourt and de Waal 1992; Byrne and Whiten 1988).

Similarly, the retributive kindly emotions ('desire to give pleasure in return for pleasure', Westermarck 1912, 93) have an obvious parallel in what we now call reciprocal altruism, such as the tendency to repay in kind to those from whom assistance has been received. Our studies of captive chimpanzees indicate a marketplace of services in which grooming, sex, food, and support in fights are exchanged on a reciprocal basis. One of our latest studies produced compelling evidence that chimpanzees tend to share more food with individuals who recently groomed them, and that this exchange is partner-specific (de Waal 1997). In another study, we found that capuchin monkeys share food more with individuals who have helped them obtain the food than with the same partners when assistance was unneeded (de Waal and Berger 2000). Even though it is unclear if in these cases we can truly speak of 'gratitude', Westermarck's concept of kindly retribution seems not far off the mark.

Westermarck adds moral approval as a retributive kindly emotion, hence as a component of reciprocal altruism. These views antedate the discussion about 'indirect reciprocity' in the modern literature on evolutionary ethics, which revolve around reputation building and perceptions within the larger community (e.g. Alexander 1987). It is truly amazing to see how many issues brought up by contemporary authors are, couched in somewhat different terms, already present in the writings of this Swedish Finn of one century ago.

When I watch primates, measuring how they share food in return for grooming, or wait for the right opportunity to get even with a rival, I see very much the same emotional impulses that Westermarck analysed. A group of chimpanzees, for example, may whip up an outraged chorus of barks when the dominant male overdoes his punishment of an underling, and in the wild they form cooperative hunting parties that share the spoils of their efforts. Although I shy away from calling chimpanzees 'moral beings', their psychology contains many of the ingredients that, if also present in the progenitor of humans and apes, must have allowed our ancestors to develop a moral sense. Instead of morality being a radically new invention, I tend to see it as a natural outgrowth of ancient social tendencies and capacities, called building blocks of morality (de Waal 1996; Flack and de Waal 2000a).

Westermarck was far from naïve about how morality is maintained: he knew it required both approval and negative sanctions. For example, he explains how forgiveness prohibits revenge but not punishment. Punishment is a necessary component of justice, whereas revenge – if let loose – only destroys. Like Adam Smith before him, Westermarck recognized the moderating role of sympathy: 'The more the moral consciousness is influenced by sympathy, the more severely it condemns any retributive infliction of pain which it regards as undeserved' (Westermarck 1912, 78). Thus, of the two layers of morality – the moral sentiments and the capacity for moral judgment – Westermarck never neglected the second, even though he emphasized the first.

The most insightful part of his work is perhaps where Westermarck tries to come to grips with what defines a moral emotion as moral. Here he shows that there is more to these emotions than raw gut feeling as he explains that they 'differ from kindred non-moral emotions by their disinterestedness, apparent impartiality, and flavour of generality' (Westermarck 1917, 738–9). Emotions, such as gratitude and resentment, directly concern one's own interests – how one has been treated or how one wishes to be treated – hence are too egocentric to be moral. Moral emotions ought to be disconnected from one's immediate situation: they deal with good and bad at a more abstract, disinterested level. It is only when we make general judgments of how *anyone* ought to be treated that we can begin to speak of moral approval and disapproval. It is in this area, famously symbolized by Smith's (1937 [1759]) 'impartial spectator', that humans seem to go radically further than other primates.

Sympathy

Westermarck was ahead of his time, and went beyond Darwin's thinking in the precision with which he described moral tendencies. In spirit, however, the two were on the same line. Darwin firmly believed that there is plenty of room within his theory to accommodate the origins of morality (Uchii 1996). He did not see any conflict between the harshness of the evolutionary process and the gentleness of some of its products. He drew a sharp distinction between how evolution operates and how the human mind operates. He expressed his views most clearly by, rather than presenting the human species as capable of breaking the laws of biology, emphasizing its continuity with animals even in the moral domain:

> Any animal whatever, endowed with well-marked social instincts, the parental and filial affections being here included, would inevitably acquire a moral sense or conscience, as soon as its intellectual powers had become as well developed, or nearly as well developed, as in man (Darwin 1871, 71–2).

It is important to dwell on the capacity for sympathy hinted at by Darwin ('Many animals certainly sympathize with each other's distress or danger', Darwin 1871, 77), because it is in this domain that striking continuities exist between humans and other social animals. To be vicariously affected by the emotions of others, including distress, must be very basic, because these reactions have been reported for a great variety of animals, and are often immediate and uncontrollable. They undoubtedly derive from parental care, in which vulnerable individuals are tended with great care, but in many animals stretch well beyond this situation, including relations among unrelated adults. Laboratory experiments on rats and monkeys confirm that the sight of a conspecific in pain or trouble calls forth powerful responses to ameliorate the situation (reviewed in Preston and de Waal 2002).

When 28-year-old Lenny Skutnik dove into the icy Potomac River, in Washington DC, in 1982, to rescue a plane-crash victim, or when Dutch civilians sheltered Jewish families during World War II, life-threatening risks were taken on behalf of complete strangers. Similarly, Binti Jua, a lowland gorilla at Chicago's Brookfield Zoo, scooped up and rescued an unconscious boy who had fallen into her enclosure, following a chain of actions no one had taught her. Her behaviour was entirely in line with what we know about empathic behaviour in the great apes. It is common among chimpanzees, for example, that a bystander approaches the victim of a recent attack to gently wrap an arm around his or her shoulder. In an analysis of hundreds of post-conflict situations, de Waal and Aureli (1996) have demonstrated such 'consolations' in apes, and speculated that they rest on perspective-taking capacities that may be restricted to the small Hominoid family (i.e. humans and apes).

Despite these conspicuous caring tendencies, humans and other animals are routinely depicted by biologists as complete egoists. It is only recently, however, that the concept of 'selfishness' has been plucked from the English language, robbed of its vernacular meaning, and applied outside the psychological domain. Even though the term is now seen by some as synonymous with self-serving, English does have two different words for a reason. Selfishness implies the *intention* to serve oneself, hence knowledge of what one stands to gain from a particular behaviour. A vine may serve its own interests by overgrowing and suffocating a tree, but since plants lack intentions and knowledge they cannot be selfish except in a rather meaningless, metaphorical sense. Unfortunately, it is precisely this sense that has come to dominate debates about human nature in complete violation of the term's original significance (Midgley 1979).

Darwin never confused adaptation with individual goals, and had no trouble seeing altruistic motives. In this, he was inspired by Smith, the Scottish moral philosopher and father of economics. It says a great deal about the distinction between self-serving actions and selfish motives that Adam Smith, best known for his emphasis on self-interest as the guiding principle of economics, also wrote extensively about the universal human capacity for sympathy.

> How selfish soever man may be supposed, there are evidently some principles in his nature, which interest him in the fortune of others, and render their happiness necessary to him, though he derives nothing from it, except the pleasure of seeing it (Smith 1759, 9).

The evolutionary origins of this inclination are no mystery. All species that rely on cooperation – from elephants to wolves and people – show group loyalty and helping tendencies. These tendencies evolved in the context of a close-knit social life in which they benefited relatives and companions able to repay the favour. The impulse to help was therefore never totally without survival value to the ones showing the impulse. But, as so often, the impulse became divorced from the consequences that shaped its evolution. This permitted its expression even when pay-offs were unlikely, such as when strangers were the beneficiaries.

In discussing what constitutes morality, the actual behaviour is less important than the underlying capacities. For example, instead of arguing that food-sharing itself is a building block of morality, the thought rather is that its underlying capacities (e.g. high levels of tolerance, sensitivity to others' needs, reciprocal exchange) are relevant to morality. Ants, too, share food, but probably based on quite different urges and motives than those that make chimpanzees or people share food (de Waal 1989b). This distinction was understood by both Westermarck and Darwin, who in their discussions of morality looked beyond the actual behaviour at the underlying motivations, intentions and capacities. In other words, whether animals are nice to each other is not the issue, nor does it matter whether their behaviour fits our moral outlook, or not. The relevant question is whether they possess the capacities for reciprocity and revenge, for the enforcement of social rules, for the settlement of disputes, and for sympathy and empathy. These capacities, which constitute the prerequisites of morality, are shared by humans and other primates even if only humans seem to put them together in actual moral systems (de Waal 1996; Flack and de Waal 2000b).

Thus, Dawkins's call, quoted previously, that we must reject Darwinism so as to build a moral society, reflects a profound misunderstanding of Darwin's thinking. Since Darwin saw morality as a logical outcome of evolution, he envisioned an eminently more livable world than the one proposed by Huxley. The latter believed in a culturally imposed, artificial morality, the maintenance of which seems virtually impossible given its separation from human nature. It is Huxley's world, not Darwin's, that is a cold and amoral place.

The *ke* willow

There is never much new under the sun. Westermarck's emphasis on the retributive emotions, whether friendly or vengeful, reminds one of Confucius's reply to the question whether there is any single word that may serve as prescription for all of one's life. Confucius proposed 'reciprocity' as such a word. Reciprocity is of course also at the heart of the Golden Rule ('Do unto others as you would have them do unto you'), which remains unsurpassed as a summary of human morality.

A follower of the Chinese sage, Mencius, wrote extensively about human goodness during his life, from 372 to 289 BCE (which makes him a contemporary of Aristotle – born 384 BCE in Greece). Mencius lost his father when he was only three, and his mother made sure he received the best possible education. The mother is at least as well-known as her son: she still serves as a maternal model to the Chinese for her absolute devotion.

Called the 'second sage' because of his immense influence, second only to Confucius, Mencius had a revolutionary, subversive bent in that he stressed the obligation of rulers to provide for the common people. Recorded on bamboo clappers and handed down to his descendants and their students, his writings show that the debate about whether we are naturally moral, or not, is ancient indeed. In one exchange, Mencius (372–289 BCE, 270–1) reacts against Kaou Tsze's views, which are strongly reminiscent of Huxley's gardener and garden metaphor:

> Man's nature is like the *ke* willow, and righteousness is like a cup or a bowl. The fashioning of benevolence and righteousness out of man's nature is like the making of cups and bowls from the *ke* willow.

Mencius replied:

> Can you, leaving untouched the nature of the willow, make with it cups and bowls? You must do violence and injury to the willow, before you can make cups and bowls

> with it. If you must do violence and injury to the willow, before you can make cups and bowls with it, *on your principles* you must in the same way do violence and injury to humanity in order to fashion from it benevolence and righteousness! Your words alas! would certainly lead all men on to reckon benevolence and righteousness to be calamities.

Mencius believed that humans tend toward the good as naturally as water flows downhill. This is also evident from the following remark, in which he seeks to exclude the possibility of the Freudian double-agenda (*avant la lettre*) on the grounds that the immediacy of the moral emotions, such as sympathy, leave little room for this:

> When I say that all men have a mind which cannot bear to see the suffering of others, my meaning may be illustrated thus: even nowadays, if men suddenly see a child about to fall into a well, they will without exception experience a feeling of alarm and distress. They will feel so, not as a ground on which they may gain the favor of the child's parents, nor as a ground on which they may seek the praise of their neighbors and friends, nor from a dislike to the reputation of having been unmoved by such a thing. From this case we may perceive that the feeling of commiseration is essential to man (Mencius 372–289 BCE, 78).

It is striking how similar Mencius's example is to the ones quoted earlier from Westermarck ('Can we help sympathizing with our friends?') and Smith ('How selfish soever man may be supposed to be . . .'). The central idea underlying these statements by men as different as Mencius, Westermarck, and Smith is that distress at the sight of another's pain is an impulse over which we exert little or no control: it grabs us instantaneously, like a reflex, without time to weigh the pros and cons. Remarkably, all of the alternative motives listed in Mencius's last quote occur in modern literature, usually under the heading of reputation-building. The big difference is, of course, that Mencius rejected these explanations as too contrived given the immediacy and force of the sympathetic impulse. Manipulation of public opinion is entirely possible at other times, he said, but not at the very moment a child falls into a well.

I could not agree more. Evolution has produced species that follow genuinely cooperative impulses. I don't know if people are deep down good or evil, but I do know that to believe that each and every move is selfishly calculated while being hidden from ourselves and others overestimates human mental powers, let alone those of other animals. Apart from the already discussed animal examples of consolation of distressed individuals and protection against aggression, there exists a rich literature on human empathy and sympathy that, generally, agrees with Mencius's assessment that impulses in this regard come first and rationalizations later (e.g. Batson 1990; Wispé 1991).

Interesting additional evidence comes from child research. Both Freud, B. F. Skinner and Jean Piaget believed that the child learns its first moral distinctions through fear of punishment and a desire for praise. Similar to Huxleyan biologists, they conceived morality as coming from the outside – the same way it is imposed by culture upon a nasty human nature, it is imposed by adults upon a passive, naturally selfish child. Children were thought to adopt parental values to construct a super-ego, the moral agency of the self. Left to their own devices – like the children in William Golding's (1954) *Lord of the Flies* – they would never arrive at anything close to morality.

We now know, however, that at an early age children know the difference between moral principles ('do not steal') and cultural conventions ('no pyjamas at school'). They apparently appreciate that the breaking of certain rules distresses and harms others, whereas the breaking of other rules merely violates expectations about what is appropriate. Their attitudes don't seem based purely on reward and punishment. Whereas pediatric handbooks still depict young children as self-centred monsters, we now know that by one year of age they spontaneously comfort people in distress (Zahn-Waxler *et al.* 1992), and that soon thereafter they begin to develop a moral perspective through interactions with other members of their species (Killen and Nucci 1995).

Conclusion

In this chapter, I have contrasted two separate schools of thought on human goodness. One sees people as essentially evil and selfish, and explains morality as a veneer, a cultural overlay that is not grounded in human nature or evolutionary theory. This dualistic school of thought, personified by T. H. Huxley, is still very much with us with its calls to throw out Darwinism so as to build an orderly but artificially moral society.

The second school of thought, personified by Edward Westermarck, but going back much further in time, sees morality arise naturally in our species, and believes that there are sound evolutionary reasons for the capacities involved. The question of how we came to be this way can be answered only if we broaden the evolutionary horizon beyond the dog-eat-dog theories advocated by Huxley. This more expansive evolutionary framework is nothing new: it has been in place from the beginning, since Darwin himself firmly subscribed to this second school.

In this view, the child is not going against its own nature by developing a caring, moral attitude any more than that civil society is an out-of-control garden subdued by a sweating gardener. Moral attitudes have been there from the start, and the gardener, rather, is, as John Dewey aptly put it a few years before Westermarck, an organic grower. The successful gardener creates conditions and introduces plant species that may not be normal for this particular plot of land 'but fall within the wont and use of nature as a whole' (Dewey 1898, 109–10). Similarly, without being naïve about people, Westermarck recognized that theories that explain goodness as purely acquired – or worse: pretended – will never get anywhere near offering an explanation of the universal human tendency to build moral systems. He therefore postulated and carefully specified a genuine tendency towards the moral.

How refreshingly simple!

References

Alexander, R. A.

1987 *The Biology of Moral Systems* (New York: Aldine de Gruyter).

Arnhart, L.

1998 *Darwinian Natural Right: The Biological Ethics of Human Nature* (Albany, NY: State University of New York Press).

Aureli, F., and F. B. M. de Waal

2000 *Natural Conflict Resolution* (Berkeley, CA: University of California Press).

Aureli, F., R. Cozzolino, C. Cordischi, and S. Scucchi

1992 'Kin-oriented Redirection among Japanese Macaques: An Expression of a Revenge System?' *Animal Behaviour* 44: 283–91.

Axelrod, R., and W. D. Hamilton

1981 'The Evolution of Cooperation', *Science* 211: 1390–96.

Badcock, C. R.

1986 *The Problem of Altruism: Freudian-Darwinian Solutions* (Oxford: Blackwell).

Batson, C. D.

1990 'How Social an Animal: The Human Capacity for Caring', *American Psychologist* 45: 336–46.

Byrne, R. W., and A. Whiten

1988 *Machiavellian Intelligence: Social Expertise and the Evolution of Intellect in Monkeys, Apes, and Humans* (Oxford: Oxford University Press).

Damasio, A.

1994 *Descartes' Error: Emotion, Reason, and the Human Brain* (New York: Putnam).

Darwin, C.

1981 [1871] *The Descent of Man, and Selection in Relation to Sex* (Princeton, NJ: Princeton University Press).

Dawkins, R.

1976 *The Selfish Gene* (Oxford: Oxford University Press).

1996 No title. *Times Literary Supplement* (November 29): 13.

Desmond, A.

1994 *Huxley: From Devil's Disciple to Evolution's High Priest* (New York: Perseus).

Dewey, J.

1993 [1898] 'Evolution and Ethics'. Reprinted in M. H. Nitecki, and D. V. Nitecki (eds.), *Evolutionary Ethics* (Albany, NY: State University of New York Press), 95–110.

Flack, J. C., and F. B. M. de Waal

2000a 'Any Animal Whatever': Darwinian Building Blocks of Morality in Monkeys and Apes, *Journal of Consciousness Studies* 7 (1–2): 1–29.

2000b 'Being Nice is Not a Building Block of Morality: Response to Commentary Discussion', *Journal of Consciousness Studies* 7 (1–2): 67–77.

Freud, S.

1913 *Totem and Taboo* (New York: Norton).

1930 *Civilization and Its Discontents* (New York: Norton).

Golding, W.

1954 *Lord of the Flies* (New York: Capricorn).

Haidt, J.

2001 'The Emotional Dog and its Rational Tail: A Social Intuitionist Approach to Moral Judgment', *Psychological Review* 108: 814–34.

Harcourt, A. H., and F. B. M. de Waal

1992 *Coalitions and Alliances in Humans and Other Animals* (Oxford: Oxford University Press).

Hobbes, T.

1991 [1651] *Leviathan* (Cambridge: Cambridge University Press).

Hume, D.

1978 [1739] *A Treatise of Human Nature* (Oxford: Oxford University Press).

Huxley, T. H.

1989 [1894] *Evolution and Ethics* (Princeton, NJ: Princeton University Press).

Killen, M., and Nucci, L. P.

1995 'Morality, Autonomy and Social Conflict'. In M. Killen and D. Hart (eds.), *Morality in Everyday Life: Developmental Perspectives* (Cambridge: Cambridge University Press), 52–86.

Killen, M., and F. B. M. de Waal

2000 'The Evolution and Development of Morality'. In F. Aureli and F. B. M. de Waal (eds.), *Natural Conflict Resolution* (Berkeley, CA: University of California Press).

Kropotkin, P.

1972 [1902] *Mutual Aid: A Factor of Evolution* (New York: New York University Press).

Mayr, E.
1997 *This is Biology: The Science of the Living World* (Cambridge, MA: Harvard University Press).

Mencius
(372–289 BCE). *The Works of Mencius* (English translation Gu Lu; Shanghai: Shangwu).

Midgley, M.
1979 'Gene-juggling', *Philosophy* 54: 439–58.

Preston, S. D., and F. B. M. de Waal
2002. 'Empathy: Its Ultimate and Proximate Bases', *Behavioral & Brain Sciences* 25: 1–72.

Ridley, M.
1996 *The Origins of Virtue* (New York: Viking).

Roes, F.
1997 'An Interview of Richard Dawkins', *Human Ethology Bulletin* 12 (1): 1–3.

Rothstein, S. I., and R. Pierotti
1988 'Distinctions among Reciprocal Altruism, Kin Selection, and Cooperation and a Model for the Initial Evolution of Beneficient Behavior', *Ethology & Sociobiology* 9: 189–209.

Smith, A.
1937 [1759] *A Theory of Moral Sentiments* (New York: Modern Library).

Sober, E., and D. S. Wilson
1998 *Unto Others: The Evolution and Psychology of Unselfish Behavior* (Cambridge, MA: Harvard University Press).

Taylor, C. E., and M. T. McGuire
1988 'Reciprocal Altruism: Fifteen Years Later'. *Ethology & Sociobiology* 9: 67–72.

Todes, D.
1989 *Darwin without Malthus: The Struggle for Existence in Russian Evolutionary Thought* (New York: Oxford University Press).

Trivers, R. L.
1971 'The Evolution of Reciprocal Altruism', *Quarterly Review of Biology* 46: 35–57.

Uchii, S.
1996 'Darwin on the Evolution of Morality'. International Fellows Conference, Center for Philosophy of Science, University of Pittsburgh, www.bun.kyoto-u.ac.jp/~suchii/D.onM.html

de Waal, F. B. M.
1989a *Peacemaking among Primates* (Cambridge, MA: Harvard University Press).

1989b 'Food Sharing and Reciprocal Obligations among Chimpanzees', *Journal of Human Evolution* 18: 433–59.

1996 *Good Natured: The Origins of Right and Wrong in Humans and Other Animals* (Cambridge, MA: Harvard University Press).

1997 'The Chimpanzee's Service Economy: Food for Grooming'. *Evol. & Human Behav.* 18: 375–86.

1998 [1982] *Chimpanzee Politics: Power and Sex among Apes* (Baltimore, MD: The Johns Hopkins University Press).

de Waal, F. B. M., and F. Aureli

1996 'Consolation, Reconciliation, and a Possible Cognitive Difference between Macaque and Chimpanzee'. In A. E. Russon, K. A. Bard and S. T. Parker (eds.), *Reaching into Thought: The Minds of the Great Apes* (Cambridge: Cambridge University Press), 80–110.

de Waal, F. B. M., and M. L. Berger

2000 'Payment for Labour in Monkeys', *Nature* 404: 563.

de Waal, F. B. M., and L. M. Luttrell

1988 'Mechanisms of Social Reciprocity in Three Primate Species: Symmetrical Relationship Characteristics or Cognition?' *Ethology and Sociobiology* 9: 101–18.

Westermarck, E.

1912 [1906] *The Origin and Development of the Moral Ideas*, I (London: Macmillan, 2nd edn).

Westermarck, E.

1917 [1908] *The Origin and Development of the Moral Ideas*, II (London: Macmillan, 2nd edn).

Williams, G. C.

1988 'Reply to Comments on "Huxley's Evolution and Ethics in Sociobiological Perspective" ', *Zygon* 23: 437–8.

Wispé, L.

1991 *The Psychology of Sympathy* (New York: Plenum).

Wright, R.

1994 *The Moral Animal: The New Science of Evolutionary Psychology* (New York: Pantheon).

Zahn-Waxler, C., M. Radke-Yarrow, E. Wagner, and M. Chapman

1992 'Development of Concern For others', *Developmental Psychology* 28: 126–36.

8

Theological reflections on the moral nature of nature

Nancey Murphy

Introduction

My task in this essay is to propose a *theological* understanding of morality, but with some attention paid to biology, especially to the contributions of Frans de Waal. The problem of the relation of morality to religion, of course, has a 2500-year history, and there are equally complex and long-lived problems in understanding the relations of ethics to biology. So where to begin?! This essay will take as its point of departure some of the work I have done with George Ellis, in our book titled *On the Moral Nature of the Universe* (1976). I shall not attempt to recapitulate all of the arguments of that book. Rather I shall use our account of the relations between theology, science and ethics as a point of departure for this essay.

Ellis and I began with Arthur Peacocke's model for relating theology to the sciences. Peacocke makes use of the well-accepted notion of the hierarchy of the sciences, the order depending on the complexity *or* the comprehensiveness of the systems under investigation. Theology, he argues, may be seen as the science at the top of the hierarchy, in that it studies the most complex and all-encompassing system possible: the relation of God to all that is.[1]

It is difficult, however, to order the sciences above biology. In the physical sciences the criteria of complexity and comprehensiveness tend to overlap but here they diverge. For example, cosmology studies the most comprehensive system, but the cosmos so understood is simpler than a human brain and perhaps simpler than many social structures. To evade this problem of ambiguity, Ellis and I proposed a model in which the human and natural sciences form two branches above biology.

Our more radical suggestion was the claim that ethics can be viewed as a science, and located above the social sciences, but below theology in the hierarchy of the sciences. I shall draw upon this model in describing the relations between theology and ethics, on the one hand, and ethics and biology on the other. Ethics is constrained by theology above and biology below, but the kinds of constraints are different in each case. In section 1 I shall say more about this.

In sections 2 and 3, I turn to the role of biology in ethics. My central concern will be evolutionary biology, and I shall first survey some of the history of the entanglements of evolutionary theory with both ethics and theology. In light of this history and also in light of de Waal's critique of the overly conflictual portrayals of animals in science, I shall argue that biology has been infected, since Darwin's day, by bad theology.

In section 4, I turn to theology, but now to a particular theological perspective indebted to the Radical or Anabaptist reformation, and suggest that it provides a valuable interpretive scheme for viewing suffering in the natural world. Here suffering in nature is seen as participation in the suffering of God in Christ for the sake of others.

I conclude with some philosophical reflections on the relations among ethics, science and theology.

1. Ethics in the hierarchy of the sciences

The hierarchy of the sciences is a widely accepted idealization representing the relations among the sciences. The picture that Ellis and I suggested is something like the following. Here the sciences of physics, chemistry and biology form a base; above them are two branches containing on one side the human sciences (I include psychology at the lower level, then – in no particular order – sociology, economics, political science). Above the social sciences is ethics. On the other side are scientific ecology, astrophysics and cosmology.

Most early proponents of hierarchical models assumed both the possibility and the desirability of reductionism. (Of course, I recognize that there have always been battles over the question of whether the human sciences could be reduced to or even related at all to the natural sciences.[2]) I believe we are now at a turning point in intellectual history where reductionism can no longer be assumed. We have to consider what might otherwise have seemed obvious, were it not for reductionist ideologies – the fact that the behaviour of an entity at any level is usually a product not only of the behaviour of its parts, but also of events, structures and conditions in its environment. Thus, we are at a point where claims regarding top-down causation or emergence require serious reflection.

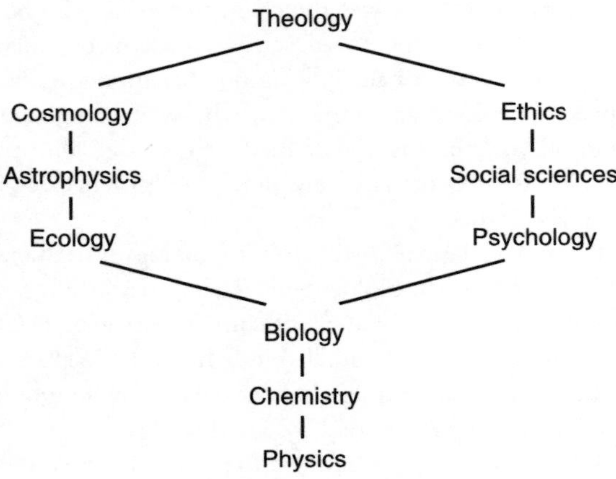

Without getting into the technicalities of these discussions, a very simple way of understanding the relations among levels is to say, first, that states of affairs at lower levels provide necessary *but not sufficient* conditions for higher-level states of affairs, while the converse does not hold. Second, however, questions arise at one level of the hierarchy that can only be answered from a higher-level perspective. Following Ian Barbour, I call these questions boundary questions. Part of my claim in this essay, then, can be stated as follows: the sciences raise boundary questions that only theology (or some other account of ultimate reality) can answer. Many of these are familiar: why is there a universe at all?; why are its cosmological constants finely-tuned for the production of life?; and so on.

In our book, Ellis and I called attention to boundary questions raised by the human sciences, and argued that these questions are largely *ethical* questions – hence, our justification for inclusion of ethics in the hierarchy. In short, the human sciences cannot describe human phenomena without some concept of what is normal for individuals and social groups. But concepts of normality are either openly or clandestinely dependent on some concept of what is *good* for humans – on an ethical vision. For example, there is the assumption in economics that self-interest, rather than benevolence, is normative and if left unchecked will lead to greater good in the end. There is the assumption in sociology that all social order is based on violence or the threat of violence and so violence is morally justifiable; in political theory there is the assumption that justice, as opposed to love, is the highest good at which government can aim; that freedom is an ultimate human good; that life, liberty, property and the pursuit of happiness are *natural* rights.

When called into question, these assumptions all raise ethical questions, which cannot be answered by any scientific means. The social sciences are suited for studying the relations between means and ends (e.g., if your goal is to avoid surpluses and shortages, the best economic system is the free market), but they are not suited for determining the ultimate ends or goals of human life. This is, instead, the proper subject matter of ethics.

Yet, at the end of the modern era we recognize that ethicists have not been able to provide answers to moral questions to which all rational people can assent. I follow Alasdair MacIntyre in taking moral reasoning to be essentially dependent upon some concept of the ultimate purpose of human life. Such concepts, he points out, are usually provided by religious traditions, although some philosophical traditions provide such answers as well (MacIntyre 1984). Thus, ethics is needed to answer boundary questions that arise from the human sciences, but ethics itself raises a central question – the purpose of human life – that can only be answered by theology or some substitute for theology.

The point of all this is to say that the positions one takes in ethics are conditioned both from above and from below. One's account of ultimate reality has a bearing on how one understands the purpose of human life. For a Christian, humans are made of the dust of the ground, but destined to be images of God. Our various subtraditions define the ultimate purpose of human life differently, for example, as the glorification of God (Calvin), the Beatific Vision (Aquinas), or carrying on the work of Jesus (my Brethren tradition). Notice that if there is no God and the evolution of human life was a huge cosmic accident, this does not get in the way of finding moral implications, as one can see from the writings of E. O. Wilson and other scientistic critics of religion.

Much that has been written in Christian ethics can be criticized for failing to pay adequate attention to the role that biology must play in determining the possibilities and goals of human life. My late husband, James McClendon, argued that Christian ethics is a three-stranded cord, constituted by attention to what God is doing in human life, to social structures, and, not least, to biology (McClendon 1986). My concern here is with the meeting of theology and biology in ethics.

2. Ethics and evolution

I recently had occasion to study some of the cultural history surrounding the development of evolutionary biology and of the social ethic called social Darwinism – *laissez-faire* economics, survival of the economically fittest, and justification for failure to assist the poor. I was quite surprised to find that there was a variety of uses made of Darwin's theory to support social programmes – not just the conservative programme that we think of as social Darwinism; it was used by socialists and by liberals as well.

I was also surprised by the history because, whereas I understood 'social Darwinism' to have been a *result* of the development of Darwin's theory, the historical causation is at least as much the reverse. Attitudes toward the poor that were prevalent during Darwin's day in fact helped to create Darwin's understanding of biology. Evolutionary theory grew out of a mixture of natural theology, Malthusian population theory, Darwin's observations, and the preceding history of the development of evolutionary ideas. All of these ingredients played a part in Darwin's theory of natural selection.

Darwin was much influenced by the work of William Paley and his design argument. Paley's work conditioned Darwin and others in his day to see features of nature as specifically and intentionally designed by God. So Darwin was predisposed to read the character, the intentions and the activities of God against the characteristics of the natural world.

A second ingredient in Darwin's thinking is found in the work of Thomas Malthus, in his *Essay on the Principle of Population* (1798). The principle of population states that population, if unchecked, will grow geometrically whereas food supply will increase, at most, arithmetically. Thus, struggle, competition and starvation are the natural result. Malthus's principle of population was the key to Darwin's thinking. It had already been proposed that one species could change into another; already the old age of the earth had been established by the geologists. So what was missing was the mechanism to get from one species to another.

Darwin came to the conclusion from the study of domesticated animals that selection was the principle of change. Then, reading Malthus, he saw how to extend this principle to the natural world: animals breed without 'the moral restraint which in some small degree checks the increase in mankind'.[3] Therefore, 'the pressure is always ready . . . A thousand wedges are being forced into the economy of nature . . . The final cause of all this wedging must be to sort out proper structure and adapt it to change.'[4] So Darwin concluded that it is the competition for food that provides the mechanism of change.

It is important to note that Malthus was an Anglican clergyman, who was working in the tradition of eighteenth-century natural theology. So his writings were not simply a scientific treatise on population growth and food supply, but rather they were, in a sense, a *theodicy* – an attempt to reconcile the goodness of God with evil and suffering. In place of Paley's 'myriads of happy beings' Malthus sees struggle, inequality, suffering and death as the basic features of the natural world. And these are interpreted by him as the result of divine providence. So Paley had set everyone up to say that, whatever the character of the natural order, it reflects God's design. Malthus's role was to say that the character of the natural world is competition and starvation. This, then, reflects on God's intentions and it is also seen as *providential.* Malthus wrote that evil produces exertion, exertion produces mind, and mind produces progress. So in the end it is *good* that there is not enough food for all.

The difference between eighteenth-century political and economic views and those after Malthus was the loss of optimism. The limits placed on economic growth by the limits on food production meant that the growing population of urban poor was seen in terms of surplus mouths rather than as an economically beneficial surplus of labour. Thus, Malthus and his followers argued that relief to the poor should be restricted, since it only postponed the collapse of those who could not support themselves. Malthus argued that a law should be passed such that no child born from any marriage more than a year after the law was passed should be entitled to parish assistance.

After Malthus it was not uncommon for other theologians to take up the cause. Thomas Chalmers, professor of divinity at the University of Edinburgh, emphasized the necessity of moral restraint, especially sexual restraint, if the poor were to avoid the miseries to which Malthus' principle of population would lead. The necessary connection between moral weakness and misery was a reflection of the very character of God. Chalmers wrote:

> It is not the lesson of conscience, that God would, under the mere impulse of parental fondness for the creatures whom He has made, let down the high state and sovereignty which belong to Him; or that He would forebear the infliction of the penalty, because of any soft or timid shrinking from the pain it would give the objects of His displeasure . . . [W]hen one looks to the disease and the agony of spirit, and above all the hideous and unsparing death, with its painful struggles and gloomy forebodings, which are spread universally over the face of the earth – we cannot but imagine of the God who presides over such an economy, that He is not a being who will falter from the imposition of his severity, which might serve the objects of a high administration (Chalmers 1833, 292f).

So, a rather gloomy view of God and God's purposes! The question then is what role Darwinian theory *actually* played in the development of social Darwinism. Historian Robert Young says that all Darwin's theory actually did was to provide a simple change in the source of the justification for social stratification. Now the basis of social stratification among rich and poor

> changes from a theological theodicy to a biological one in which the so-called physiological division of labor provides a scientific guarantee of the rightness of the property and work relations of industrial society . . .
>
> The famous controversy in the nineteenth century between science and theology was very heated indeed, and scholars have concentrated on this level of analysis. However, at another level, the protagonists in the debate were in fundamental agreement. They were fighting over the best ways of rationalizing the same set of assumptions about the existing order. An explicitly theological theodicy was being challenged by a secular one based on biological conceptions and the fundamental assumption of the uniformity of nature (Young 1985, 191).

So the theological context in which Darwin's theory was developed was largely responsible for the conflictual imagery in Darwin's language. It is not surprising, therefore, that his theory could be used to support the same social agenda as that which contributed to its development.

Now, this raises another question. If Darwin's perception of how nature works was influenced by thinkers such as Malthus and Chalmers, has this affected only his theory of natural selection, or has it affected his and subsequent scientists' perception of nature itself?

3. Good-natured nature?

The image of nature 'red in tooth and claw' was not an adequate account of Darwin's own perceptions. Besides the 'battle of life' of one organism against another, Darwin recognized additional, non-conflictual elements in the mechanisms driving the evolutionary process. One was 'sexual selection', which refers to competition within the species for mates. This sometimes involves conflict, such as between male elk, but it sometimes involves only differences in appearance, such as tail displays of male peacocks.

The Russian naturalist and anarchist Petr Kropotkin recognized that in Darwin's *Descent of Man* (1871) the term 'struggle for existence' was used broadly to include the evolution of social and moral faculties as well as the everyday battle for survival against the environment. He set out to elaborate these insights in depth, and came to view sociality, rather than life-and-death struggle between individuals, as typifying the animal world (Heyer 1982, 156).

Textbook accounts of evolution have long been expressed in much less loaded language than were the theories of Darwin and Wallace. Natural selection is defined simply as the differential reproduction of alternative genetic variants, that is, as higher rates of reproduction for individuals with certain useful characteristics. Commenting on the uses of Darwin's theory to justify war, aggression, classism, and unrestrained economic competition, the great synthesizer of evolutionary and genetic theory, Theodosius Dobzhansky, points out that in nature the struggle for life does not necessarily take the form of combat between individuals. Among higher animals combat is often ritualized and victory may be achieved without inflicting physical harm. Plants 'struggle' against aridity not by sucking water from one another but by developing devices to protect against water loss. Thus, '[i]t is no paradox to say that under many circumstances the most effective "struggle" for life is mutual help and cooperation' (Dobzhansky *et al.* 1977, 98).

So 'altruism' among animals has become an important topic of research. 'Altruism' here means any behaviour that puts the individual at risk or disadvantage but favours the survival of other members of its species, such as a bird's warning call when predators approach. This is not altruism in a moral sense, of course, but it is a far cry from the old image of intraspecific conflict.

Frans de Waal's book, published in 1996, titled *Good Natured*, mounts a powerful critique of images of nature that overemphasize conflict. De Waal points out that

> [i]n biology, the very same principle of natural selection that mercilessly plays off life forms and individuals against one another has led to symbiosis and mutualism among different organisms, to sensitivity of one individual to the needs of another, and to joint action toward a common goal. We are facing the profound paradox that genetic self-advancement at the expense of others – which is the basic thrust of evolution – has given rise to remarkable capacities for caring and sympathy (de Waal 1996, 5).

De Waal concludes that Malthusian influences have indeed biased scientists' perceptions of animal behaviour. In the minds of many, he says, 'natural selection' has become synonymous with open, unrestrained competition. This raises the question of how such a harsh principle could ever explain the concern for others and the benevolence that humans display. Thus, there has developed the subdiscipline of sociobiology – the study of animal (and human) behaviour in an evolutionary perspective. The core explanation of altruistic behaviour is 'kin selection'. It is hypothesized that behaviour patterns favouring the survival of kin, even at cost to the individual, could have been selected since the survival of kin results in the survival of close approximations to the individual's genes. So, for example, if an individual animal possesses a gene that predisposes it to bring food to its offspring, this will contribute to the survival of the offspring, who are likely to carry the same gene and, as a result, that gene will spread. So sociobiologists such as Richard Dawkins find themselves explaining apparently altruistic behaviour as a result of the operation of 'selfish genes'. De Waal sees this paradox (selfish altruism) as the result of an unfortunate refusal to countenance genuine sympathy and care in the natural world; he attributes it to the influence of Thomas Malthus and his principle of population.

De Waal notes that even the language used by most ethologists to describe animal behaviour is negatively biased. '[A]s a corollary to the belief in a natural world red in tooth and claw, there remains tremendous resistance, both inside and outside biology, to a terminology acknowledging beauty in the beast . . . The current scientific literature routinely depicts animals as suckers, grudgers, and cheaters, who act spitefully, greedily, and murderously.' Yet, if animals show tolerance or altruism, these terms are placed in quotation marks lest their author be judged hopelessly romantic or naïve. Alternatively, positive inclinations are given negative labels, such as when preferential treatment for kin is not called love for kin, but nepotism (1996, 18).

De Waal is careful not to go to the other extreme of providing romantic characterizations of animals. He shows due caution in asking whether terms used to describe desirable human traits can legitimately be applied to similar traits in animals, asking, for example, if animals should be described as displaying 'sympathy', or merely 'caring behaviour'. His wealth of descriptions of animal behaviour, drawn from his own and others' observations, includes a series of increasingly complex abilities that go into caring behaviour. The most basic is mutual attachment, which occurs among pack animals such as wolves and sea mammals such as dolphins and whales who will beach themselves collectively out of reluctance to leave a disoriented group mate. He reports a striking example of attachment observed in a dwarf mongoose colony.

> A British ethologist, Anne Rasa, followed the final days of a low-ranking adult male dying of chronic kidney disease. The male lived in a captive group consisting of a pair and its offspring. Two adjustments took place. First, the sick male was allowed to eat much earlier in the rank order than previously . . . Second, the rest of the group changed from sleeping on elevated objects, such as boxes, to sleeping on the floor once the sick male had lost the ability to climb onto the boxes. They stayed in contact with him, grooming him much more than usual. After the male's death, the group slept with the cadaver until its decay made removal necessary (1996, 80).

Another element involved in caring behaviour is emotional contagion – vicarious arousal by the emotions of others. Human babies display this trait – crying at the sound of another's cries – and so do a variety of animals. When infant rhesus monkeys scream, other infants rush to them to make physical contact.

The example of the mongoose above illustrates yet another element of caring behaviour: learned adjustment to others' disabilities. A further example is the case of Azalea, a rhesus monkey born with a condition comparable to Down's Syndrome in humans. She was slow to learn climbing and jumping and also slow in social development. Her troupe adjusted to her handicaps; for example, an elder sister carried her long beyond the age for such sisterly care, often pulled her out of physical entanglements and defended her against attacks by other monkeys (1996, 49).

Finally, de Waal gives examples of caring behaviour among higher primates. Chimpanzees excel at 'so-called *consolation*'. For example, after a fight, bystanders hug and touch the combatants, pat them on the back and groom them. It is interesting that their attentions focus more on the losers than the winners. If such behaviour does not occur quickly enough, loser chimpanzees resort to a repertoire of gestures – pouting, whimpering, begging with outstretched hands – so that the others will provide the needed calming contact.

So is nature better captured in Paley's phrase, 'myriads of happy beings', or in Tennyson's 'red in tooth and claw'? Obviously *both* are natural, and the picture is complex: the same animals that comfort one another and share food also cooperate in hunting and killing prey. De Waal points out that animals that share food tend to do so when the foodstuff is highly valued, prone to decay, too much for individual consumption, procured by skill or strength, and most effectively procured through collaboration – in short, the food most likely to be shared is meat killed in a hunt. He speculates that this tendency, shaped among social animals by evolutionary necessity, creates a predisposition among humans for sharing. While a natural tendency among animals to share food is not equivalent to human generosity, human morals cannot be entirely independent of our evolutionary past: 'Of our own design are neither the tools of morality nor the basic needs and desires that form the substance with which it works. Natural tendencies may not amount to moral imperatives, but they do figure in our decision-making. Thus, while some [human] moral rules reinforce species-typical predispositions and other suppress them, none blithely ignore them' (1996, 39).

This point aptly illustrates de Waal's 'profound paradox', noted above, that genetic self-advancement at the expense of others has given rise to remarkable capacities for caring and sympathy. He concludes: 'If carnivory was indeed the catalyst for the evolution of sharing, it is hard to escape the conclusion that human morality is steeped in animal blood. When we give money to begging strangers, ship food to starving people, or vote for measures that benefit the poor, we follow impulses shaped since the time our ancestors began to cluster around meat possessors' (1996, 146).

4. An Anabaptist theology of nature

If both Paley's and Tennyson's accounts of the biological world have turned out to be simplistic, perhaps the account of God associated with each is equally simplistic – both Paley's benevolent designer and Chalmers's sovereign God who will not 'falter from the imposition of any severity, which might serve the objects of a high administration'. In this section I intend to pursue an image of God both more complex and, I believe, more Christian than either of these alternatives. I hope to show that it is consistent with, even if not entailed by, the more complex and balanced accounts of nature presented by recent biologists such as de Waal.

My reflections are based on theological resources from the tradition that was once pejoratively called 'Anabaptist'. These were the radical reformers who rejected church–state alliances. Their rejection of the use of violence has led to a somewhat different perspective on suffering that than of the mainline Churches.

It is now rather common to talk about the suffering of God on behalf of humankind. But for Christians in the Radical-Reformation tradition, the suffering of God in Christ is in a very important way the intended model for all human faithfulness. In anabaptist thought, the suffering of Christians is not seen so often as punishment for sin but as costly participation with Christ in the likely consequences of such obedience to God in the midst of a sinful world. Anabaptist leader Hans Hut proclaimed 'the Gospel of Christ crucified, how He suffered for our sake and was obedient to the Father even unto death. In the same way we should walk after Christ, suffering for his sake all that is laid upon us, even unto death'. It is interesting to note that several anabaptist writers extended this account of human suffering to include 'the gospel of all creatures'. Hut himself taught that the suffering of animals and the destruction of other living things conforms to the pattern of redemption through suffering, and in its own way preaches the gospel of Christ crucified.[5]

Baptist theologian James McClendon describes creation itself as travail. The theme of God's own struggle in creation is found in Old Testament and New, from Isaiah's likening creation to a woman giving birth (Isa. 42:5, 14) to the claim that the suffering Messiah is the very one through whom all things came into being. Paul, in Romans, asserts that the Christian's sufferings are but a part of the groaning of the whole created universe in all its parts (Rom. 8:22) and all of this is associated with the labour of God to bring forth something 'we do not yet see' (Rom. 8:25).[6]

Philosopher of religion Holmes Rolston has developed similar insights with particular reference to the suffering inherent in the evolutionary process. Rolston emphasizes our continuity with the rest of the biological world and at the same time reconciles the suffering in nature with a Christian concept of God. In both the life Christians are called to live as followers of Jesus and in the biological realm there is an analogy with the self-sacrificing character of God. The key to his interpretation of nature is his recognition that *God identifies not with the predator, but with the prey.* I quote his beautiful prose at length.

> The Earth is a divine creation and scene of providence. The whole natural history is somehow contained in God, God's doing, and that includes even suffering, which, if it is difficult to say simply that it is immediately from God, is not ultimately outside of God's plan and redemptive control. God absorbs suffering and transforms it into goodness . . . [N]ature is . . . cruciform. The world is not a paradise of hedonistic ease, but a theater where life is learned and earned by labor, a drama where even the evils drive us to make sense of things. Life is advanced not only by thought and action, but by suffering, not only by logic but by pathos . . . This pathetic element in nature is seen in faith to be at the deepest logical level the pathos in God. God is not in a simple way the Benevolent Architect, but is rather the Suffering Redeemer. The whole of the earthen metabolism needs to be understood as having this character. The God met in physics as the divine wellspring from which matter-energy bubbles up . . . is in biology the suffering and resurrecting power that redeems life out of chaos . . .
>
> The secret of life is seen now to lie not so much in the heredity molecules, not so much in natural selection and the survival of the fittest, not so much in life's informational, cybernetic learning. The secret of life is that it is a passion play. Things perish in tragedy. The religions knew that full well, before biology arose to

> reconfirm it. But things perish with a passing over in which the sacrificed individual also flows in the river of life. Each of the suffering creatures is delivered over as an innocent sacrificed to preserve a line, a blood sacrifice perishing that others may live. We have a kind of 'slaughter of the innocents', a nonmoral, naturalistic harbinger of the slaughter of the innocents at the birth of the Christ, all perhaps vignettes hinting of the innocent lamb slain from the foundation of the world. They share the labor of the divinity. In their lives, beautiful, tragic, and perpetually incomplete, they speak for God; they prophesy as they participate in the divine pathos. All have 'borne our griefs and carried our sorrows.'
>
> The abundant life that Jesus exemplifies and offers to his disciples is that of a sacrificial suffering through to something higher. There is something divine about the power to suffer through to something higher. The Spirit of God is the genius that makes alive, that redeems life from its evils. The cruciform creation is, in the end, deiform, godly, just because of this element of struggle, not in spite of it. There is a great divine 'yes' hidden behind and within every 'no' of crushing nature. God, who is the lure toward rationality and sentience in the upcurrents of the biological pyramid, is also the compassionate lure in, with, and under all purchasing of life at the cost of sacrifice. God rescues from suffering, but the Judeo-Christian faith never teaches that God eschews suffering in the achievement of the divine purposes. To the contrary, seen in the paradigm of the cross, God too suffers, not less than his creatures, in order to gain for his creatures a more abundant life (Rolston 1994, 218–20 *passim*).

So here in the writings of Hut, McClendon and Rolston is an account of the moral character of a God who participates with creatures in a world where suffering is inevitable, and who brings good out of evil in all imaginable ways – even creating the capacity for sharing in the midst of 'carnivory'.

It should go without saying that an appreciation for the possibility of participating in Christ's suffering does not absolve us from the need to alleviate the suffering of others, but my experience in talking about these things suggests otherwise. So, I state categorically, the responsibility of anyone who hears and accepts the 'Gospel of All Creatures' is to be willing *oneself* to suffer for the good of others, and that includes, in so far as possible, freeing them from pain.

A central thesis of this paper, then, is that biology is not only a potential shaper of theology, but in fact has been shaped by the alliance between the (misguided) natural theology of Darwin's day and Malthusian justifications for the suffering of the poor. Here, very briefly, is an alternative view of God and of God's relation to those who suffer, a view that more nearly reflects the gospel of Jesus Christ than does Chalmers's (merely) sovereign God. Happily, it can be shown, as well, to better reflect the character of the biological world as it has come to be known in our own day. If Rolston's account of God was shaped by biologists' accounts of nature, it is not far-fetched to say that some current biologists' views of nature have been shaped by theology as well – de Waal's critique of sociobiology is in a section whose title is 'Calvinist Sociobiology', and he speculates that the dark mood in which nature has been perceived since Darwin's day goes back not only to Malthus but, before him, to (certain) Calvinist doctrines of original sin (1996, 17).

Conclusion

Earlier in this paper I endorsed Alasdair MacIntyre's account of ethics and its relation to theology. MacIntyre argues that, in contrast to ancient and mediaeval ethics, modern ethics is in disarray. Ethics used to be a discipline that taught how to act in order to reach humankind's ultimate goal. The concept of humankind's *telos* was provided by either a metaphysical or a theological tradition, which informed the ethicist of the nature of ultimate reality.

When Enlightenment ethicists severed all ties between morality and tradition (here, largely the Christian tradition) they kept fairly traditional lists of moral prescriptions, but lost all concepts of the end for which those prescriptions were the means of achievement. So a consequence of the 'autonomy of morals' was confusion about the very nature of ethics as a discipline, about the very nature of moral truth. Modern representational theories of language and knowledge led ethicists to ask what kind of 'objective realities' moral prescriptions or ascriptions might represent. Failing to find any such 'realities' it seemed necessary to reduce moral claims to some other kind of claims that could be verified (e.g., utility); yet there was the cultural memory that moral claims must be something more than that, and so we memorize and repeat Hume's law as an incantation – 'one cannot deduce an "ought" from an "is" ' – and worry about committing 'the naturalistic fallacy' (Macintyre 1984).

All of this confusion is regularly taken up into discussions of biology and ethics. It is due to having forgotten that the 'ought' statement – 'you ought to do (or be) *x*' – is only half of a moral truth. The original form of an ethical claim (implicitly, at least) is, 'if you are to achieve your *telos*, then you ought to do (or be) *x*'. This latter sort of ethical claim can be straightforwardly true or false; the 'ought' is no more mysterious than the 'ought' in 'a watch ought to keep good time'. Furthermore, it can and in fact *must* be derived from certain sorts of 'is' statements: about the nature of ultimate reality, about regularities in human life regarding the achievement of ends as a result of adopting certain means – the latter being amenable to empirical study.

So it is quite true to say that ethics cannot be derived from biology, but this is not because of the universal rule that an 'ought cannot be derived from an is'. It is due to the fact that biology is but one of many layers of description needed for an adequate account of human life. In the model I have presented, there are also the levels of psychology, the social sciences, ethics itself, and theology – or some other account of ultimate reality.

Thus, the debates among scientists about the roots of morality in animal nature are extremely important. But, in line with de Waal's suggestion, I have argued that biology itself is not pure description; it is, as we say in philosophy of science, theory-laden. This is no surprise – all scientific observation is theory-laden. What may have been surprising is my claim that the theories affecting scientists' views of nature include economic *and theological* theories as well as biological theories.

I have also given attention here to the ways in which biological science affects theological interpretation. Christians have, rightly, been challenged to give an account of the moral character of a God who would choose to create through the process of evolution. My response has been twofold: first, to reject as one-sided the picture of the evolutionary process as relentlessly cruel, but second to draw upon the teachings of a minority Christian tradition in which suffering, both human and animal, is given meaning by seeing it as participation in the sufferings of Christ. It is, in Rolston's terms, suffering through for the sake of something higher.

The inclusion of animal suffering in the work of the cross makes it clear, as Paul says, that it is not only we ourselves, but the whole of creation groaning while we await the final transformation of the cosmos.

Notes

1 See especially Peacocke 1993.
2 Those who argued for the independence of the human sciences generally did so on the basis of a dualistic anthropology, which has been severely questioned in the past generation.
3 Darwin, quoted in Young (1985, 41).
4 Darwin's notes, quoted in Young (1985, 41).
5 Quotations from Armour (1966, 78–82).
6 McClendon 1994, 160–76.

References

Armour, Rollin S.
1966 *Anabaptist Baptism: A Representative Study* (Scottdale, PA: Herald Press).

Chalmers, Thomas
1833 *The Adaptation of External Nature to the Moral and Intellectual Constitution of Man* (2 vols.; Bridgewater Treatises; London: Pickering).

Darwin, Charles
1981 [1871] *The Descent of Man and Selection in Relation to Sex* (London: J. Murray; 1981 edn with an introduction by John Tyler Bonner and Robert M. May, Princeton: Princeton University Press).

Dobzhansky, Theodosius *et al.*

1977 *Evolution* (San Francisco: W. H. Freeman).

Heyer, Paul

1982 *Nature, Human Nature, and Society: Marx, Darwin, Biology and the Human Sciences* (Westport, CN: Greenwood Press).

MacIntyre, Alasdair

1984 [1981] *After Virtue* (Notre Dame, IN: University of Notre Dame Press, 2nd edn).

Malthus, Thomas R.

1970 [1798] *An Essay on the Principle of Population and a Summary View of the Principle of Population* (ed. A. Flew; Harmondsworth: Penguin Books).

McClendon, James Wm. Jr.

1986 *Ethics: Systematic Theology Volume 1* (Nashville: Abingdon).

1994 *Doctrine: Systematic Theology Volume 2* (Nashville: Abingdon).

Murphy, Nancey, and George F. R. Ellis

1996 *On the Moral Nature of the Universe: Theology, Cosmology, and Ethics* (Minneapolis, MN: Fortress Press).

Peacocke, Arthur

1993 *Theology for a Scientific Age: Being and Becoming – Natural, Divine, and Human* (Minneapolis, MN: Fortress Press, enlarged edn).

Rolston, Holmes, III

1994 'Does Nature Need to Be Redeemed?' *Zygon* 29.2 (June 1994): 205–9.

de Waal, Frans

1996 *Good Natured: The Origins of Right and Wrong in Humans and Other Animals* (Cambridge, MA: Harvard University Press).

Young, Robert M.

1985 *Darwin's Metaphor: Nature's Place in Victorian Culture* (Cambridge: Cambridge University Press).

9

Is it suitable to translate Christian anthropological topics into genetic and cognitive categories? The case of original sin

Lluís Oviedo

Recent years have seen several attempts to fit traditional Christian concepts concerning human nature into the new anthropological framework provided by such disciplines as evolutive psychology, genetics and the cognitive sciences. The importance of this enterprise lies in the possibility of translating the old language of Christian theology – with all of its values and truths – into the new language of science. Science being the presently acknowledged standard of rationality, theological discourse can benefit by the plausibility and respect provided by modern scientific disciplines.

Among many possible examples, two of the most striking trials in this field have dealt with the idea of 'soul', as an explanation of the essence and value of the human persona and, in terms of the tradition of 'original sin', as a way to tackle the problem of limitations and evil present in the human condition. Both of these have been submitted to different proofs of translation according to the new scientific background. The consequences of these essays are obvious: what is at stake is the possibility of keeping an axiomatic framework where the so-called 'Christian values system' can still work and yet be able to cope with new ethical challenges.

This paper will examine both the potentialities and limitations of such an enterprise by focusing on the topic of 'original sin'. The traditional theological way of understanding human negativity is subjected to new interpretations, which take into account the genetic structure of human beings, the socio-biological constraints of evolution, and our neurological and cognitive rules. The possibility of better understanding a category, which has suffered intense criticism in recent years, opens the way for a new synthesis, even if – as in any endeavour at translation – there is a price to pay.

The present situation shows a 'work in process', which needs maturation and is subject to further revision. Nevertheless, this deepening of the dialectic between science and theology has already borne many fruits. Yet, the success of these attempts depends on a willingness to exercise some degree of 'theological restraint' based on the conviction that we cannot, at the present time, achieve a 'complete translation' of Christian anthropologic categories into natural ones, without falling prey to the dangers of 'secularization'.

Original sin at the proof of time

At the present time, we are aware of various past and ongoing attempts to understand the topic of 'original sin' – or a similar stance of egoism and anti-social tendencies – in a socio-biological and genetic perspective, deepening some ideas already formulated in recent decades, for example, the well-known 'selfish gene' of Richard Dawkins. In this field we find explicit developments that show the fecundity of this approach.

The second approach to original sin from a scientific standpoint is less explicit, but can profit from some developments in the field of 'cognitive sciences'. We can envisage, at the present state of research, at least two different applications of such disciplines: the neuro-physiological theories concerning the area in the brain 'responsible' for egoistic tendencies, and Boyer's suggestions on 'mythic and religious answers to misfortune and negativity'.

The dialogue between science and the theological topic of 'original sin' offers an opportunity to test some strategies in the field of interdisciplinary or 'cross-disciplinary' studies, in order to ascertain the value of their contributions. It is not easy to take into account the outcomes of the new sciences, as a kind of *loci theologici*; they should work inside the theological elaboration of the causes of evil. This is an unavoidable step before we engage in the discourse of Christian salvation. Many years ago John Henry Newman proposed that one test of the truth of the Christian message is its ability to 'assimilate' foreign truths – in the scientific realm as well – a principle recently re-edited by Bruce Marshall (Newman 1989; Marshall 2000, 147). Theology has, therefore, a constant responsibility to engage in the exercise of cultural and scientific 'assimilation'. This represents one of its most important challenges.

The project of establishing a more interdisciplinary theology is an open question, which can be answered only through concrete trials and the outcomes we manage to obtain in the ongoing exchange with the new sciences. Theological endeavour is much more 'comfortable' working from within the hermeneutics of texts from the Christian tradition, without being challenged by new research in foreign fields of empirical science. Even so, in the revision of subjects such as theological anthropology, we cannot avoid taking into account the results of the sciences concerned with the state of the human person, even if it is hard to obtain the right balance between biblical inspiration and other sources of knowledge that pertain to the human being.

A brief history of biological explanations of original sin

Since at least the seventies, there has been pioneering work available that has tried to understand the old topic of human sinfulness with the help of the life sciences. The argument was proposed by Donald Campbell (1975) on the basis of the 'conflict between social and biological evolution'. In a simple way, he hypothesizes two means in which evolutionary constraint works: one individual or genetic, and a second social or cultural. The human social-complex is the outcome of both forces acting simultaneously, and human sinfulness expresses, at a 'mythic level', the unavoidable struggle between the pro-social tendencies and the biological imperatives genetically coded. The biological approach to human nature has experienced, since its origins, the challenge to integrate in the evolutive scheme both social and cultural influences, and has tested some solutions: *genes* and *memes* (Dawkins), *genotype* and *culturtype* (Burhoe). It is obvious that such a relationship is problematic and that, even for Burhoe, conflict is unavoidable and requires a 'symbiotic regulator' (Burhoe 1981).

This kind of argument has known several versions and re-editions. One of them appears in the anthropological work of Philip Hefner (1993, 133ff.). He relies on diverse material and research to develop his thesis. Indeed, he finds useful the quoted work of Paul MacLean (1973) on the 'triune character of the human nervous system' (reptilian, paleo-mammalian and neocortex), the evolutive studies on human values by George Pugh (1977), and the theological reception of socio-biological theories by Ralph Burhoe (1981). All of this points to a 'sense of discrepancy' between different impulses or imperatives presiding over human behaviour; a stress hard to bear, which often brings fatal consequences.

Other contributions to this line of thought take advantage of developments in the field of genetic studies, and the possibility of linking aggressiveness and violence to some strand of the genetic code. Such a path has been followed by Marjorie Suchocki (1994), Ted Peters (1997) and Audrey Chapman (1999). The first author attempts to understand sin as an expression of instinctive human violence, embedded in social culture and transmission. The second refers more explicitly to the theological consequences. The third develops a concept of human violence more clearly rooted in our genetic constitution. Chapman actually makes use of the study of some authors who emphasize, not only the genetic 'selfish' tendency – as Dawkins declared some time ago (1976) – but the role played by 'patrilineal selection' favouring those males who are more affirmative and dominant in order to defend a limited territory and scarce resources (Wrangham and Peterson 1996). Another source that could lead to the same conclusions is found in certain attempts to demonstrate the link between cases of persistent violence in some subjects to genetic traits. Even if the collected evidence is quite poor, there could be a basis for a 'genetic theory' of violence and sin.

In general, the presently available explanations use a model of conflict between inside and outside forces: genetic and social-cultural. Sinfulness relates to the hard-to-manage complexity of the personal constituency, compelled to play on several fields at the same time, and very prone to making the wrong move. The element of violence and aggressiveness, as long as this disposition has a positive defence function, contributes to that complexity when the function is misused in the interplay between one's own and another's interest.

Sometimes genetic ideas have been used in order to support some traditional views of sinfulness. A good example is offered by Steve Jones (Jones 1997, 207–42), who reconstructs some traits of the Christian understanding with the help of genetics: concupiscence and a natural inclination to the 'bad side' are seen as being compelled by the influence of some genes. In the same way, the hereditary character of our inclination to sin, and the determinism which follows, makes good fellows between Augustine, Calvin, John Knox and some geneticists of recent times.

The final – until now – attempts to understand original sin in the light of biology are presented by Patricia Williams (2000, 2001). Her scheme is a little different. First, she approaches human nature from the 'diploid' principle that guides our genetic heritage. This implies a sharing of genetic material from our ancestors, which is never unilateral in its outcome, but contains tendencies of self-interest and altruism as well. The fact of altruism – present in diverse degrees in some animal species and in humans as well – as opposed to the self-assertive genetic basic orientation, opens the way to a different biological interpretation of the tensions that humans endure, but this time transferred from an inner-outer conflict, to an inner-inner one.

In her latest study, Williams proposes we prescind entirely from the topic of original sin. She champions a theology of atonement 'without Adam and

Eve', as the base of socio-biological studies. Of course, there is the problem of evil and guilt that cannot be ignored, but we don't need the biblical narrative of human origins in order to propose a theologically relevant interpretation of sinfulness and suffering. Indeed, socio-biological anthropology offers a different narrative, which shows the deep ambiguity of our natural constituency, where the once-named 'concupiscent appetites' play an essential role in the struggle for survival, but at the same time, and due to the more flexible, free and complex character of human nature, these tendencies can revert to their opposites, and become destructive and self-defeating. We do not find anything like 'original sin' or an 'ancient guilt' at the base of natural, human or social distress, but only a counterpart to the positive potentialities of our species that should be taken into account, a kind of 'price to pay' or of 'the lesser evil' for the great advantages our species enjoys: selfhood, freedom and a sophisticated knowledge. The theological scheme of atonement has to do with natural limits, not with self-inflicted punishments (Williams 2001, 180ff.).

The biological translation of original sin does not intend to offer a scientific apology for this Christian topic, but to stress the possible contact points between both views: the theological and the socio-biological one. Williams has made clear, more than others, at what point theology and biology meet and agree, and where they disagree (Williams 2000, 148ff.). In the first list one finds the nature of 'concupiscence', the heredity of selfishness, and the universality of some human traits. However, the idea of an attributable first sin with subsequent guilt, as the cause of all further distress, is not seen to be compatible. The same can be said for the theologically postulated historical, and substantial, difference in the human condition between a pre- and post-lapsarian reality.

At the end of these attempts to understand better from a scientific point of view the idea of original sin, we have less to do with real translations and more with an unavoidable biological displacement of Christian doctrine, which is deemed irrelevant in the light of the new biological knowledge. The Christian topic still works as a 'symbol' or 'cipher' concerning the limits of human nature, but not as a normative idea or an objective explanation for what has 'gone wrong' with the origins and development of the human condition. Following this path, it is understandable that even a socio-biologist – the most quoted – so distant from the Christian background as Edward O. Wilson offers his own version of original sin, in the terms of a 'fundamental misalignment' in evolution, 'that produced a human brain with the capacity to understand in far greater depth than is needed for survival' (Wilson 1998, 61). In this case there is not a need for Christian atonement, because the 'proper task of the scientist is to diagnose and correct this imbalance'. In this way we see accomplished the cycle that results in the complete secularization of a

Christian topic, which concludes with a 'scientific' substitution for a Christian scheme of salvation (Midgley 1986; 1992).

The main danger of any project of scientific reconstruction of Christian topics is, indeed, to ignore the essential circularity that affects all the attempts to 'understand' religion from a more rational or scientific point of view (Olivetti 1995). It has happened with the philosophical, psychological and sociological theories of religion, and it will happen again with the biological attempts, when they seem unable to distinguish between the objective and the subjective levels of religious meaning, and when the 'rational explanation' reduces religion to only that. At the end the already mentioned characteristic of circularity becomes obvious in the continuous and mutual remittance between the genetic and the cultural dimension of religion in some of its biological interpreters: between present outcomes and past evolution and selection of archeological religion, or between 'religious fitness' and the overcoming of religion by science, as a better factor of 'fitness'. In conclusion, the very problem of incompleteness is not only an anthropological one, but a scientific one as well. It expresses the incapacity of scientific knowledge to manage all of the aspects that integrate the complex world that makes up human and social reality. 'Original sin' is not only a doctrine that speaks of the limits and negativity of the human person, but also about the limits and ambiguities of our cognitive tools.

Further possibilities for scientific interpretations of original sin

There are surely other resources – not yet fully tapped – that will make plausible some aspects of original sin in the 'economy of knowledge' that manages to integrate the new sciences, or better the 'new anthropological synthesis' composed of evolutive biology, genetics, evolutive psychology and the cognitive sciences. The following suggested examples are much more hypothetical and immature than the aforementioned. First, I propose to take advantage of some neurological studies. Second, the cognitive theories on religion, which provide a very fertile field for the understanding of negativity and its management. Third, some trends in cognitive psychology that alert us to the flaws in the human mind.

A first case-scenario, and actually quite obvious considering the theories already explained, makes good use of some developments in neurophysiological research mixed with evolutive categories. A recent study of Gerald Cory (2000) deepens and provides a new insight into the idea formulated years ago by MacLean of the 'triune brain'. The ongoing research shows the presence of two contrasting programs in our brain: a 'self-preservation programming' and an 'affectional programming'. The first has a reptilian origin, and the second a mammalian. Both structures are linked to interconnected neurons, placed in physical brain locations. One represents the self-interested or egoistic orientation, while the other is the cooperative or empathic. Among them is a continuous dynamic interaction, never completely resolved, that allows for better decision-making in very different environments. At this point, it is not difficult to formulate a theory of sinfulness based on the 'irresolution' of the mentioned tension, or, still worse, resulting from an imbalance, that gives more ground to the egoistic programming. Such a theory would be nothing more than a neurological extension and confirmation of the evolutive interpretations already mentioned, but offering a more resolute scientific basis for a view overly affected by both internal and external criticism.

The second way to understand, in a more scientific fashion, the topic of original sin is provided by the cognitive approach of Boyer (1994; 2001) – among others – to religious cognition. It is relatively simple to apply the same axiom to beliefs in supernatural beings and to beliefs in the mythic causes of evil and suffering. Even if the principle applied uses concepts found in evolutive philosophy, the attempt is not to show the biological roots of a religious conviction, but to show – from a cognitive point of view – how these beliefs are constructed and how they gain plausibility. Its meaning is, therefore, more reflexive. The basis of such an approach is the concept of 'agency', which articulates in a more logical way the frame of reference that ordinates the many events happening within human life and society. Those events that lack a more explicit and immediate agency-explanation, resort to 'supernatural' and 'anthropomorphic' agents, such as gods, angels and demons, depending on the quality of the event. In this way humans manage to articulate their environments and to cope better with the dangers continually arising. A very similar strategy has been proposed by P. Williams with the concept of 'canalization', resorting to the cognitive and evolutive theories of M. Gazzaniga and Walter Burkert. There is a repeated pattern of reaction to all kinds of catastrophes, fixed by a normal tendency to find personal agents either for the causes of the evil, or for rescue and atonement (Williams 2001, 19).

Boyer has applied the cognitive theory of religion to the 'causes and reasons of misfortune' (2001, 196ff.), and concludes that attributing to anthropomorphic supernatural agents the causes of negative events allows individuals and populations to compose an appropriate strategy of response, which includes the revision of what has been wrong with us or what caused the spirits' anger against us. Such a theory is subjected to an extension – at least partially – to the Judeo-Christian view of an originating sin, as a plausible explanation in order to cope with the ill-fated destiny of human nature, and to envisage some remedies, obviously religious. The 'epidemology' of Sperber (1996) can help to explain the diffusion of such ideas.

This way of 'naturalizing' religious ideas does not refer to the real or biological limits and constraints of human nature, but deals with the cognitive usefulness of the religious view, which surely has been 'selected' because it did help entire populations to cope with their distresses and difficult situations. The question of the 'truth' of such a view is misleading or wrongly posed. Anyway, from a theological point of view, it is true that the Christian narrative of the origins and causes of evil tries to 'personalize' the problem – which is not exactly the same as to 'anthropomorphize' – as an attempt to manage it and to develop a strategy of redemption.

For Williams, the natural cognitive tendencies raise a different question, because the mechanism of 'canalization' always contains – in her opinion – a suspicion of unscientific knowledge. This represents a false way to solve the real problem, which is never properly understood or identified. The question is how to avoid this cognitive trap or how to offer a better explanation, which does not resort to mythic or archetypal ideas, but remains true to scientific models or maps. The question goes much deeper, and what is at stake, finally, is the problem of which maps are better able to cope with the struggles and stresses which reality and history place upon us, especially when we confront insurmountable or exceptionally dramatic problems that take us beyond the abilities of scientific understanding and management. It is not only a question of competing narratives or explanations of the old tensions between myth and reason, or their enlightened versions, but a self-referential, which identifies a radical problem concerning the possibility of 'total understanding'.

The last possibility to explore corresponds to the cognitive psychiatric awareness of the causes of 'psychic suffering'. So-called 'cognitive psychotherapy' has developed not only a healing praxis to cope with a wide range of psychic illness, but a theoretical framework worthy of more detailed consideration. Indeed, in this scheme, 'psychic suffering' is a symptom of distortions in our cognitive system and functions: wrong information processing, wrong judgments of events, over-generalizations, misplacement of emphasis ... (as a first source, consult the work of Bruno Bara 1996).

The cognitive interpretation of psychic suffering offers an ulterior opportunity to shed new light on the topic of human sinfulness, this time linked not so much to biological-evolutive causes – even if this is not completely excluded – but to the wrong functioning of our cognitive capacities. Indeed, the biblical narrative also expresses the meaning of sin in cognitive terms: the anxiety to acquire greater knowledge and the challenge to distinguish between good and evil. Human sinfulness may be understood in both cases as a hereditary distortion in human cognitive functions, that makes it more difficult to implement that basic distinction, with all the wrong decisions, deeds and suffering that follow. The idea should be carefully examined, not only because of the new plausibility it concedes to some biblical intuitions, but because the cognitive limits perceived in any exploration of human thinking, feeling and behaving are part of a complex history in the interplay between nature and nurture, between genetics and a socio-cultural context. In this way it is easier to rescue the Christian topic of sinfulness from an excess of naturalization, and to acknowledge a greater degree of influence from other factors: human decisions, social tendencies and cultural environments; factors decisive for a recovering of the Christian understanding of evil. Original sin – from this point of view – does not belong only to the genetic limits of human nature, that which provokes suspicion on the causes of such an imperfect nature, but is a component of human evolution, in the sense of decisions, options and deeds that determine and direct its evolution. It is an opinion shared in some measure by Richard Swinburne, who considers the weight of genetic selfish influence, but links, in a decisive fashion, sinfulness, moral belief and decision, as conditions *sine qua non* to proper speech on original sin (Swinburne 1985).

A theological balance

The challenge to theology, considering our review of several attempts to translate or re-conceptualize the topic of original sin, consists in the ability to still provide a theological understanding of the origins and causes of evil, distress and suffering in our world. There has always been a link between the theological interpretation of sin and suffering, as a break or trauma in the relationship between humans and God, and the Christian understanding of salvation, which has a religious or transcendent meaning to impart, even in today's world. This link seems much less evident, or even pertinent, in the wake of a new understanding of the 'human factor' and its incompleteness, which refers not to a broken 'covenant' with God, but to the natural status of the human race, forever involved in the unfinished process of self-assertion and the struggle to survive and to cope with new challenges arising in the environment.

The theological panorama of the history of salvation, which has included – from the very beginning – moments of obedience and of rebellion in humanity's relationship with God, is not universally accepted today, and what once was taken as a premise seems now to require a demonstration. It is not clear that such a view should be the only authorized interpretation or narrative of the 'facts' of the human drama. Still, what else can we offer as an explanation? Can science change the basic narrative, derived from biblical patterns, that speaks of a kind of universal struggle between the impulse to sin and the possibility of redemption?

What is at stake poses a fundamental challenge to theology. The problem is fraught with theological consequences; if any scientific project would ultimately lead to a complete naturalization of the causes and development of human negativity. We are conscious of dealing with two different 'codes' of understanding this reality, and it is often troublesome to incorporate one into the other: the bio-cognitive scheme and the theological. First, in order to ascertain and diagnose the limitations imposed on the human condition, and second in order to discover at last some solutions. Indeed, the naturalization of the anthropological constituency carried out by socio-biology and other sciences has profound consequences for the Christian view, which perceives itself to be ever more limited in its ability to offer explanations and to represent a sense of 'reality'. Theology cannot remain indifferent to the sense of 'displacement' caused by these scientific explanations.

The case of the 'fallacy of projection', denounced by S. J. Kline (1995) in an interdisciplinary exercise, is more than apparent in the reviewed theological reception of biological outcomes. The same may be said concerning the problem of 'incommensurability' (Sankey 1994, 220). Both arguments alert us to the dangers of an overly simplistic exercise of translation between very different sciences or theories because the nature of the explanations or the axiomatic used in each field make sense only in that field. Furthermore, the important question is how to maintain the theological identity of a discourse, which has been overly influenced by naturalizing views which risks a consistent loss of the aspect of 'transcendence'. In other words, how can we still propose a theological understanding of human nature despite the continuous impact of science and alternative anthropological explanations, which impose ever more stringent limitations on the transcendental dimension that forms such an essential component of what theology has to contribute to the discussion?

It would seem that the aforementioned danger can, indeed, be overcome in various ways. The first – and the most obvious – consists in accepting the scientific view as the only true explanation of human nature and limits, and to conclude that we should ignore the biblical narrative of Adam and Eve. This solution has been proposed not only by Williams, but by other theologians who deem today as indefensible the traditional doctrine. For these authors, the meaning of Christian salvation is no longer linked to the scheme of ancient sin, guilt and its consequences, but to other, diverse, aspects of human nature that call for redemption.

Some representatives of process theology stress the 'kenosis' of God within the work of creation, God's involvement in the process of reality, even in the negative dimension of it, and the freedom of all things. Such a theological view can be usefully applied to implement the aforementioned possibility of creating a theology without the concept of original sin.

There is also a second path, which attempts to cope with the problems arising from a theological confrontation with biology. In this alternative strategy, theology proclaims the need for a conscious restraint, which includes the mysterious character of evil, as a human trait, and accepts the scientific explanations of evil only as a part of the story, while still justifying the need for supernatural means to overcome it. Scientific explanations cannot adequately describe the perceived reality of evil, and its dramatic negativity, with historical and experiential manifestations that go far beyond our abilities to reduce them to a 'natural theory of evil'.

It seems far more useful in this context to resort to the systems theory of Niklas Luhmann and his particular understanding of religion as the way to name and to go through the 'dark side', the excluded part after any last distinction, which allows us to understand and to communicate. Original sin is, in this context, the expression of the limit of reflexivity, the way to name the darkest side of the real experience, of any semantics, or of reality's map (Luhmann 2000).

Even so, does all of this mean that the scientific contributions are useless for theology? Can we still do theological anthropology without socio-biology and cognitivism? Not at all – the problem is how to move between the extremes of complete assimilation and displacement of theology by science, and a totally fideistic attitude, which deems scientific outcomes to be irrelevant to Christian faith. One way to avoid both extremes might be found in the Luhmannian scheme of 'interpenetration': a kind of relationship between different systems, in which the complexity of one becomes part of another. In this sense, the contributions of science contribute to an increased complexity for theological elaboration, of new elements which must be taken seriously. It is possible to understand the theological answer to the challenge coming from new biological and cognitive theories, as a constant attempt to maintain the difference between nature and supernature, immanence and transcendence, or between naturalistic explanations and theological 'restraint': an acknowledgement that we do not know everything that there is to know concerning the human condition. Resistance to the complete naturalization or secularization of the maps of human nature becomes the main task of a theological anthropology engaged in a difficult and very serious dialogue with scientific views.

Finally, what is really at stake is which view has the last word: the scientific, which distinguishes between true and untrue representation, or the theological, which distinguishes between what saves and what does not save. In the wake of recent secularization, and before the vindication of some theologians (John Milbank, for example), who strive for a more conscious theological appropriation of some areas that have been lost (the body, society, sexuality . . .) the real challenge facing Christian thought is the necessity to maintain a clear theological profile regarding the most relevant aspects of present personal and social life. This means that even subjects perceived to be within the realm of scientific knowledge may be read, interpreted and critiqued, at the same time, from a theological perspective.

References

Bara, B. G.

1996 *Manuale di Psicoterapia Cognitiva* (Torino: Bollati Boringhieri).

Boyer, P.

1994 *The Naturalness of Religious Ideas: A Cognitive Theory of Religion* (Cambridge/New York: Cambridge University Press).

2001 *Religion Explained: The Evolutionary Origins of Religious Thought* (New York: Basic Books).

Burhoe, R.

1981 *Toward a Scientific Theology* (Belfast: Christian Journals).

Campbell, D. T.

1975 'The Conflict between Social and Biological Evolution and the Concept of Original Sin', *Zygon* 10: 234–49.

Chapman, A. R.

1999 *Unprecedent Choices: Religious Ethics at the Frontiers of Genetic Science* (Minneapolis, MN: Fortress Press).

Cory, G. A.

2000 'From Maclean's Triune Brain Concept to the Conflict Systems Neurobehavioral Model: The Subjective basis of Moral and Spiritual Consciousness', *Zygon* 35.2: 385–414.

Dawkins, R.

1976 *The Selfish Gene* (Oxford: Oxford University Press).

Hefner, P.

1993 *The Human Factor: Evolution, Culture and Religion* (Minneapolis, MN: Fortress Press).

Jones, S.

1997 *In the Blood: God, Genes and Destiny* (London: Flamingo).

Kline, S. J.

1995 *Conceptual Foundations for Multidisciplinary Thinking* (Stanford, CA: Stanford University Press).

Luhmann, N.

2000 *Die Religion der Gesellschaft* (Frankfurt a.M.: Suhrkamp).

MacLean, P.

1973 'The Brain's Generation Gap: Some Human Implications', *Zygon* 8: 113–27.

Marshall, B. D.
2000 *Trinity and Truth* (Cambridge Studies in Christian Doctrine; Cambridge/New York: Cambridge University Press).
Midgley, M.
1986 *Evolution as Religion: Strange Hopes and Stranger Fears* (London/New York: Routledge).
1992 *Science as Salvation: A Modern Myth and his Meaning* (London/New York: Routledge).
Milbank, J., and Ward G. Pickstock
1999 *Radical Orthodoxy* (London/New York: Routledge).
Newman, J. H.
1989 *An Essay on the Development of Christian Doctrine* (1845) (Notre Dame, IN: University of Notre Dame Press).
Olivetti, M. M.
1995 'Filosofia della religione', in P. Rossi (ed.), *La filosofia I: Le filosofie speciali* (Torino: Utet), 137–220.
Peters, T.
1997 *Playing God? Genetic Determinsm and Human Freedom* (London/New York: Routledge).
Pugh, G. E.
1977 *The Biological Origin of Human Values* (New York: Basic Books).
Rolston, H. III
1999 *Genes, Genesis and God: Values and their Origins in Natural and Human History* (Cambridge/New York: Cambridge University Press).
Sankey, H.
1994 *The Incommensurability Thesis* (Aldershot/Brookfield: Avebury).
Sperber, D.
1996 *Explaining Culture: A Naturalistic Approach* (Oxford: Blackwell).
Suchocki, M. H.
1994 *The Fall to Violence: Original Sin in Relational Theology* (New York: Continuum Books).
Swinburne, R.
1985 'Original Sinfulness', *Neue Zeitschrift für systematische Theologie und Religionsphilosophie* 27: 235–50.
Williams, P. A.
2000 'Sociobiology and Original Sin', *Zygon* 35.4: 783–812.
2001 *Doing Without Adam and Eve: Sociobiology and Original Sin* (Minneapolis, MN: Fortress Press).
Wilson, E. O.
1998 *Consilience: The Unity of Knowledge* (New York: Knopf).

Wrangham, R. and D. Peterson
1996 *Demonic Males: Apes and the Origins of Human Violence* (Boston: Houghton Mifflin).

PART III

MORALITY IN A TECHNOLOGICAL SOCIETY

10

Ethical issues of AI and biotechnology

Margaret A. Boden

There are many ethical issues associated with artificial intelligence (AI) (Boden 1977–87, ch. 15; anon 1989). And there are many ethical issues associated with biotechnology. All of these still arise, in the context of the combination of AI and biotechnology. But are there any 'extra' ethical issues which arise with the *combination*?

What's happening already?

I'll start by saying a little about how AI and biotechnology are already being combined. That is, I'm ignoring futurology and science fiction. There are more than enough examples already to engage our attention – and our ethical sensibilities.

The many examples include (1) applications of visual pattern recognition by computer. For instance, automatic recognition of chromosomes has been possible for over 40 years, though its efficiency has of course increased over that time. Similarly, much work has been done on the automatic interpretation of X-rays for medical diagnosis.

A relatively recent variant has been developed by some of my colleagues at the University of Sussex, in cooperation with the universities of Birmingham and Edinburgh (Du Boulay *et al.* 1999). This is a system called MEDIATE: an acronym for MEDical Image And Training Environment. MEDIATE deals with MRI (magnetic resonance imaging) data of the brain. The aim, here, is not to relate ongoing brain activity to specific thoughts or moods, as is done in cognitive neuroscience. Rather, the aim is to diagnose various diseases and tumours of the brain. Or rather, the aim is to provide diagnostic *assistance* to human doctors, and also to train radiologists to interpret MRI brain-scans.

MEDIATE has a large database of MRI images, and various statistical models that are used to analyse the data. The system shows typical cases, or prototypes, of a variety of diseases, highlighting the overlap between specific diseases so as to help pre-empt and resolve confusion. The degree of similarity between cases can be illustrated visually, and also measured statistically. Diagnostic concepts, like most concepts, have fuzzy boundaries. MEDIATE takes account of this – and illustrates it, for the benefit of medical trainees. In general, the program tells the user what is the *probability* of diseases X or Y, given the images relating to the patient in question.

The program can be used by both novices and experts, and works differently in either case so as to allow for their cognitive differences. The visual cues for a range of diseases are based on medical knowledge about the development and the histology of distinct types of lesion. And, of course, diagnosis depends not only on the nature of the lesion-image itself, but on its anatomical location in the brain.

I've described this system, albeit briefly, in more detail than the others mentioned here. The general points – about assistance, training, user-variance, and assessments of probabilities – should be borne in mind when thinking about other AI applications. Not all are as sophisticated as this one. But the point, here, is that these complexities are possible in principle, and in some cases already being used in practice.

Another use of AI is (2) for the computer search of DNA sequences in the genome, and the comparison of DNA sequences across species. The huge advances in recent years in mapping the genomes of fruit-fly, mouse, and man depended heavily on this technology – here used largely for its 'brute force' strengths.

(3) Robots are already being developed, and in some cases regularly used, for cybersurgery. There are two classes of robot involved. One type is free-standing, or (as the jargon has it) autonomous. An example would be a tiny machine, manufactured not with hammer and chisel but by nanotechnology, for 'eating' the fatty deposits laid down over the years in blood vessels. The second type is a robot that produces a scaled-down version of a human surgeon's movements. This technique can be used for keyhole surgery, or for 'distance surgery', where the patient doesn't even have to be in the same room as the surgeon. This involves the remote manipulation (via radio communication) of a robot many miles, perhaps a whole continent, away from the originating action.

Virtual reality (VR) is an AI technique that's widely used for (4) teaching anatomy without requiring the student to dissect actual human bodies. When

I was a medical student in the 1950s every two students would dissect an entire body. Now, there is much more reliance on VR simulation (as well as on 'illustrative' dissections done by professional anatomists). Similarly, VR is being used (5) to enable trainee surgeons to 'practise' their surgery, on computer programs rather than real patients. In all these cases, however, and in the robotic-surgery cases too, the human being loses the information that's normally available from the pressure-sensors. (In principle, robotic sensors could compensate to some extent – but at present, that's more science fiction than reportage.)

A further VR application, used not for medical surgery but for medical research, is (6) the simulation of various physiological systems so that biochemical experiments can be carried out *in silico*. The development of AI models of this type has been sponsored for many years by an organization called FRAME: Fund for the Replacement of Animals in Medical Experiments. It's now being widely used by pharmaceutical companies as well as university research laboratories. Indeed, no research scientist in the UK can get a licence from the Home Office to experiment on living animals unless he or she can convince the inspectorate that no simulation experiment exists as a practical alternative. Such VR systems can also be used to help suggest future experiments. Indeed, one of the very earliest practical applications of AI was in planning and suggesting experiments in genetics, using an expert system overseen by the Nobel prize-winner Joshua Lederberg. As you might expect, (7) genetic diagnosis and counselling are also done with the aid of AI programs giving access to the relevant data.

Evolutionary AI, using genetic algorithms (GAs) are employed (8) in the development of new drugs. On the one hand, the GAs can help in designing new molecules. On the other hand, AI enables these (virtual) molecules to be tested in simulation before the real molecules are let loose on animals or human patients.

A rather different application involves (9) electronic 'implants' in cockroaches' brains, instructing the six legs to move in a nicely coordinated fashion so that the cockroach can walk in a normal or near-normal way. Similar experiments have recently been carried out with rats. The hope is that this research may provide applications for helping human paraplegics, or even quadraplegics.

(10) Entire neural systems can be modelled by AI techniques. For example, there's a discipline known as computational neuroethology. This goes to the 'classic' neuroethologists for data on the nervous (and/or neuromuscular) system of a particular species – usually insects (such as crickets, hoverflies and cockroaches), but sometimes fish or amphibia too – and on the relevant species-specific behaviour (navigation, mate-finding, swimming movements etc.). Or computational analysis and AI modelling can be used (as it has been

since the 1960s) to study how the mammalian cerebellum learns to control bodily skills (Willshaw and Buckingham 1990).

Human psychopathology includes some cases of 'strange' behaviour that can be better understood in terms of computational theories of the psychological processes going on – and, in some cases, of the associated neural mechanisms too.

For instance, some patients have a pathological tendency to get trapped in errors of various types, which all of us commit occasionally but which are so common in these patients as to be debilitating. Most of us, for example, while intending to drive the car to place A, have inattentively found ourselves arriving at place B – perhaps the office, or some point on the route to the office. The reason is that there is a partial overlap between the routes to place A and place B, and the visual cues (a familiar roundabout, perhaps) are so strongly associated with the much-travelled route to place B that the B plan 'captures' the driver's activity. Such capture-errors, and other familiar categories of error, have been modelled by AI simulations that also connect them with theories about the specific types of brain process that are occurring (Norman and Shallice 1986; Cooper, Shallice and Farringdon 1995).

In addition, AI models have been applied in various areas of psychiatric theory, diagnosis, and even psychotherapy. And, of course, expert systems have long been available as diagnostic aids in physical medicine.

These examples are just a few of the many I could have mentioned. I hope their range and variety makes clear, however, that virtually all aspects of biotechnology can *already* be fruitfully linked to AI. What we must consider now is whether the fruits of that research taste pleasant on the ethically sensitive tongue.

What sorts of ethical issues are involved?

The ethical issues that are involved here are also diverse. They include seven broad classes, each of which has many instances.

First, there's the area of respect for animals. Indeed, respect for animals was a main motive behind FRAME's sponsorship of the VR biochemistry I mentioned above. There's no doubt that this computational technology has saved many animals from experimentation in the physiologist's or pharmacologist's laboratory. Many thousands of animal experiments are performed annually as a matter of law: new commercial products have to be tested for toxicity before going on sale. If some of these tests can be done using AI models, the animals will benefit.

Whether animals can properly be said to have 'rights' is highly controversial. After all, they don't have responsibilities, not being moral creatures.

But even if they don't, literally, have rights, many questions remain about the degree of respect, or consideration, we ought to show towards them. Killing isn't the only issue: there are disputes about the degree to which animals' natural lifestyles should be interfered with by us.

We normally believe – and some religions make a point of stressing – that respect is due to living beings *as such*. Certainly, we don't necessarily show the same degree of respect to one species as to another. Most car-drivers, for instance, would run over a dog or a squirrel without hesitation, if the alternative were killing a child. I assume that much the same applies even to Jainists, whose respect for life is so great that they try to avoid stepping on the tiniest ant, and wear masks to avoid swallowing (i.e. killing) bacteria.

Nevertheless, by and large we accept that life deserves respect. Sentient life, above all – but we don't have to be sure about the sentience. (Have you never got out of your comfortable armchair to rescue a ladybird, or even a spider, trapped on the window-sill?) Many of us don't even think it right to destroy *plants* wantonly. I'm not talking about objections to polluting pesticides, nor about the potential medicinal drugs that are being lost with the destruction of the Amazon rain-forests. I'm not even talking about the delicate balance of the Earth's ecosystem. All those considerations could be regarded as human-centred utilitarianism. No, I'm talking about the feeling that many people have that *life as such* deserves our respect – and animal life, in particular. If we're convinced we have good reason to destroy a living thing, fair enough. But if we don't, we should leave it alone to do its own thing.

Closely associated with this issue is what's often referred to – in an attempt to downgrade it as irrational – the Yuk-factor. For instance, you may have experienced some disgust when I mentioned the electronic implants in the cockroach's brain, forcing its legs to move in human-intended ways. (I almost said 'human-designed': but, as I explained, this type of research attempts to keep as close as possible to the biological reality of the creature's nervous system.) The question here is whether your wince of disgust had any *moral* dimension, and if so whether that was ethically *justified*. Is it immoral to do this sort of thing to cockroaches? And what about rats? The human paraplegics, of course, will be able to give their consent. But rats can't. If it is immoral to treat any or all animal species in this way, why is that? Or rather, is it any *more* immoral than vivisecting rats or cockroaches without any thought of AI? (Don't forget, we're trying to concentrate on the ethical issues that arise when biotechnology is combined with AI.)

The second class of ethical problems concerns AI's use in decision-making, where the human being(s) should accept responsibility.

These issues were explicitly forefronted many years ago, in a simple expert system produced by the British Medical Association (BMA). The program, made available to medical and para-medical personnel across the UK, was called COMET: COnsent for MEdical Treatment. Its point was to aid medics and paramedics facing difficult decisions about just who may, or must, be asked to give consent for a particular medical treatment. (Suppose the patient is a minor? Or in a coma? Or the parents are abroad . . . ?) This program embodied *both* legal rules *and* ethical conventions, namely those recommended by the BMA's Ethical Committee. COMET constantly reminded the users that *they* had the responsibility for whatever decision was taken. It also reminded them from time to time that 'I'm just a computer program', and that 'You may have extra knowledge that I don't have'. That last phrase, of course, covered not only missing data that could in principle have been supplied, but also knowledge of a type that couldn't have been represented in the program even if someone had tried to do so. (One might argue that these reminders were in order only because most people at that time were unfamiliar with computers, and utterly ignorant of AI. Now – so this objection goes – such constant reminders are not only annoying, but unnecessary. We'll come back to that point later.)

This example leads neatly on to the third class of ethical problems, concerning *which* human should accept the responsibility. Put more colloquially: whom do you sue?

Suppose, for example, that someone uses MEDIATE to make a diagnosis, and that diagnosis is wrong. Whose fault is that? Perhaps the person actually *misused* the system. That could range from pressing the wrong button to putting too much trust in the 'advice' the program gave. But perhaps the system itself was faulty. In that case, who's to blame? The programmers? The medical user? The hospital that employs him or her? The company that sold MEDIATE to the hospital? (At present, it's not for sale. But many medical AI applications are.)

One can even foresee a situation in which someone might be justly blamed for *not* using an AI program. After all, some of them are very good: much better than the average family doctor, and in some cases better than most consultants too. In brief, even if we take for granted that only human beings can take moral responsibility for decisions, the *degree* and *locus* of that responsibility is often debatable. To be sure, analogous problems arise with the use of any technology. What if a heart pacemaker fails? Whom do you sue . . .? The difference is that the failure is likely to be very much easier to locate, and to explain, in a physical mechanism such as a pacemaker. In the complex interaction between a complicated AI program and an even more complicated human being, this is usually much more difficult.

These problems are related, in turn, to the fourth class of ethical issues, which arise from a failure to understand the *limitations* of AI systems in general and any given system in particular. (COMET was an attempt to flag some of these. And the problem remains with us, for the limitations of AI systems still aren't widely recognized.) Increasingly, as AI applications enter our lives, the education of ordinary people – and especially of doctors, nurses, medical counsellors and researchers – must stress these limitations. Some are merely temporary: in 10 or 20 years, they can be forgotten. But some are, in principle or in practice, unavoidable.

For instance, the more a program uses (and/or accepts) 'natural' phrases in English (or French . . .), the more the naïve user may be misled. Suppose that the program is provided with a range of vocabulary with which to express (numerically calculated) statistical probabilities, for instance. Granted, this is unlikely in programs written for use by highly educated professionals. But programs designed to be bought 'off the shelf' by the general public are different. The man on the Clapham omnibus, arguably, has a better chance of understanding the terms *practically impossible*, *very unlikely*, *evens*, *a good bet* and *highly probable* than of distinguishing statistical measures such as *0.0001*, *0.01*, *0.5*, *0.75* and *0.90*. And other items could be added too: *impossible*, *possible*, *just possible*, *virtually certain* . . . one could go on. If naïve users see the program coming up with phrases like this, they're likely to assume that its use of language (which is to say, its judgments) in other areas is comparably subtle. In general, however, it won't be – and it *can't* be. Outside very limited and strictly defined domains, there's no practical possibility – some would say, no possibility *in principle* – of our writing AI programs that will use natural languages with anything approaching human subtlety. The user who doesn't realize this may therefore be seriously misled.

This, of course, is an argument suggesting that ethically sensitive programmers should *desist* from making their programs deceptively user-friendly. Indeed, some AI professionals have argued exactly this (Whitby 1988). In the biomedical context, particular issues – such as those surrounding medical consent – arise which just aren't relevant in the general case.

A further difficulty here is that it's often difficult for AI professionals to understand the *success* of their program, never mind its limitations and failures. A famous case of the early 1980s concerned a neural network, or connectionist system, called NETtalk (Sejnowski and Rosenberg 1986). This was hugely impressive for its time. What it did was to learn to pronounce English words correctly, by reading them off a page and being told whether one pronunciation was better than another. The result, especially evident if one heard only every 300th 'try', was an increasingly humanlike pronunciation that reminded one inescapably of a young child's progression from babbling to 'proper' speech. Significantly, it took the programmer only 18 months to build and test the program. It took him another two years to understand it.

The technical details needn't concern us. To cut a long story short, the programmers had to find three new ways of analysing the network's performance, in order to grasp just what was going on. Of course, they knew what the basic learning-rule was, for they'd built that in from the start. The mystery was to understand, at a higher level of description, what – in effect – the learning-rule was enabling the program to do. The researchers found three ways of studying this. They could 'partition' the performance statistically, to see which sound-discriminations were being made most often, and which depended on which (the class of vowels, for example, or the sub-class of labial consonants). They could 'injure' the network temporarily, by deactivating specific parts of it, and watch to see what difference this made to the overall behaviour. And third, they could track the activation of particular individual units.

The general moral (no pun intended!) here is that many AI systems are close to being 'black boxes': devices whose input-output relations are reliable, even useful, but whose inner workings are unknown. In so far as they really are 'reliable', there's no problem. But if one doesn't understand how they work then there's no way of knowing how they'll react to an *unusual* situation without actually trying it. And in many medical and/or biological contexts, that may be too late. This problem is especially severe with neural-network systems (too often thought by the general public to be near to magic). But even traditional AI programs, if they're complex enough, and especially if they're able to learn and/or accept new data, can be difficult to understand and predict.

The fifth class of ethical problems is highly relevant here. They relate to the morality of giving advice in contexts where people are required to assess, and to accept, some degree of risk. Risk assessment is notoriously difficult, in technical terms. More to the point, people's attitude to risk varies.

Sometimes it varies with the context: a general anaesthetic is risky, but if the alternative is death or great discomfort then it's readily accepted. But what *counts* as 'great discomfort'? John may be less able to tolerate pain than Mary – so an AI adviser shouldn't be accorded equal strength in both cases. Again, what counts as *acceptable* risk? Financial advisers know that John may be more tolerant of risk than Mary – and this difference may cross from the stock market into medical contexts. Genetic counsellors, and doctors prescribing drugs or recommending surgery, have to take these individual differences into account. An AI model should be able to allow for them also – or at the very least, to flag them for consideration. Some patients, of course, wouldn't want to know the risk. This leads us to our sixth class of problems: how much should an AI program be able to tell the non-professional user? Someone with a life-threatening disease may want to know the medical statistics *even if they're not favourable*. Others will want to know only if they're 60 per cent or above. Yet others won't want to think about such measures at all, preferring to rely on willpower, or prayer, or just plain luck. Similarly, some patients faced with having an operation will want to know exactly what's going to be done, and maybe also how. Others won't want to know *anything at all* about it.

Doctors face such problems every day, in deciding just how much to tell their patients. And legal issues sometimes get in the way. If one has an eye operation in the USA, for example, one may have to sign a consent-form which (for the protection of the hospital in case of mishap) lists all possible negative outcomes. Obviously, one possibility, in the worst case, is 'loss of the eye'. I've seen someone very seriously worried by the prospect of an operation in which this was very unlikely indeed. So, legal protection aside, *should* he have been informed of this possibility? And should an AI program list it as a possible outcome of that particular type of surgery?

These questions lie at the heart of the doctor–patient relationship. One may not like one's doctor. She may not be a model of tact. And one may suspect that she's fobbing one off with pleasantries, instead of being 'straight' about the medical issues. But at least the doctor is a fellow human being. She's persuadable – maybe. And there are some undesirable things that she can, presumably, be trusted not to do. After all, she – as a human being – shares the general background of human interests. An AI program doesn't.

Imagine a greengrocer needing to hire people to pick 50 kilos of blackberries. He knows from past experience that an 18-year-old woman can pick (let's say) two kilos an hour, and that a 22-year-old man can pick three. So he consults his computer-calculator, which tells him to hire them for ten hours. – Fine. But if he sends them out *together*, he won't get 50 kilos. He'll either get much more, because they're both showing off to each other, or he'll get much less – for reasons we needn't go into, but which no computer-calculator could ever suspect. 'Background human interests', it seems, can even override arithmetic.

Finally, biotechnology in medical contexts raises concerns about 'quality of life'. This concept itself is highly problematic. And it's linked with ethically controversial matters such as abortion and euthanasia – we shan't reach general agreement on those in a hurry. In principle, however, quality of life (QOL) issues could be included in AI programs. Provided that we'd agreed on a certain QOL 'menu', that menu could be represented by an AI adviser. In other words, it's not just 'medical-technological' issues that can be involved. And the QOL priorities could be made more or less explicit, more or less visible to the user and/or the patient concerned.

An illustration of this point caused something of a scandal in the late 1980s (anon. 1988). St. George's Hospital in London decided to use a computer program to do the initial 'weeding-out' of the hundreds of applications for medical school which they received each year. Only objective facts were to be dealt with by the program, of course: exam results, for instance. The program was written, and tested on experimental batches of application forms until it could select the same 'second-stage' candidates that the human interviewers did. Then, it was left to get on with it. The only human input needed was from a clerk, keying-in the information from the forms. Meanwhile, the doctors could relax: they had nothing to do until the actual interviews. Everyone was happy.

This situation lasted for four years. Then, someone suspected that it might be biased. This wasn't clear from an initial inspection of the program, but was confirmed when the gender and/or ethnic group of several candidates were changed and the data re-run – with the result that applicants previously selected were now refused, and vice versa. Eventually, it became clear that the program was applying numerical weightings that affected the probability of the candidates' getting through to the interview stage. And they were disadvantaging women and blacks. They'd been put there in the first place in order that the program should select the very same applicants as the human admissions-staff would have done. Since the staff, unknowingly, were prejudiced, their prejudices had to be implemented in the program if it was to give the same results.

The point, here, is that irrationalities of many different kinds *can* be represented in AI models if we wish. As the COMET program showed, ethical values can be represented too. And so can judgements about the quality of life, or the desirability/undesirability of abortion or euthanasia. But it has to be done *by us*. The program, in and of itself, can never do it.

In sum: the new moral problems arise partly because of the location of human responsibility. This concerns the design, the sale and marketing, the recommendation, the use and the misuse of AI systems. But ethical problems also arise because of the many differences between human thinking and perception and AI. It follows that one can't discuss them seriously without a good knowledge of what AI can and can't do, and *why*. Some forms of AI are apt for doing one thing, others for another. Indeed, their strengths and weaknesses are largely complementary. Neural networks, for instance, are very good at pattern recognition. But they can't do sequential reasoning or hierarchical planning: for that, one needs the more traditional type of AI program. In that sense, the ethics depends on the science. For sure, there's no quick and easy answer.

References

Anonymous

1988 *Report of a Formal Investigation into St. George's Hospital Medical School* (London: Commission for Racial Equality).

Anonymous
1989 *Benefits and Risks of Knowledge-Based Systems: Report of a Working Party of the Council for Science and Society* (Oxford: Oxford University Press).

Boden, M. A.
1987 [1977] *Artificial Intelligence and Natural Man* (London: MIT Press, 2nd edn).

Cooper, R., T. Shallice and J. Farringdon
1995 'Symbolic and Continuous Processes in the Automatic Selection of Actions', in J. Hallam (ed.), *Hybrid Problems, Hybrid Solutions* (Oxford: IOS Press), 27–37.

Du Boulay, B., B. Teather, G. H. du Boulay, N. P. Jeffrey, D. Teather, M. Sharples and L. Cuthbert
1999 'Towards a Decision Support Training System for MR Radiology of the Brain', *AI in Medicine (AIMD '99)*, 93–102.

Norman, D. A., and T. Shallice
1986 'Attention to Action: Willed and Automatic Control of Behavior', in R. Davidson, G. Schwartz and D. Shapiro (eds.), *Consciousness and Self Regulation: Advances in Research and Theory* vol. IV (New York: Plenum), 1–18.

Sejnowski, T. J., and C. R. Rosenberg
1986 *NETtalk: A Parallel Network that Learns to Read Aloud* (Johns Hopkins University Electrical Engineering and Computer Science Technical Report JHU/EECS-86/01; reprinted in J. A. Anderson and E. Rosenfeld (eds.), *Neurocomputing: Foundations of Research* (Cambridge, MA: MIT Press, 1988), 663–72.

Whitby, B.
1988 *Artificial Intelligence: A Handbook of Professionalism* (Chichester: Ellis Horwood).

Willshaw, D. J., and J. T. Buckingham
1990 'An Assessment of Marr's Theory of the Hippocampus as a Temporary Memory Store', *Philosophical Transactions of the Royal Society: Series B*, 329: 205–15.

11

Co-creation or hubris? Responses to biotechnology in Christianity, Judaism and Islam

Ulf Görman

Introduction

Biotechnology offers new possibilities for dealing with life. But these options for action also create ethical problems. Not least this constitutes a challenge to religion, for different reasons. First, religion tends to look back at its sources for guidance. Although it seems important for religion to take a standpoint, these sources do not give any direct guidance for thinking about how to act responsibly with respect to the courses of action opened by microbiology and its applications. Second, through biotechnology, religion meets not only a theory of reality but also a vision for the future. Technology is a tool for doing things, for achieving goals and for causing effects. A religious understanding is also connected to a vision, and the relation between these two imaginations will need consideration.

In this article I will investigate some religious reactions to modern biotechnology. I will not only deal with a few different interpretations of Christianity, but also look at other religions of the book, i.e. Judaism and Islam. It will be evident that, not only are there great differences between various religions, but also that there is strong diversity within them. Each religion embraces several different views on how to understand the religious tradition in relation to modern society, the worldviews in modern society, and the tools offered by technology for realizing the ideals of that worldview. Some understand religious sources and tradition as literally applicable and directly normative. Others perceive the tradition as an authority that needs to be understood and reinterpreted in every new situation, not least in the current world. Still others look upon religious sources as relative to their time and culture, but expressions of some very general ideas, which we today must apply freely by means of our own worldview, intellect and experience. This means that within each religious tradition we can find a variety of different standpoints and arguments.

It is often argued that positions in ethical matters are achieved by the application of very general principles. However, I will try to make clear that it is often more enlightening to look upon such views and arguments as efforts to use earlier standpoints in important questions as tools for dealing with the new situation. This is a kind of casuistry in the sense that what I will call *profile standpoints* are used as guides in new but similar situations.[1]

Some historical comments

Early religious responses to biotechnology tended to be reluctant. In my early theological studies I discovered the book *Fabricated Man*, published in 1970 by theologian Paul Ramsey. He discussed reproductive technology of his time, like artificial insemination, and looked into other techniques he could foresee for the future. In general he was critical about the separation between reproduction and sexuality he could discern in all these future visions, and his general conclusion was that humans ought not to 'play God'. He was not the only one to use this phrase as a warning against biotechnology.[2]

A number of years later I looked at the treatment of bioethical issues in different Churches and in the ecumenical movement. The World Council of Churches (WCC) may serve as an illustrative example. In 1982, biotechnology was discussed in a WCC booklet, *Manipulating Life: Ethical Issues in Genetic Engineering*. A major concern in this report is the risk involved in these new techniques and the social issues connected to their use. The central committee of WCC adopted more precise interpretations and recommendations in 1989, documented in the report *Biotechnology: Its Challenges to the Churches and the World*. This report focuses on the dilemma created by the potentials and dangers of biotechnology: technology is not only a scientific tool, but also an ideology. The Churches are encouraged to offer within their societies an alternative vision for the future, based on their commitment to the integrity of creation as God's gift.

The WCC identifies the extraordinary social and ethical concerns raised by prenatal diagnosis. The possibility of using prenatal genetic analysis for sex selection is described as most disturbing, and the WCC calls for the prohibition of genetic testing for sex selection. The report draws attention to ways in which knowledge of an individual's genetic makeup can be abused, for example in work, health care, insurance and education. The WCC proposes a ban on experiments involving engineering of the human germ-line, which affects also an individual's descendants, and urges strict control of somatic gene therapy, drawing attention to the potential misuse of both techniques as a means of discrimination. In vitro fertilization (IVF) has been developed to correct or circumvent the problem of infertility. But IVF may also result in suffering by creating pain and unfulfilled promises, exploitative uses of women by the sale of ovum, foetus or childbearing, and the separation of parenthood from the sexual act, which can pose challenges to traditional understandings of the family. Embryo research raises difficult questions about the status of the human embryo as a potential human being. The WCC calls for the ban of commercialized childbearing as well as the commercial sale of ovum, embryos and sperm, and advises governments to prohibit embryo research, with any experiment, if agreed, being undertaken only under well-defined conditions.

These examples illustrate that early religious responses to biotechnology were in general very reluctant. At the end of the 1980s the WCC still saw its main task as being to put a brake on the use of biotechnology, which was understood as an ideological enemy to religion. At that time, however, others had begun to look upon biotechnology in a more open and diversified way. It is evident that we can see a development in the religious reactions to the new challenges created by biotechnology. Immediate reactions have often been characterized by scepticism. Successively we can see more diversified, balanced and complex responses. Common to the many different Christian, Jewish and Muslim reactions is the reverence for the world and especially the human being as the creation of God. But when it comes to the understanding of this in relation to the new biological knowledge and its technological applications we can see a world of differences. Let us first look at two examples from the Christian tradition.

Roman Catholic Church

According to the Roman Catholic Church marriage is a sacrament, a divine mystery that provides the grace of God. Among the gifts God gives in marriage are love and procreation. Marital love reaches its completion in the matrimonial act, which always implies the possibility of procreation. This means that in the tradition of the Catholic Church human procreation is strongly connected with the sexual act. This is connected to a definite understanding of the conception as the beginning of individual human life. Every human life is holy and inviolable. Consequently, the embryo is considered as having full human value from the time of conception, and it should be protected like any human being.

Critics have raised the objection that a human embryo or a foetus is evidently not yet a fully developed human being. In response to this the Catholic tradition has used the concept of potentiality. Even though the foetus is not fully grown, it is potentially a human being, and when it is allowed to develop naturally its potentiality will be realized. Because of this it ought to be fully respected as a human being from its first individual existence. The standpoint of the Vatican in these matters can be understood as a consequence of the belief that conception is the time of the infusion of the soul. Although there is no official doctrine saying this, this is an idea with a large influence in the Catholic tradition.

This has evident connections with the official standing of the Catholic Church concerning abortion. Abortion is described as a detestable atrocity. Any instance of produced abortion is a deliberate and direct killing of a human being in the beginning of its existence. In several encyclicals, among others *Evangelium Vitae*, the Pope declares that any deliberate abortion, whether it is considered as a goal or as a means to something else, is a serious moral violation, because it kills an innocent human being (John Paul II 1995).

Stark statements like these within a religious community with a strong central power might be expected to create unity. However, this has not been the case. Instead there is a forceful discussion within the Church. Some critics, among others some Catholic moral theologians, question whether the standpoint of the Pope is in line with Catholic tradition. Another important conflict concerns the question of how to apply the standpoint of the Church in its pastoral practice. This became evident in the recent conflict on the abortion advice clinics in Germany.

In Germany abortion legislation became a matter of debate when the former German Democratic Republic was integrated with Germany. The legislation on abortion in the two countries had been very different. The debate resulted in a compromise, according to which abortions are in principle prohibited, but may still be executed if the woman in question has received advice concerning abortion. Consequently, a certificate of abortion advice was a step towards an abortion. Around 1700 abortion advice clinics were started around the country, and the Catholic Church ran one out of six. This created a conflict within the Church. The Vatican urged the closure of the clinics, while the majority of the German bishops wanted them to continue. Finally the Vatican had its own way. However, the clinics are not closed but taken over by others.

This example is not only an illustration of the fact that there are contrary standpoints within the Church, but also that it is not evident how a principle should be applied in practice. And not least it seems to illustrate a dilemma in the Catholic Church: should it be the long-term goal for the Church to require its members to act according to its doctrines, or should the Church focus on giving advice and leave the decision to the individual?

Assisted reproduction, handling of embryos, and embryonic stem cells

The official teaching of the Catholic Church is not to accept assisted reproduction.[3] It is argued that it separates procreation and the sexual act. The Church warns that excessive embryos are destroyed or misused in connection with assisted reproduction. In dealing with assisted reproduction, the Church says, human life is reduced to biological material.

However, on these matters there is a strong disagreement within the Church. A number of leading Catholic moral theologians and medical doctors argue that assisted reproduction, by using the gametes of a married couple, should be accepted. This applies to artificial insemination as well as IVF. Their main argument is that this will help an infertile couple to procreate. When such a treatment results in a child, this is a fruit of the intimate relation between the husband and wife, even if it is not the result of a sexual act.

As a clear consequence of its official understanding of conception and the foetus, the handling of human embryos and foetuses is acceptable according to the Vatican if it aims at protecting the individual foetus, improving its health or curing a disease, provided that it does not involve disproportionate risks. However, a number of activities made possible through assisted reproduction, such as use of embryos for research and use of embryonic stem cells, are strongly argued against. Pope John Paul II commented publicly on these matters a number of times. Not least he strongly opposed the creation for research purposes of human embryos, destined to be destroyed in the process. For similar reasons, cloning, and especially reproductive cloning of human beings, has been banned by representatives of the Church.

Genetic intervention

In 1996 British Catholic bishops presented a 'Report on Genetic Intervention on Human Subjects'. They especially focus on germ-line intervention, and their attitude is reluctant. It is interesting to see how they argue in detail and what conclusions they arrive at. They point out a number of questionable steps: germ-line intervention must be done by means of IVF. They expect that in the development of this technique embryos must be used for experimentation and discarded, and abortion may be necessary on foetuses where the therapy is not successful. But if germ-line intervention could be made on eggs or sperm instead of embryos, and if conception could take place through intercourse, then they would not find any serious problems with germ-line intervention. Consequently, the main problems that the Catholic bishops find with germ-line intervention are that it separates conception from marital intercourse, and that embryos will be disposed of. Their main concern is neither the change in the genetic set-up itself nor the risks involved (anon. 1996).

But even a strong authority does not change the fact that there are a large number of different understandings of Christian belief within the Catholic Church. A number of Catholic moral theologians do not think of the early human embryo as an individualized human entity. They refer to embryological studies indicating that fertilization is a process, and that the embryo is not sufficiently individualized to be considered a person. So there is a certain opposition within the Church, arguing for an orientation that is more open to the benefits of biotechnology when applied to the beginning of human life, and which looks at its possibility to promote future human well-being.[4]

In sum, the connection between the 'matrimonial act' and procreation, the infusion of the human soul at conception and the principle of goodness are such profile standpoints for the official Catholic Church. But even if the Catholic Church has a very restrictive official attitude to the use of biotechnology at the beginning of life, there are a number of divergent views behind the official façade and a discussion is certainly going on.

Organ transplantation

The official ban on most use of biotechnology at the beginning of life, however, does not mean that even the official Catholic Church is against any use of biotechnology. When the beginning of human life is not involved, the Church can be very open in these matters. The example of organ transplantation may illustrate this.

Organ transplantation is a recent technology, which has been highly controversial. Problems that have been discussed are, among others: Is it right to use the body of another human being as a tool to save or improve life for a person with a malfunctioning organ? Is there a risk with organ trading, and should this be accepted? What risks are involved when the transplanted organ is rejected or does not function properly in another body? We have two kidneys but can live with one. A donor can live on with only one kidney, but with a higher risk. However, the heart or lungs can only be taken from a donor with no future life. Should then brain death be accepted as a death criterion?

All these problems could certainly be able to create hesitation and misgivings as to the appropriateness of organ donation and organ transplantation. However, the Catholic Church has taken a clear standpoint in favour of organ donation, which is not only accepted, but also recommended. The Church recommends individuals to be willing to donate their organs, and states are recommended to presume willingness to donate organs in their legislation. In Germany the bishops of the Catholic Church have even managed to make a common statement with the Lutheran bishops to this effect, a statement that proved to become controversial within the Lutheran Churches in Germany (anon. 1990).

Modern Lutheran tradition

Modern Lutheran tradition focuses on the capacity of every human being to understand and decide on ethical matters, even difficult ethical problems. Ethical knowledge is available in the Bible, which can in principle be read and understood by everybody. The community of Christians as well as human rationality and culture are other sources of ethical knowledge. Christian ethics cannot be definitely and finally defined by church leaders, as standpoints are temporal, and morally relevant situations are complex and to some extent unique. The responsibility and burden of an ethical decision lies to a certain extent on the individual Christian. 'Humans are God's created co-creators' has become a common wording among modern Lutherans for expressing the understanding that humans when serving God are to take an active and creative role in the world.

Prenatal genetic analysis and selective abortion

In Lutheran tradition there are different understandings of the rights of the foetus. Some argue that the fertilized egg and the foetus should be ascribed full human dignity, respect and rights already from conception. Others look upon human dignity as something that should be gradually ascribed to the foetus. But this question is not decisive for resolving the matter of an abortion, as the interest and situation of the mother is involved as well. Abortion is considered to be a complicated question, precisely because of the sometimes contrary interests of the mother and the foetus. Today abortion is often seen as an emergency solution to a conflict in a difficult situation, which means that abortion is generally accepted if the pregnancy is considerably in conflict with the interests of the mother.

These traditional deliberations can be used as a clue to understanding arguments among Lutherans on prenatal genetic diagnostic and selective abortion. The question whether the discovery of a genetic deviation should result in an abortion is often described as a dilemma, where the foetus' right to protection is weighed against the risk of a short life with severe suffering, and where the responsibility of the parents and their desire to have a child are compared to and contrasted with their limitations in taking care of a severely handicapped child. It is common to argue that decisions for selective abortions are often based on too weak arguments. Sex selection based on prenatal diagnostic is heavily criticized. Many Lutherans point out that a life is valuable even with a handicap, and there is no right to have a child without a handicap. However, prenatal diagnostic is always welcomed when it is used as a basis for medical treatment of the foetus.

Other uses of biotechnology

Artificial insemination, IVF and other means of assisted reproduction are often accepted in principle as methods to overcome childlessness. Some representatives of Lutheran Churches tend to focus on the problems involved and caution that treatments like these can involve suffering and frustrated hopes. It can lead to exploitation of women through trading of eggs and embryos and surrogate motherhood. Other Lutherans are much more affirmative, focusing on the benefits of assisted reproduction and its possible contributions to human well-being, including, among others, the bestowal of a blessing to a childless couple. The Swedish Lutheran bishop Bengt Wadensjö explicitly talks about 'the principle of blessing' as a tool for evaluating new technologies, such as stem cell research. We should welcome technologies that can improve human life and understand them as 'blessings' (Wadensjö 2001).

Some Lutherans, like the American theologian Ted Peters, are very optimistic as regards the future of biotechnology, including gene therapy. The possibilities of human self-transcendence and a creativity that leads to something new 'belong to human nature', he says. He argues from the idea of man as created co-creator, and describes his position as a theology of freedom. Rather than discussing whether we should play God he wants to have us think about how we should play human (Peters 1997).

In the Lutheran Churches and among Lutheran theologians we can see a large variety of responses to biotechnology, from fairly sceptical attitudes to very positive and anticipating approaches. An important profile standpoint in the modern Lutheran approach is that the final decision in ethical dilemmas is left to the individual.

Judaism

In Jewish belief, the Jewish Bible and the *Halaka* tradition are strong authorities, but the extensive and ever ongoing discussion underscores the necessity to reinterpret the tradition. Judaism is a tradition of interpretation, based on the idea that there is no divine revelation after the divine message on

Sinai. According to this belief, rabbis have a great freedom of interpretation, and it is legitimate for new understandings to develop over time. The Jewish tradition of interpretation is explicitly casuistic, in the sense that similar cases in history are identified and applied to the new situation (Zetterholm 2004).

A leading idea in Jewish ethics is that life is a gift from God. Life itself is not in our command. It is not up to us whether we want to live or not, and neither what we should use life for. Instead we are the stewards of life. It is our duty to respect and preserve all life. Every human being has an eternal and highest value. Because of this, any step towards the shortening of human life is unacceptable. But there is also openness for influencing life in order to improve the circumstances for every human being.

To procreate is a divine command according to Jewish religion. A Jew is supposed to be married, to be sexually active, and to strive for having at least two children, preferably a boy and a girl, according to a common interpretation of the Jewish tradition. Sexual communion as well as procreation are both central aspects of marriage. For instance, if a pregnancy should be dangerous, then abstinence is not a desirable solution, because then the couple would have to abandon both these aims of marriage, instead of only one. As a consequence of this, whenever a pregnancy must be avoided, the use of contraceptives is not only accepted, but in fact required, because otherwise the sexual communion would be prevented.

An important problem is the 'improper emission of male seed'. This idea refers to the story of Onan in Genesis 38, who was supposed to marry his brother's widow and give offspring to his dead brother, but spilled his seed on the ground and was blamed and killed by God for this. In Jewish religion this story is understood as a prohibition against *coitus interruptus* as well as masturbation. This divine command has been an important factor in Jewish discussion for deciding on contraceptives and other aspects of sexual life.

In Jewish tradition the foetus is a human being in the making. It is not yet an independent human being, and not even fully a human being as long as it is in the womb. This is expressed by the standpoint taken by some rabbis, that the mother has a kind of ownership of the foetus, or that it is still a part of its mother.

The moment of birth, carefully defined, is the decisive instant when the foetus becomes an independent human being. Now it is fully human, and the value of its life is on a par with the mother. However, even during the first 30 days after birth, this is still conditional. When a child dies within 30 days after birth, it is considered as stillborn, perhaps as a result of the fact that the pregnancy was not fully completed.

By tradition, this understanding of the foetus has influenced Jewish opinions in relation to abortion. The attitudes to abortion are very different, and they vary from very restrictive to fairly liberal. However, the arguments used have similarities and tend to illustrate and clarify the Jewish way of arguing. Arguments on abortion are generally oriented towards the situation of the mother. In the orthodox tradition, abortion is only accepted when the life of the mother is in danger, but when this is the case abortion is not only accepted, but even a duty. The main reason for this is the understanding that the mother is a full human being, while the foetus is not yet so. In the liberal tradition also a number of weaker needs on behalf of the mother have been accepted as reasons for abortion, up to the modernist position that any undesired pregnancy creates an unacceptable burden for the mother.[5]

Assisted reproduction

The debate on assisted reproduction has created an interesting and typical dilemma in the Jewish religion. On the one hand the duty to procreate is often described as the first divine command. On the other hand the prohibition against the improper emission of male seed has entailed a critical attitude to other sexual activities than correct intercourse as defined in Jewish tradition. The evident character of the dilemma is that assisted reproduction can assist in fulfilling the first of these commands, but it can violate the second one.

The common method to achieve sperm for IVF or artificial insemination is through masturbation. Evidently there is a strongly negative attitude to this among Jewish scholars. However, the Jewish discussion is, as always, characteristically practical and adjustable. Many authorities have argued that in the case when artificial insemination is the only way of effecting procreation, then procuring the semen is not 'in vain' and therefore acceptable. Sperm can also be extruded by means of a needle from the spermatic duct. This is a method that has been accepted and recommended by some authorities.

An example can illustrate how traditional problems can be treated today. Rabbi David Bleich in New York discusses IVF: How can the duty to procreate be understood in the light of modern technology? It cannot be a duty to have children, but only to have intercourse. Further, it is only a duty to do what is natural. Because of this, IVF is allowed and may be welcome, but cannot be a duty (Bleich 2000).

There is more or less a consensus among rabbis that neither donation of eggs or sperm can be accepted. A child born in this way would be illegitimate according to Jewish law. Some authorities are willing to accept artificial insemination or IVF with the gametes of a married couple, because it helps them to procreate, while some are against this, because a child born in this way has not been conceived through a normal sexual relation.

Stem cell research, gene therapy, and cloning

The traditional understanding of the status of the embryo is used to take a standpoint in relation to embryonic stem cell research. With current techniques an embryo outside the womb cannot develop into a human being. Because of this it is considered to have a lower status than an embryo within the womb, and consequently the duty to cure disease is more important than the respect for the embryo. It is accepted to destroy embryos remaining after IVF, but rabbis are divided when it comes to the question of creating embryos especially for research purposes (anon. 2001; anon. 2002).

Somatic gene therapy and even germ-line gene therapy is accepted by a number of authorities as long as it is an aid to cure diseases, because of the duty to heal, but standpoints are divided and reluctant when it comes to the question of improving or changing human properties. Therapeutic cloning in connection with gene transfer is clearly accepted by the conservative movement as a means to cure diseases (Wahrman 2002; Zetterholm 2004).

Reproductive cloning is much more problematic. Some sources look upon reproductive cloning as a possible last resort to help a childless couple to procreate, but most authorities find it unacceptable, often based on the argument that a child with only one parent is illegitimate. Rabbi Feldman (1998) tries to avoid this problem by arguing that it would be acceptable to divide an embryo in order to help a couple obtain two children, in this case a pair of twins, provided that this is the last chance for a couple to fulfil the duty to procreate. Rabbi Bleich, on the other hand, does not accept reproductive cloning to help a childless couple, because of the danger for the foetus. He accepts, however, the possibility of creating a twin from a terminally ill child by reproductive cloning, if tissue from the cloned child can be used to cure the diseased child (Bleich 1998). According to Rabbi Dorff it is a danger that humans may try to reach immortality by reproducing themselves, but he accepts different kinds of cloning for research and in order to cure diseases (Dorff 1998).

As in other religious traditions, we find a large variety also in Jewish responses to biotechnology. This is partly in line with Jewish self-understanding, which involves the idea that the interpretation of Jewish belief is an ever ongoing and unending discussion. A number of characteristic Jewish profile standpoints make the Jewish discussion distinctively different from the Christian.

Islam

The traditional understanding is that Islamic ethics is based upon a kind of casuistry. In a morally difficult question, similar cases are identified in the

Quran or the tradition of *Sunna*. These cases are then propounded as exemplary in order to interpret the new situation. In practice, however, the situation is much more complicated. The tradition of interpretation involves contradictory standpoints. In the current situation several different authorities compete on the right to make interpretations. By tradition, interpretations have been made by the *'Ulama*, the collective of the religiously learned. In *fiqh* academies, groups of learned authorities try to reach consensus in interpretation. However, their sole authority is being questioned today.

When it comes to the way of interpretation itself, the *'Ulama* has been eager to take its own long tradition of interpretation into account and to suggest solutions to new problems that are in line with this tradition. Others, however, go around this history of interpretation and look directly at the texts of the *Quran* and the *Hadiths* themselves. This has been a frequent approach in modern feminist Islam. In the current discussion a number of other approaches for interpretation can also be found, such as appeal to general Islamic moral principles, appeal to current scientific knowledge, and so on (Svensson 2000; 2004).

In principle, Islam has a positive opinion of human knowledge. Knowledge is a gift from God, and human beings have a duty to use knowledge in order to communicate with God and serve other human beings. In practice, however, different representatives, traditions and schools tend to apply this idea in different ways. Some put the main emphasis on the Quran and the tradition as the source of knowledge and look with scepticism at the modern Western understanding of knowledge. Others point out the importance of the continuous search for knowledge and look upon this as a task and an opportunity that God has given to humans. In this case biological and medical knowledge are in general looked upon as good. The decisive question is whether the use of knowledge is in line with or contrary to basic Muslim ethical ideas. God is the ruler of the human life span. Death is inevitable in time. However, this does not mean that it is wrong for human beings to intervene. Physicians are considered to be in the service of God.

According to Islamic belief, everything that happens is a result of the will of God. This strong belief has resulted in a discussion as to whether efforts at birth regulation would be improper and an expression of distrust for God. Are not *coitus interruptus*, use of contraceptives, and assisted reproduction different attempts to prevent God's predestination? Those who believe that this is not the case have quoted the *Hadith*, which tells about a man who went to the mosque and left his camel outside. The camel walked away. The man complained to the Prophet and said that he had left the camel and trusted God to take care of it. The Prophet answered: '[You should] bind it and trust God.' The lesson, of course, is that we should not only trust God, but also act adequately ourselves.

Assisted reproduction

On assisted reproduction Islam has a fairly homogenous view. A disease should always be cured. Infertility is regarded as a disease, and consequently medical treatment against infertility is not only accepted but also recommended. The keeping of family bonds is one of the most important values that have to be kept and guarded according to Islamic belief. To procreate is strongly recommended, but this is a duty for a married couple. This has also been an important argument when Muslim authorities have discussed assisted reproduction. Generally they accept artificial insemination as well as IVF, as long as sperm and eggs from the married couple are used. They are against donation of sperm as well as eggs, surrogate motherhood and any other procedure that dissolves the idea that two married persons should be the parents of a child. This is also the reason put forward when Muslim authorities tend not to accept reproductive cloning.

Blood transfusion

A number of questions are of special interest in a Muslim context and give an interesting insight to the specific presuppositions and arguments in Islam. One of these is blood transfusion, where Islam faces a dilemma. Blood outside the body is impure, and, more specifically, blood poured forth is forbidden to eat, like dead meat or flesh of swine is also forbidden to eat. And if something is forbidden to eat, then it is also forbidden to deal with it, like selling or buying. Should then the well-known technique of blood transfusion in order to save life be accepted or not?

Mufti Shafi in Pakistan argues that in principle blood transfusion is forbidden, because it is a part of the human body, and outside the body it is impure. However, in extraordinary life-threatening circumstances it can be permissible. Here he draws an analogy to breast milk. This is a part of the female body, but in normal circumstances it is even an obligation for a mother to give milk to her child. It is also permissible for an adult to use breast milk as nourishment as a form of medicine. The analogy to breast milk is specific for Mufti Shafi, but a number of authorities are willing to accept blood donation in the case of urgent need.

Interesting are the comments about the donor. It is considered to be in line with human dignity to make the humane gesture to assist a fellow human being. Because of this, voluntary donation is accepted, but it must be without economic compensation. However, some authorities are not willing to accept blood transfusions or organ donations from donors who are not Muslims. There are different arguments for this: by not being Muslims, they are *shirk* i.e. they ascribe partners to God, and as such they are religiously impure. Or they are looked upon with suspicion because they may have consumed impure food. Mufti Shafi even points out that Islam discourages parents from having their children breast fed by women known to be of bad character. Because of reasons like these some authorities recommend a Muslim avoids having a blood transfusion from a non-Muslim (Ebrahim 2001).

Organ transplantation

Classical Islam regards the human body as a trust from God, and because of this it is not allowed to use or sell parts of the human body. The possibility of organ transplantation has challenged this view. Muslim scholars have been divided when facing the opportunities opened by the possibilities of organ transplantation. Those who are willing to accept this generally look upon transplantation as an act of altruism. They find arguments in the *Quran*, such as in *Sura* 5: 'Help one another in righteousness and piety', as well as in the *Hadith*, which states that the believers are like a whole body: when one part is affected with pain the whole of it responds in terms of wakefulness and fever. A number of restrictions are applied: consent must be given, no other treatment must be available, organs must not be sold, and organs from non-Muslims should be avoided (Ebrahim 2001).

Stem cell research and cloning

In Muslim tradition the development of the foetus goes through a number of stages of 40 days each – a drop of water, a lump of blood, and a lump of meat, followed by ensoulment after 120 days. Based on this understanding most Islamic authorities regard embryonic stem cell research, based on left-over embryos, as unproblematic, as stem cells are produced from embryos before this time.

Human striving for knowledge is in general considered to be a good thing. Health is also worth aiming at, and it is a divine decree to cure diseases. Modern gene technology, however, involves a risk for mischief and depravity. Reproductive cloning is described as 'copying' a human being and is condemned by almost all authorities. It is described as hubris because it is an effort of human beings to step outside the limits set by God (Anees 2002). The main argument against reproductive cloning is that it is a threat to the idea of the family. It is also considered dangerous and unsafe for the cloned individual, a violation of human dignity, and an example of the spread of Western decadence, which Muslims should resist (Saheb 2001).

The idea of the family as the basic human community, and the belief that a child is a divine creation based upon the unity of contrasts, i.e. male and female, are central to the religious Muslim family law. An individual who is the result of reproductive cloning has an unclear identity and kinship, as he or she is not a result of the family community of man and woman. But in extreme cases, some authorities argue, reproductive cloning may still be acceptable, if it is the only way to fulfil the duty to procreate, but only if gametes from the couple involved are used.

Concerning human cloning the Islamic discussion points out a number of benefits, such as the possibility of curing diseases and infertility, and of producing organs for transplantation. It may also open the possibility of reversing the ageing process. However, this may contradict the *Hadith* where the Prophet is reported as saying that God created a cure for every disease except for old age. The largest problem, however, is the threat to family relations. As a result of its considerations, the Islamic *Fiqh* Academy of the Muslim World League at its tenth meeting in Jeddah, 1997 stated that the cloning of humans is un-Islamic and forbidden, no matter what methods are used to produce identical humans, and that all biotechnological manipulations involving human procreation whereby a third-party element is introduced outside the marital bounds, be that in the form of womb, egg, sperm or cell, are unlawful. This is, however, allowed on micro-organisms, plants and animals.[6]

It should be evident from this paper that Islamic discussion of biotechnology finds it important to relate heavily to the Islamic tradition and its holy sources, especially the *Quran*. In practice, however, the tradition can be understood in many ways, and a large part of the discussion focuses on the current application of Islamic profile questions.

Summary

Even if initial reactions mainly expressed scepticism, this paper has given evidence that religious responses to biotechnology today are much more well-informed and diversified than in the early days. The large differences between, as well as within, different religious traditions are evident. I have tried to clarify the differences between traditions by pointing out that many arguments are related to profile standpoints. There are also large differences within religious traditions. To a great extent they can be understood as depending on different attitudes to the final truth and authority of the original religious sources, and in contrast, to the variability of the human situation and the possibility of new insights in the modern world.

Notes

1 Jonsen and Toulmin (1988) give good evidence that different kinds of casuistic arguments have been much more influential in the history of moral reasoning than we generally expect.

2 Chapman (1999) as well as Peters (1997) both comment on the use of the phrase 'playing God'. It seems that this phrase was first used by the biochemist Leroy Augenstein in *Come, Let Us Play God*, in 1969, then as a recommendation, but it was quickly taken over by sceptical theologians and used as a warning.

3 To begin with, the matter was still to some extent open to discussion. This was evident when Societas Ethica in 1985 had its annual meeting in Palermo on 'Problems in Bioethics: The Paradigm of In Vitro Fertilisation'. See Hemberg and Görman 1985.

4 Interesting examples of this standpoint can be found in *The Human Embryonic Stem Cell Debate: Science, Ethics and Public Policy* (Holland *et al.* 2001), where Margaret A. Farley ('Roman Catholic Views on Research Involving Bioethics and Research on Human Embryonic Stem Cells') and Michael M. Mendiola ('Human Embryonic Stem Cells: Possible Approaches from a Catholic Perspective') both argue for a more open Catholic view in these matters.

5 For summaries of Jewish ethical thinking, see for instance Feldman (1998), and Rosner and Bleich (2000).

6 For discussion on the Islamic treatment of these problems, see Omran (1992) and Ebrahim (2001).

References

Anees, Munawar A.

2002 'Human Clones and God's Trust: The Islamic View', in Glenn McGee (ed.), *The Human Cloning Debate* (Berkeley, CA: Berkeley Hills Books, 3rd edn).

Anonymous

1990 *Organtransplantationen. Erklärung der deutschen Bischofskonferenz und des Rates der Evangelische Kirche in Deutschland* (Gemeinsame Texte, 1; Bonn: Sekretariat der Deutschen Bischofskonferenz).

1996 *Genetic Intervention on Human Subjects. The Report of a Working Party of the Catholic Bishops' Joint Committee on Bioethical Issues* (London: Linacre Centre for Health Care Ethics).

2001 'Human Stem Cell Research', Reform Responsa 5761.7, http://data.ccarnet.org/resp/ (accessed 24 March 2005).

2002 'Stem Cell Research', unpublished Conservative Responsa accepted by Committee on Jewish Law and Standards, 13 March 2002.

Augenstein, Leroy

1969 *Come, Let Us Play God* (Evanston, IL: Harper & Row).

Bleich, J. David

1998 'Cloning: Homologous Reproduction and Jewish Law', in *Tradition: A Journal of Orthodox Jewish Thought* 32: 47–86.

2000 'Test-Tube Babies', in Fred Rosner and J. David Bleich (eds.) *Jewish Bioethics* (Hoboken, NJ: KTAV Publishing House).

Chapman, Audrey R.

1999 *Unprecedented Choices: Religious Ethics at the Frontiers of Genetic Science* (Minneapolis, MN: Fortress Press).

Dorff, Elliot N.

1998 *Matters of Life and Death* (Philadelphia/Jerusalem: Jewish Publication Society).

Ebrahim, Abul Fadl Mohsin

2001 *Organ Transplantation, Euthanasia, Cloning and Animal Experimentation: An Islamic View* (Leicester: The Islamic Foundation).

Feldman, David M.

1998 *Birth Control in Jewish Law: Marital Relations, Contraception, and Abortion as Set Forth in the Classic Texts of Jewish Law* (Northvale, NJ/Jerusalem: Jason Aronson).

Hemberg, Jarl and Ulf Görman (eds.)

1985 *Societas Ethica, Jahresbericht 1985* (Lund: Societas Ethica).

Holland, Suzanne, Karen Lebacqs and Laurie Zoloth (eds.)

2001 *The Human Embryonic Stem Cell Debate: Science, Ethics and Public Policy* (Cambridge, MA and London: MIT Press).

John Paul II

1995 *Evangelium Vitae: encyclical letter addressed to all the bishops, priests and deacons, men and women religious lay faithful and all people of good will on the value and inviolability of human life* (London: Catholic Truth Society).

Jonsen, Albert R., and Stephen Toulmin

1988 *The Abuse of Casuistry: A History of Moral Reasoning* (Berkeley, CA: University of California Press).

Omran, Abdel Rahim

1992 *Family Planning in the Legacy of Islam* (London and New York: Routledge).

Peters, Ted

1997 *Playing God? Genetic Determinism and Human Freedom* (New York and London: Routledge).

Ramsey, Paul

1970 *Fabricated Man: The Ethics of Genetic Control* (New Haven: Yale University Press).

Rosner, Fred, and J. David Bleich (eds.)

2000 *Jewish Bioethics* (Hoboken, NJ: KTAV Publishing House).

Saheb, Muhammad Saeed Motara

2001 'Human Cloning', http://www.islam.tc/ask-imam/ (accessed 30 March 2005).

Svensson, Jonas

2000 *Women's Human Rights and Islam: A Study of Three Attempts at Accommodation* (Stockholm: Almqvist & Wiksell International).

2004 'Muslimska perspektiv och attityder', in *Etik och genteknik. Filosofiska och religiösa perspektiv på genterapi, stamcellsforskning och kloning* (ed. Carl-Gustaf Andrén and Ulf Görman; Stockholm: Nordic Academic Press).

Wadensjö, Bengt

2001 'En etisk debatt är nödvändig', *Svenska Dagbladet* (18 October): 26.

Wahrman, Miryam Z.

2002 *Brave New Judaism: When Science and Scripture Collide* (Hanover/ London: Brandeis University Press).

World Council of Churches (WCC)

1982 *Manipulating Life: Ethical Issues in Genetic Engineering* (Geneva: World Council of Churches).

1989 *Biotechnology: Its Challenges to the Churches and the World* (Geneva: World Council of Churches).

Zetterholm, Karin

2004 'Judiska förhållningssätt till medicinsk etik', in *Etik och genteknik. Filosofiska och religiösa perspektiv på genterapi, stamcellsforskning och kloning* (ed. Carl-Gustaf Andrén and Ulf Görman; Stockholm: Nordic Academic Press).

12

The human being a co-creator? Theological reflections on reproductive cloning of human individuals

Jan-Olav Henriksen

What science develops in terms of possibilities for action and new ways of dealing with the world cannot be seen as ethically neutral. It is closely interrelated with our understanding of what it means to be a human being, and what we perceive as the determining elements of our existence. Moreover, science can present us with new opportunities for being human, and confront us with possibilities of expressing ourselves that have not hitherto been realizable. The possibility of realizing some of the options with which science presents us thus creates possibilities for our way of living as human beings. Such life can never be ethically neutral, but needs assessment in relation to what we see as the moral and theological dimensions of human life. A theological understanding of the relationship between freedom and moral responsibility can consequently be a crucial factor in how we interpret the interaction between science and theology.

This paper is an attempt to present and discuss the implications of some basic elements in systematic theology as regards how they will have impact on the understanding of the issue of cloning and modification of cells of human beings. Hence, it deliberately takes its point of departure in theological tradition, and not in what can be assumed as acceptable viewpoints for everyone. The point of departure is rather simple: Are humans 'playing God'[1] in a non-legitimate way when they make efforts to improve the life-conditions of others, for example, by means of therapeutic cloning? Can there be assessed a difference, ethically and theologically speaking, between therapeutic cloning of cells on the one hand, and reproductive cloning of human individuals on the other? Are there any elements in the theological understanding of what a human being is, and how he or she is related to God, that could provide us with some guidelines on how we are to address these issues? Can and should we be seen as co-creators to God when dealing with such challenges, or should cloning of human individuals be perceived as an attempt to compete with God?[2] Finally, how is one to understand the status of a cloned human individual, theologically speaking: is it possible to say that he or she is created in the image of God?

By affirming how there is a close relation between ethics and the underlying understanding of what a human being is, I tacitly recognize that not every kind of ethical problem can be solved with reference to values that are shared by everyone irrespective of their religious stance and worldview. What is at stake here is a question about how we understand the human being in its relation to the world, and whether or not we understand it in its relationship to God. I try to discuss the problem about human cloning in a perspective that also involves how the human being is created in the image of God, that is, called to reflect *God's* love and purposes for the world. Hence it is not an ethical assessment as such, but how a theological position can influence such assessments, that I want to explore in the following.

The following presentation is thus intended to be somewhat experimental and openly reflecting. It does not aim to present a fully worked through argument, but will imply an identification of important elements in an approach to reproductive cloning as it is seen from the viewpoint of theological anthropology. Hence, what I suggest in the following is simply to offer some resources for further discussion of the issue.

The conditions of freedom: the infinite creator as the giver of finite life

From a theological stance, human freedom does not primarily consist in our ability to choose whatever we like from a neutral point of view. It is constituted by our relationship to God. How we relate to God, and how our relation to him is shaped, opens up different other elements that guide human life and identity: the self-understanding that develops from this relationship, be it positive or negative, also guides our choices, actions and life-fulfilment. When humans are living in a true relationship with God and recognize God as the infinite source of their own being, this provides humans with a specific basis for life and the realization of freedom in the world: it establishes a self-understanding from which humans can see themselves as not fully determined by any *finite* being. Hence we are able to live on the basis of trust and faith in something infinite, something that transcends the very finite experiences and situations in which we find ourselves. This basis of our life in the trust towards the infinite makes it possible for humans to understand life within a larger horizon than the one provided by our occasional aims, desires and needs. However, it does not exclude such elements from human life, but integrates them into a larger horizon where they are not the solely determining factors. This horizon is constituted by the relationship with God, recognized as something different from, something other than, the world.

Negatively, a human being who does not see God as something to whom she relates positively, tries to avoid any relation to God that makes God a formative factor in her life. This is the life of the sinner: the sinner tries to live without God and, ultimately, she is her own master and orients herself toward aims based on her own interests. The sinner does not want to give God praise and glory for all that is – and sometimes she even tries to grasp some of that glory for herself.[3] A sinner will try to ignore the fact that she is a finite being, not able to grasp and control the very life-conditions that are given prior to her life, and still determines it. Her freedom is thus also a limited one: always determined by the very finite factors to which she relates in her life.

In concrete life, even anyone who believes in God still lives a life where both of these dimensions appear: we are both sinners and believers, and, accordingly, the tendencies to relate to ourselves and our finite aims on the one hand, and towards the infinite God on the other hand, shape a basic tension in human life.

From this follows several implications: first, humans believing in God have to realize that they are finite, and that finitude is one of the characteristics that makes them different from God. God is the infinite, and the source of our finitude. However, as long as we recognize both our own finitude and God's infinity, we have the possibility for being free, i.e., for not being determined in our lives by solely finite factors. God provides us with a point of departure for life that is not constituted by the finite.

Second, this means that the basis of human life and life-fulfilment is constituted by our relationship with God. True human freedom consists in living and acting based on this relationship. Freedom in a true sense is unconditioned by a finite relationship to something finite; instead it is conditioned by a relationship to the infinite (God).

Third, this means that human freedom is based on our relation to someone who is *other* than ourselves (God). The point of *otherness* or difference is necessary to recognize as important to freedom. But otherness is relevant both in relation to God and to humans. Other humans can influence our life and our abilities to live as free and responsible people. That we recognize each other as *others*, i.e., as individuals or subjects that have the right and possibility of being self-determined, is a constitutive element in how freedom can flourish among humans. If this is not so, the other and her relation to me is made into *sameness*, a sameness that does not allow me to see her as someone with a right in herself. Then I understand her solely from my own interests, perspectives, desires, needs, concepts, ideals, and so on. However, when I understand her as *other*, she transcends what is given in and by me. Consequently, my relation to her is then also marked by transcendence, or to say it more Levinasian-like: through her is given openness to the infinite and transcendent.

This goes for God as well. God transcends what is in my finite world. Only that God is not an other like other humans are to me, but an other that is only represented in the world, but never fully present there in the way others are.[4] God is one with whom I cannot immediately suppose any kind of similarities. Hence, to ground my life in God is to ground it in someone that I can suppose is transcending the different human needs, desires, and so on, but as said, without excluding them from the totality of my life. God offers me a life where I can relate to something else than what is given – but at the same time, he is the source of what is given in my life.

God is infinite. In Christian theology, God is also the source of life. Hence, God is the infinite source of life. This is interesting also because life itself seems to be infinite, in a certain sense: the phenomenon of life can only pass on from other forms of life and other living beings.[5] It does not arise out of that which is not alive. In this sense, we can also say that life is the source of freedom, or a condition for freedom, since it is something that we as finite human individuals are not the ultimate source of. The only way *we* can get *control* over life is by restricting it. When we improve the life-conditions of others or ourselves, this is based on a life already given – already existing. How life flourishes, we cannot control, although we can improve the *possibilities* for it to flourish.[6]

God is the giver of life. This does not only mean that Christian theology sees him as the source of life, but that he offers us life, and all that comes with it. Life is *given* to us – and it is up to us what we make out of it. The gift of life is also in this sense a condition for freedom. With this gift humans get access to the possibilities for self-determination. Since life is something that has its source outside us, but at the same time is *given* to us, no one else other God and we ourselves should be (note the normative element here!) the determining factors of our life. Hence, life from the infinite source of God is flowing towards us as finite beings, and no *other* finite beings are legitimately to take total control over what exists in that exchange. To do that, be it by taking another person's life or by forcing him or her to relate solely and exclusively to the finite interest and desires of others, is not to respect human dignity. Such control, modification or restriction would not only ruin freedom, but also other elements such as personality, responsibility, the capacity for true love, and so on. Hence any action taken by a human being that interferes with the human being's relation to the infinite must be precautions as not to eliminate the integrity of that creation. This point – the integrity of creation as constituted by the relation between the finite and the infinite – I will now try to develop with reference to some present challenges.

The challenges from science

For a long time, humans have accepted that we interfere with the genetic material of animals and plants when we try to breed better cattle or grow better crops. As growing knowledge about DNA also has made it increasingly more likely to use modified cells for different purposes, these previously established practices of 'changing' or 'modifying' nature now seems to be surpassed by new, more radical ones. One of these actions goes under the name 'cloning'.

Do we 'play God' if we clone a cell? Or a human individual? Are we able, on the basis of the presentation above, to present a more nuanced assessment than one simply stating that this is the case, and thus, by inference, saying that this should not take place?

I suggest that we differentiate between different forms of cloning: we should make a distinction between reproductive and therapeutic cloning. Most of what I say in the following refers to the former. First, however, some words on the latter. Therapeutic cloning is the cloning of, or generation of, sequences of cells in order to treat diseases such as Parkinson's or Alzheimer's. Such cloning seems to make it possible that in the future we will be able to cure such cases by generating/producing cells that replace corrupted or destroyed tissue with healthy tissue. Although we here replace what is ill by cells that have been multiplied for the aim of making a person well, this is not in any qualified sense different from what we do when we give people medicine in order to recover, or operate on them after a cardiac arrest. The aim of recovery or health is an aim that is intrinsically linked to the person's own life and well-being, and it is not something that is dominated or determined by aims or purposes other than those who already express themselves in their own lives and struggles toward recovery.

Therapeutic cloning implies no *creation* of life. The cell used is participating in life already, although it is modified in a way that makes it possible for the features of the person to develop in a more healthy way than without. Hence, human actions cannot be said to generate life as God does or be the source of life in the way that God is. To clone cells in order to heal a person is thus also a practice that does not interfere with his or her relation to the infinite source of all life, i.e., God. At its best, it can help that person to live a better life in which he or she is more able to fulfil the purposes that are set for her life by herself or by God. It is not from here on only a question of being totally determined by a finite other.

What, then, about the cloning of individuals? From what has been presented so far, also in this respect, it would imply no actual creation of *life*. A cloned individual also would have her origin in living cells derived from other persons as we all do. She would also have her origin in the life of another person, just like all of us have. That the cloned individual would have her origin in a process that can be described as artificial would not in itself be an argument against her 'production', at least not as long as we would allow for similar artificiality when it comes to the overcoming of problems for couples suffering from infertility by means of in vitro fertilization (IVF). Thus, a case against reproductive cloning of individuals must be developed along other paths, if we want to make it.

Such a case, I would argue, should be made by taking the point of departure in the question *Why perform a reproductive cloning of individuals?* The reason for stating the question like this is twofold: first of all, in this case, we are not talking about an already existing individual who is in need of some kind of therapy. An answer to the question would thus not be given by pointing to the benefit for somebody who was to be given better life-conditions that she or he presently had. Second, this way of stating the question allows us to see how a possible answer would have to be given by pointing to limited and finite reasons, thus initially not offering any transcendence-open framework for the individual being made. A human clone would be made for the sake of other humans, and thus not be given the aim-free and open-ended life like the one other humans can assume and live.

So, if we assume the role of a co-creator, i.e., of one that produces individual life out of the concrete living cells that stem from the source of life we call God, what would justify such an action? Could any argument be offered except a reference to our own self-interest? The problem with reproductive cloning seems to be that the production of a cloned individual would have an origin in the aims, interests, needs, ideas and ideals of other humans. Hence, by the very constitution of the individual's life, the conditions would be limited; they would be finite, and the answer to the question 'Why am I?' would be presented with reference to finite instances represented in other people.

One could, of course, try to parallel cloning of individuals with what couples do when they conceive children. Nevertheless, there would be some important differences here. Although there might be elements of self-interest also involved in the couples, this interest should not count as ethically justifiable, and, consequently, imply that we accept such motivation as justifiable for the action in question. However, if the couple experience a *need* to have a child, this does not make the conception of a child ethically problematic: they can still conceive it with the aim of having a child that they want to love *for its own sake*, and that has independent dignity or worth. I stress here that the child is something that is loved for its own sake. That element is hard to see paralleled in a clone – where the purpose would be to make an individual in whom you can see yourself, and where the worth is related to its similarity to its origin, giving witness to his or her excellence. The clone could be seen as an extreme case of narcissistic gratification – and such gratification is hard to justify morally.

Theologically speaking, it is at this point that to clone another human individual seems to be a possible candidate of action suitable for the criticism of 'playing God'. Such cloning would not be for the benefit of the cloned individual in question, but it would be for some imagined benefit of others that such clones were produced. This is problematic as long as the benefits of the cloned individual are not related to the possibility of acting on an infinite basis and thus express the origin of her own freedom and responsibility. Instead, the reference for existence and action would be that of finite producers' aims and interests. Hence, to be a co-creator who clones individuals seems to exclude the possibility of letting the cloned person be free in the sense described above. Such freedom would imply a basic relation to *God* that allows the individual to be grounded in an infinite relationship and thus to act upon something that is not set as absolute conditions by other human beings.

Cloning consequently seems to imply a practice in which human finitude is attempted to be made absolute and where humans at the same time seem to strive for becoming even more like God – now in trying to make individuals – and not only in healing that life which is restricted in the fulfilment of its potentialities. We cannot talk here about the co-creator as being the image of God, expressing and giving witness to his love and purposes. Instead, here the co-creator expresses in the clone something that only gives witness to herself and her interests and purposes. This is what C. Gestrich claims to be one of the features of sin: that we steal from God the glory that should be given to him by humans – and try to keep it for ourselves.[7]

Whereas we claim respect for our own dignity and rights, can we claim that a cloned individual should be treated with the same kind of respect? Theologically this claim is grounded in the belief that humans are created in the image of God. But can we say of a clone that she is created in the image of God? Is it not more likely to claim that she is created in the image of the human, i.e., created to represent other humans and their interests in among humanity in a way that is structurally similar to how humans are created in the image of God? Being created in the image of God is to have freedom, to be able to participate in the life of the infinite to represent and give witness to God's goodness, love, mercy and grace. Can humans be represented in the same manner, or isn't that something we should restrict for one who is truly and *infinitely* good, merciful, loving and full of grace? Can a cloned individual be said to represent the same? Regarding the respect for individuality and personality that is connected to human dignity, this is not to be understood in the same manner for a clone: instead a clone seems to be the ultimate expression of *sameness*, excluding the basic recognition of otherness that is necessary to protect human dignity.

Having said this, however, there are a couple of other reflections to be made: theologically speaking, a clone should still be recognized as an image of God. She is, in the same way as anyone else, able to call attention to the infinite source of all life – despite that she has an origin in a human that for some reason made her for his purposes, and not as related to God's will. Hence, also a clone can give the glory to God that the sinner who reproduces the clone wants to keep for himself. Moreover, anyone who has the possibility to bear witness to God as the one who creates and sustains life expresses in this their destiny as being an image of God – thereby transcending every finite human attempt to restrict this destiny.

Second, one should also be open to allowing that, given the spontaneous way life expresses itself among human persons, it would be hard to imagine a case in which a clone lived solely by being referred to the finite aims of its producer. Most of us are able to forget such origins in the ongoing flow of communication and participation in each other's lives, and at some point it is likely to assume that also a clone would be regarded as someone with her own dignity and loved for who she was in herself. This, in turn, leads us to another way of answering the initial question in the negative: There are no good reasons for reproducing clones of human individuals, since we sooner or later probably would have to experience and realize the clone for what she is in herself. To be human is to live in such a multidimensional world that the clone would very soon be recognized as what she was becoming in that world – namely, an individual.

Conclusion

The previous argument has shown that we, at least on the basis presented here, can allow therapeutic cloning for the sake of improving the life of individuals. In this respect, we would be co-creators who simply bring to fulfilment what God has created and given life to. The ultimate reference and life-horizon for the person in question would still be her relationship to God. However, by cloning individuals there seems to be another issue at stake: the source of origin for the cloned person in question would not be the loving will of a God who is infinite, but it would be the interests, aims and purposes of the finite human being. This would mean the absolutizing of finitude. Theologically speaking, neither freedom nor responsibility in a qualified sense is here initially seen as desirable for the clone, as that would immediately make her a distinct individual. Moreover, the individual in question is not rooted in an infinite source of life, but in the interest of other humans that for some reason or another want to promote their own identity, thereby also attempting to establish themselves as the ultimate reference for another individual's (the clone's) life. In this, the producer does not act as the image of God (bearing witness to God's love and glory), but acts in a way that seems narcissistic; i.e., wanting to see himself and his own interests and ideals expressed and reflected in the world for his own sake, and not for the sake of any other. That the producer of the clone does not express in his action the destiny of being *imago Dei* does not exclude the possibility that the clone, to the same extent that she bears witness to God instead of her finite producer, must also be recognized as an image of God. Also from the point of view of *altruism*, cloning of individuals would be problematic: it is not something that is done for the sake of the individual in question (as therapeutic cloning could be), but for the self-interest of those who produce the clone.

Notes

1 To 'play God' is not a very precise term, as Peters (1997) points out. Hence, in the following I try to construct an argument that is not based on this metaphor, although it is not without significance for what I am arguing.
2 For the idea of humans as co-creators, cf. Hefner (1993).
3 For this, cf. Gestrich (1996).
4 Cf. for this idea of God as represented, my article 'Creation and Construction', *Modern Theology* 2 (2002), where I develop this more extensively, based on work by R. Williams.
5 In a sense, this implies that the continuation of life is given with the continuation of genes. On this level, however, the continuation is not on the level of species. On the other hand, the continuation of genes cannot be without being related to the participation in a concrete organism (a species). Hence, the continuation of life is linked to the existence of species, but cannot simply be understood as the life of that individual species – as it is also related to a broader sphere of living entities that interact with each other.
6 This should not be read as that we cannot control procreation – we are certainly able to do that. However, in a certain sense also the prevention of procreation is a restrictive action.
7 Cf. Gestrich 1996, *passim.*

References

Gestrich, Christoph

1996 *Die Wiederkehr des Glanzes in der Welt. Die Christliche Lehre von der Sünde und ihrer Vergebung in gegenwärtiger Verantwortung* (Tübingen: Mohr [Siebeck]).

Hefner, Philip

1993 *The Human Factor: Evolution, Culture, and Religion* (Minneapolis, MN: Fortress Press).

Henriksen, Jan-Olav

2002 'Creation and Construction', *Modern Theology* 2: 153–69.

Peters, Ted

1997 *Playing God? Genetic Determinism and Human Freedom* (New York/ London: Routledge).

13

When astronomers and environmentalists clash over a sky island

Christopher J. Corbally, SJ

The situation

There are many ways to tell the story of Mount Graham, as Leslie Sage points out (2003). I shall try to sketch the generally agreed-upon facts, but since I write as an astronomer, a biologist's perspective, as found among the workshop papers collected by Istock and Hoffmann (1995), would also be good to bear in mind.

Advances in astronomy closely follow advances in technology; just think of Galileo's application of the telescope to the heavens. It is also true that an astronomical institute that does not foster and embrace new technologies will decline. So in the late 1970s we find astronomers, based at the University of Arizona's Steward Observatory, beginning to develop 'spin-casting' as an ingenious way of making a new generation of telescope mirrors. There was no room on existing mountain sites around Tucson for the large telescope that would derive from this technology (dual 8.4 m. diameter mirrors on the same mechanical mount), certainly no site with the optimum sky conditions to take advantage of such a telescope, so a new location was needed.

In 1981, the Smithsonian Institution and the University of Arizona requested permission from the United States Forest Service (USFS) to test a location on Mount Graham. This long-ridged mountain in south-eastern Arizona is 3200 m. at its highest point and well-forested. It stands high above the surrounding desert floor, isolating those biological species living on it that cannot make the journey from one 'sky island' to another. This mountain tested well as an observatory site. In this test period its value also as a biological preserve came to the notice of biologists and particularly environmentalists. The ingredients for an international clash were in place.

The opposition was not anticipated by the astronomers. True, there had been initial reluctance in the 1950s by the Tohono O'odham Native Americans, then known as the Papagos, to the construction of the Kitt Peak National Observatory on their mountain, west of Tucson. But this reluctance had vanished once the Tohono O'odham had realized, when looking through a telescope at the night sky, that astronomers were 'the people with long eyes'. So astronomers were confirmed in their opinion that their subject was in essence benign and in harmony with nature. In finding that Mount Graham provided the best in the south-western United States in terms of clear dark skies, dry stable air, and convenient access to Tucson, they pretty much assumed everyone else would agree that this was where they should build the new observatory.

On the other hand, to a biologist the mountain presented a variety of habitats ranging from desert to Canadian forests, a fact obvious to anyone driving up its road. The isolation, given by the surrounding desert, of these habitats compared with the equivalent ones on other mountains – the sky island effect – presented a particularly unique opportunity to learn how the habitats interact and evolve. Indeed it was proposed, though even now not confirmed (Sage 2003), that a subspecies of red squirrel existed uniquely on Mount Graham. This red squirrel became the symbolic focus of the opposition to the Mount Graham International Observatory (MGIO).

There was opposition to MGIO other than from a purely biological perspective. Hunters value the challenge of hunting in difficult terrain (Sage 2003), and they were suspicious of the restrictions an observatory would bring. Hikers, campers and nature lovers find Mount Graham to be a beautiful place, bringing welcome coolness to relieve the heat of desert summers. For some, the presence of telescopes would change their relationship to the beauty and mystery of the mountain. From my experience of those involved, I confirm Davis's sense (1995, 133) that it is here that the environmentalist opposition finds root.[1] That and a conviction that development on mountains must stop, and this halt must begin some place. In the 1980s for the Sierra Club and Audubon Society, that place was Mount Graham.

As in any story, this account of the opposing sides has been over simplified. Not only are individual personalities involved, there are corporate personalities too. On the side of the MGIO there is the University of Arizona, which includes both the astronomy department and the biology department, with a spectrum of personal opinions in each. There are also the Smithsonian Institution, the international partners from Italy, from the Vatican and from Germany, and the somewhat ambiguous National Optical Astronomy

Observatory. In the opposition to the MGIO, there are elements from the Arizona Game and Fish Department (AGFD) and the United States Fish and Wildlife Service (USFWS), as well as the Sierra Club and Audubon Society, and the eco-terrorist Earth First! group. The agency caught in the middle, so it seemed, was the United States Forest Service, which has the job of assigning the 'multiple use' activities for the mountain.

For the curious, how did it all turn out? In November 1988 President Reagan signed into law the Arizona-Idaho conservation act, which contained a rider establishing the MGIO within an 8.4 acre area of the mountain to contain initially three telescopes, the Large Binocular Telescope (LBT), the Heinrich Hertz Submillimeter Telescope (HHT), and the Vatican Advanced Technology Telescope (VATT), subject to compliance with 19 mitigating measures. Though with this legislation the legal battle had only just begun (85 legal activities are listed by Sage 2003), nonetheless construction of the MGIO started in October 1989. The first two telescopes, HHT and VATT, were dedicated in September 1993, and scientific observations started a couple of years later. The LBT construction, begun in 1996, is expected to result in first observations in 2006.

The interplay of values

There are people for whom all science and technology is to be spurned, the modern-day Luddites. For most though, the knowledge gained from science adds a significant value to civilization, both in itself and for the technology that it promotes. Among the sciences, astronomy has a unique place. The night sky is accessible to everyone who can get away from city lights; and everyone who, as a child, experienced the starry sky has felt a sense of wonder at what is out there. This wonder is the beginning of science (and poetry, and music, and contemplation, and religion, and . . .). In this way, astronomy can attract students to the way of looking at the world scientifically. In itself, the knowledge from astronomy can be called useless; but in the context of our civilization, astronomy has a unique value in helping to show us where we stand in the history and scope of the universe.

For our knowledge of the universe to come closer to the truth, the tools of astronomy have to become more capable, more sensitive, more refined. Hence advances in science bring advances in technology, which in turn bring better astronomy. Technology and astronomy are partners together. If the one has a value, so does the other.

What brings a pause in this idyllic partnership is when the technological needs of advances in astronomy impinge on the limited resources of this planet. That is the case when new, large telescopes need to be built on the Earth.[2]

That is certainly the case on Mount Graham. Despite the prominence given to the plight of the red squirrel there (what to astronomers seemed more of a 'red herring' than anything else), the real issue for biologists was the degradation and fragmentation of the delicate habitat on top of the mountain (Sage 2003). If you build telescopes in multiple locations and run roads between them, then you fragment the forest and hinder the interconnections that allow species to survive.

Survival of species is a biological value, but in the context of evolution there are periodic extinctions of particular species. Evolutionary change is inevitable. But for there to be change significantly for the better there must be significant diversity in the species present at any one time. Hence, a higher biological value than survival is biodiversity.

Astronomers, as scientists, cannot deny this value. What they objected to, in regard to their use of Mount Graham, was what seemed to be the unsubstantiated opinion of their opponents that the proposed telescopes would significantly affect the biodiversity on the mountain. After all, they were asking for the use of just 0.0017 per cent of the coniferous forest (Sage 2003). What biologists objected to was the perceived haste of the astronomers in getting their telescopes on the mountain without allowing due investigation.[3] This lumped astronomers in with the developers with whom the agency biologists had traditionally battled.

Values springing from science and technology were present on both sides of the clash. The entanglement came from whatever put different priorities on the values. So, might there be a common origin to these values, and in that origin might there be reconciliation?

The grounding of values

For the scientists' sense of wonder, the grounding is in our search for truth. When Pope John Paul II celebrated the Jubilee of Women and Men from the World of Learning on May 25, 2000, he insisted that rigorous scientific research is a genuine way to the source of all truth revealed to us in the Scriptures. 'The exploration of both the micro and the macro cosmos is a song to God's glory which is reflected in everything in the universe.' That is why the true scientist is drawn, even unknowingly, to be surprised and to marvel at every new discovery. They are both 'astonished and humbled' at the immensity and complexity of the universe, and at times are brought to a 'silent gasp'. In this sense, every true scientist is a contemplative (Coyne 2000, 6).

If the enchantment of science springs from the reflection of God's glory in all creation ('The heavens declare the glory of God . . .' Ps. 19:1), then another reflection of God in creation evokes appreciation of biodiversity and so respect for every kind of life itself. Within the Earth's biosphere there is an amazing number of species, conservatively between 5 and 15 million. From the 1.7 million of those that have been described and named (Basset *et al.* 2000, 28) two characteristics stand out: amazing diversity and wondrous interconnectedness. For people such as Belden Lane (2001) these characteristics are no accident but reflect the Creator as a Trinitarian God. Within God there is both diversity, expressed as the separate integrity of the Three Persons of the Trinity, and interconnecting unity, expressed as the mutual relationship of love in the One God. Everyone, especially the evolutionary biologist, who is struck by the exuberant diversity of plants and animals and yet marvels at their interdependence, is in touch with the natural expressions of a Trinitarian God. Ecological thinking and, more significantly, its practice, respect the interrelatedness of diverse life, and so celebrate the presence of God in the world.

This celebration is a very Christian response to nature, but it is also a response that the traditions of Native Americans have recently helped emphasize. For this reason, in the clash that we have been considering, it should not have been unexpected that, when the red squirrel was found to be thriving moderately well on the mountain, the non-agency opposition discovered that some members of a local Apache reservation wanted to bring up the objection that Mount Graham was a sacred mountain and so should remain undisturbed by telescopes. The USFS had anticipated such concerns and had written to local tribes to ask them about the potential use of the mountain for astronomy purposes. Two tribes responded, from the Zuni and the Hopi, and their concerns were accommodated. Only later (1991) did the objections of some Apache people emerge. I say *some*, because from personal experience other Apaches are able to accommodate an observatory on the mountain providing that due respect for nature continues to be shown there by the USFS and the MGIO.[4]

I have written that a respect for the sheer beauty of the mountain seemed behind the initial opposition to telescopes on Mount Graham, an opposition that came first from Anglos rather than Native Americans. There is something about a mountain that lifts the spirit, that puts one in touch with the spiritual as one ascends away from the cities below. What were the specific experiences of those opposed I can only guess, though I too have always loved to climb mountains. From a strange incident of collaboration between opponents, both of whose four-wheel-drive vehicles were stuck in the same winter snow, I understood a certain possessiveness about the mountain for those deeply affected by it: it is theirs, their source of the spiritual, and nothing shall disturb it. I could resonate with that feeling while up there, though the mutual confrontation returned once the vehicles were freed and both parties were down in the valley.

We are suddenly back down from the contemplative and celebratory heights of the mountain, where we find God and the spirit, to local politics. That is the way we live. Our goal is always to harness the insights of theology to help us live more considerately among each other and more responsibly in our technologically impacted world. What then can the diverse and inter-related Creator of a glorious universe teach us?

Is reconciliation possible?

With 20/20 hindsight the resolution to the clash seems obvious: it should never have been allowed to start. But it did, and the two main parties, astronomers and environmentalists, went their respective ways, without reconciling their differences. That the situation persists became clear when in 2001 a power line was being laid from the valley to the observatory to save not just electricity costs, but any accidental spillage from trucks supplying diesel fuel to the original generators at MGIO. Not only was the power line opposed in court, but on Earth Day that year the part-completed line and its installation equipment were sabotaged. Rather than the power line being understood as a protection to the environment, it was 'unnatural' and so 'unholy' to the observatory's opponents, much like the telescopes themselves. A permanent block seems to prevail between the parties against being really able to understand the fundamental values of the other side.

The source of these fundamental or deontological values is, at least implicitly, spiritual. As outlined in the section above, the astronomers find in the Creator's 'heavens' a source of the awe that is an inspiration and just has to be pursued; the environmentalists must respond to the Trinity-reflecting biodiversity around us. When the biodiversity, at least as far as the red squirrel was concerned, appeared unaffected by the presence of telescopes, then the emphasis for environmentalists shifted elsewhere, to other values. Thus it seems that the real starting points of the clash are not grasped, or at any rate not acknowledged. Until they are, mutually and with some humility, no reconciliation will happen.

What might help? A reappraisal – by both sides, of their deontological values and of what grounds these values are based on – seems essential. That reappraisal should discover a common source, implicitly God, for the seemingly opposed values. This insight could, in turn, lead to a reformulation of the relevant, consequentialist values, i.e., those based on results, which can be reviewed and prioritized in the light of better data. This interplay between the best data from science and the shaping of consequentialist values seems crucial. If that interplay can be achieved, and mutually understood, then any plan for a solution will be, not a compromise, but an implementation of our better stewardship for creation – or, as those following Lynn White (1968, 93) would prefer, a solution arising from within our understanding of nature, of which we are an intricate and equal part.

Now, none of this will happen without skilful mediation. Frans de Waal spoke engagingly to the ECST IX's participants about how female chimpanzees will mediate, for the good of the group, when two males are in conflict. We can at least hope for some similar, enlightened intervention to resolve the conflict over Mount Graham and other sky islands.

Acknowledgements

I am grateful to Leslie Sage for access to his manuscript before publication, to the helpful comments of ECST IX's Workshop E participants, and to clarifications suggested by the late Charles Polzer, SJ.

Notes

1 If professional astronomers still carried portable telescopes and sketched what they saw, there would be no resistance. The 'artificial' machines are seen to endanger the sacredness of nature, and the concrete foundations irreparably to mar the landscape. This can become a 'bucolic idolatry' (O'Donoghue 2002).

2 Space-based telescopes are not the solution to this dilemma. They are expensive and technologically fragile. So if observations can be done from Earth, this is preferred.

3 In the opinion of Lawrence Heaney (1995, 188), 'The Pinaleños have the potential to become the classic case study of biological diversity in the entire Southwest.'

4 Mount Graham is not in fact on any present reservation, though it has recently become 'eligible for listing' on the National Register of Historic Places as a traditional cultural property of Western Apache tribes (Stauffer 2002). Interestingly, there is a very similar conflict situation over telescopes on top of Mauna Kea, Hawaii. Its 2000 Master Plan tried to address that conflict, though some environmentalists feel that the Plan acknowledges the sacredness of that mountain to the Hawaiian people at the expense of understanding the true cost of telescopes to the environment (Tytell 2001).

References

Basset, Libby, John T. Brinkman, and Kusumita P. Pedersen,

2000 *Earth and Faith* (New York: UN Environment Programme).

Coyne, George V.

2000 *Vatican Observatory Annual Report 2000* (Castel Gandolfo: Vatican Observatory Publications).

Davis, Russell

1995 'The Pinaleños as an Island in a Montane Archipelago', in C. Istock and R. S. Hoffmann (eds.), *Storm over a Mountain Island: Conservation Biology and the Mt. Graham Affair* (Tucson: University of Arizona Press), 123–34.

Heaney, Lawrence R.

1995 'Population Vulnerability of Mammals in Isolated Habitats', in C. Istock and R. S. Hoffmann (eds.), *Storm over a Mountain Island: Conservation Biology and the Mt. Graham Affair* (Tucson: University of Arizona Press), 179–92.

Istock, Conrad A., and Robert S. Hoffmann (eds.)

1995 *Storm over a Mountain Island: Conservation Biology and the Mt. Graham Affair* (Tucson: University of Arizona Press).

Lane, Belden C.

2001 'Biodiversity and the Holy Trinity', *America* 185.20: 7–11.

O'Donoghue, Aileen A.

2002 *Loving the Universe* (private communication).

Sage, Leslie J.

2003 'A Brief History of the Controversy Surrounding the Mount Graham International Observatory', in A. Heck (ed.), *Organizations and Strategies in Astronomy* (Dordrecht: Kluwer Academic): IV, 75–91.

Stauffer, Thomas

2002 'Historic Status Set for Mount Graham', *Arizona Daily Star* (Tucson), 21 May.

Tytell, David

2001 'Sharing Mauna Kea', *Sky & Telescope* (August 2001): 40–8.

White, Lynn

1968 'The Historical Roots of Our Ecological Crisis', in *Machina Ex Deo: Essays in the Dynamism of Western Culture* (Cambridge, MA: MIT Press), 75–94.

14

The crisis of ideologies and the need for a new anthropology: values education in a technological and pragmatic age

Angela Roothaan

Values education and the crisis of ideologies

Over the years I have taught several philosophy courses for non-philosophy students. In the 1980s, when I started teaching, the goal of those courses was generally defined as either broadening the view of the students through general education, or strengthening their professional view by teaching them the methodological foundations of their own field. Nowadays yet another aim is introduced: students should be taught to reflect (philosophically) on professional as well as personal values and norms. This may mean that one teaches methodology, or general philosophy, or ethics, but in all cases this should lead to a qualitative increase in the choices or the articulations made by the student regarding values and norms (cf. Boschhuizen and Noordegraaf 2000).

The interest in philosophy, as a means to educate students from all disciplines in the ability to make critical evaluations of professional and practical dilemmas, is not limited to Dutch academic life. The issue, although put in different terms, received a lot of international attention when Martha Nussbaum's *Cultivating Humanity* appeared in 1997. According to its author, philosophy can fulfil this educating task because it has developed from an elitist discipline into a discipline that addresses questions concerning 'justice and rights, questions about love, fear, and grief, questions of medical and legal and business ethics'. It has 'returned to the focus on basic human interests that it had in the time of John Dewey and William James' (Nussbaum 1997, 42).

Although Nussbaum's characteristic does not apply to all present-day philosophy, it is certainly true that a lot of academic philosophy teachers have put philosophy to a more practical use in courses that may be labelled as values education. Interestingly, we see a rise of such courses in a cultural situation of crisis for ideologies. I use the term 'ideology' in a broad and neutral manner to refer to religious as well as non-religious worldviews. Of course ideologies do exist in our present-day culture, and in some contexts they even flourish. With an expression such as 'the crisis of ideologies', I do not indicate their dissolution, but their powerlessness in deciding publicly on questions regarding the right way to live. This powerlessness is due to the fact that they cannot refer to a publicly shared rationality from which they might defend their particular view on a certain question. This situation is called pluralism: there is a plurality of conflicting worldviews and values, among which one cannot rationally decide. Therefore, one cannot use philosophy to prove the truth of one worldview over another.

Using the term 'pluralism' in fact expresses a position which is bound to lead to a stress on dialogue, but which also asks for the recognition that human beings can never fully understand each other's (or even their own) motives and reasons. We cannot rationally understand a person's motives and reasons, for instance, by referring to an ideology to which that person commits him- or herself, because the reasons for committing to this ideology cannot entirely be articulated in a rational manner. This also means, to my view, that it is impossible to decide rationally on the boundaries and the content of a certain ideology. We may commit ourselves to a worldview, we may act inspired by the beliefs expressed in it, but what this worldview is exactly about will remain a matter of dispute, even among its adherents.

In taking this position I part company with Nussbaum, who prefers the notion of 'multiculturalism' to that of pluralism. For a multiculturalist, the problem is not so much to decide upon values and beliefs, but rather to guarantee peaceful relations between members of different traditions or cultures, that is, between individuals who already have decided upon the values and beliefs to which they are committed. In this view, establishing the boundaries and content of a certain culture, or of a worldview which belongs to a culture, is not seen as something problematic. The multiculturalist can believe in some sort of public rationality that allows us to draw boundaries, as well as to transcend them. Not surprisingly, Nussbaum holds the view that, although we, human beings, come from different cultures, we still share a common humanity which transcends cultural differences (cf. e.g. Nussbaum

1997, 9) and which we can cultivate. With this claim she revives the classical ideal of cosmopolitanism as a solution for problems of the multicultural society.

Her view, however, has two shortcomings. The first one is the reification of the multifaceted affiliations of human beings into well-defined 'cultures'. The second one is blindness to the ideological element in the cosmopolitan ideal itself. The kind of education through philosophy that I will consider here is not directed to cultivating a general humanity, which would have to transcend particular cultural values, but rather towards coping with the particular evaluative aspect present in all human knowledge and morality.

Furthermore, I do not consider it to be illuminating to classify people as members of clear-cut cultural wholes. I consider the more realistic description of our human predicament to be that of holding positions that are the unique personal embodiment of several overlapping cultural or ideological or traditional affiliations. This predicament may be called 'differential situatedness' (Radder 1996, 186). We do not choose or construct our point of view, but rather assemble it out of 'given patterns of meanings', like a *bricoleur* (Reinders 2000, 197).

Ideological pluralism, as I see it, goes along naturally with a pragmatic attitude, although it does not make questions of meaning superfluous. When concerned with meaning, the bricoleur will not ask for an absolute or final meaning, which, ideally, should be shared publicly, but rather for the personal and relative meaning of specific events, trying to fit them into narrative patterns which are never complete (Roothaan 2001, 28), and sharing them with others who then can relate their own life's events to them. The bricoleur will not conceive of his or her life as one great construction, to be wrought after a personal blueprint, but may rather experience his or her life project as a series of (discontinuous) goals to be achieved and of problems to be solved.

Our present era, now, has often been called the technological one. The essence of technology, however, does not lie in technical instruments and technical processes, or even in technological models and procedures of research. We find it in the pragmatic interest for establishing and solving problems. The technological worldview is concerned with the pragmatic question as to whether and how things work, rather than with the hermeneutic question of the meaning of what we do and experience. This attitude works very well in the pluralist situation: being concerned with the workings of things, one can avoid ideological differences about their meaning. I do not consider pragmatism, however, to be our exclusive viewpoint, because that would make it impossible to explain the fact that people do also have an interest in interpreting their lives (and even the technologies they use) in meaningful ways and in sharing that meaning.

The pragmatic attitude, however, has meant success for the natural sciences, especially in their applied versions, and crisis for classical theology. The quest for rational insight in religious beliefs is considered doubtful in the condition of pluralism and is not seen as very pressing in a pragmatic age. As a result, theological knowledge has lost most of its public interest. In addition, most theology students I have met in my philosophy courses seemed more interested in practical skills than in systematic reflection. Orienting themselves towards their professional future, they prefer training in argumentation techniques, or in application of moral theories to pastoral practice, to studying the structures of philosophical systems. Even in science education we see a pragmatic shift. New generations of students crowd practical or 'applied' studies such as biomedical technology, or technology management, but skew the classical 'pure' sciences. Young people nowadays seem less interested in meanings, or even in general explanations, than in problem solving.

Yet, despite the crisis of ideologies, we see a growing interest for values education. Academic policy-makers and governors feel that in our pragmatic and pluralist condition the student should be equipped with reflective skills, enabling him or her to make deliberated personal valuations and choices, in his or her future profession as well as in life in general. For even the individual who adheres to a traditional religion, or to some non-religious ideology, has to choose his or her own values. If, in these conditions, courses in values education are to be effective, they should be designed to fit the pragmatic attitude of young people, while at the same time they should stimulate the hermeneutic reflection of the students on the *meaning* of their practical relations to the world.

Individual reflection and evaluation

In the pluralist situation, when we compare it to the cultural condition in which clear-cut ideologies dominated public life, more is asked of the evaluative and reflective potential of the individual. Nowadays, one has to account not only for one's adherence to a tradition in general, but also for the extent of that adherence and the way in which it is given shape (cf. Van Harskamp 2001). Describing oneself, for instance, as a Roman Catholic could be considered quite a clear statement in the 1950s. Nowadays, the person describing him- or herself as such can (and will) be asked to articulate his or her stance in several ecclesiastical and theological disputes. The same goes for other ideological affiliations. Those who care about formulating a worldview at all are painfully aware of all kinds of subtle differences in these matters. This awareness brings with it the need to be able to articulate one's personal values in such a way that they can be communicated to others, as well as be discussed with them. Finally one has to be able to critically evaluate one's own values and those of others. These skills are especially asked of those who are academically trained and in the business of producing or communicating knowledge.

In the newly developed courses in values education, methods are offered to trace the moments of (moral, political, epistemological) choice in the production and communication of knowledge, in order to teach students to critically evaluate possible choices. For example, students are offered texts that are classical in their field, and they have to reconstruct some of the dilemmas that the producers of those texts faced. They may also be confronted with some dilemma that they could meet in their professional career, and be asked to find various ways to handle this dilemma, aided by the study of philosophical ethics. Such courses provide students with strategic instruments to handle ambiguous scientific and moral situations (Boschhuizen and Noordegraaf 2000).

In order to understand the aims, in terms of personal development, of didactic procedures like those described, we should reflect on their anthropological basis. That is, we should ask if they fit some theoretical explanation of the development of human individuals, as well as of the possibility of personal education. I will show what is required of the anthropological model for which we are looking, by discussing two classical views of development and education, those of Aristotle and Descartes. These important views still inspire many present-day anthropological views of development. As I will show below, however, they fail to explain the complex situation in which individuals nowadays have to orient themselves.

In his search for a new method for scientific and philosophical reasoning, Descartes comes to the conclusion that we can trust our own reasoning ability more than all traditional knowledge. Therefore he proposes to ignore systematically what he had learned in his school and university training. So we read in his *Discourse on Method*: 'But regarding the opinions to which I had hitherto given credence, I thought that I could not do better than undertake to get rid of them, all at one go, in order to replace them afterwards with better ones, or with the same ones once I had squared them with the standards of reason' (Descartes [1637] 1985, 117).

In so doing, he denounces the paradigm of personal development, dominant in what seventeenth-century intellectual rebels called the scholastic period. In the scholastic view on development, the relationship between a pupil and his or her teacher was deemed central. Where the teacher was seen as the one who had already mastered what was to be learned, he or she could be understood to be the trainer of the student. The student was not supposed to develop him- or herself by performing an independent evaluation of the content of what the teacher offered him or her, but rather by trusting the authority of the teacher in a field in which the student was not yet knowledgeable.

Descartes repudiates the scholastic paradigm, because he wants to find a criterion for deciding independently which knowledge is certain and useful, instead of having to trust the authority of teachers, who, in their turn, got their knowledge from other teachers, and so on. The criterion he searches has to be found by and in reason itself, that is, by and in the normal, sound reasoning capacity which every person possesses: 'for, as regards reason or sense, since it is the only thing that makes us men and distinguishes us from the beasts, I am inclined to believe that it exists whole and complete in each of us' (Descartes [1637] 1985, 113).

Descartes' approach has been very influential. In fact it formed what can be called the modern paradigm of learning by making use of natural reason. Characteristic for this paradigm is a strong faith in the individual's ability to judge the quality and usefulness of knowledge. At the same time, the Cartesian approach has made it difficult to do justice to the dimension of tradition in learning and in knowledge. Nothing that has been handed down from the past under the authority of teachers can be trusted any more in its own right. According to the modern paradigm, every piece of knowledge should be scrutinized with regard to its rationality. In terms of personal development, this has led to a view in which the primary goal of education is seen as raising people to a level of independent rationality.

For our present purpose this model therefore does not satisfy. Although the new values education shares with the Cartesian view on personal development the importance of an independent, individual appropriation of knowledge, it differs from it in stressing that knowledge cannot be judged solely by something called reason. It presupposes, namely, that knowledge is always, to a certain extent, value-loaded. This value aspect can be made explicit and can be reflected upon in values education. This asks, however, for a procedure which not only takes rationality as a criterion, but which may also refer to practical and spiritual standards.

The Aristotelian model of personal development and of education has gained new popularity in the frame of a renewed interest in virtue ethics (cf. MacIntyre 1981). In his *Ethics*, Aristotle distinguishes between intellectual learning and habitual learning. The first is directed solely towards gaining theoretical knowledge; the other has for its aim technical skills and practical (moral and political) knowledge. 'Intellectual virtue owes both its inception and its growth chiefly to instruction, and for this very reason needs time and experience. Moral goodness, on the other hand, is the result of habit' (Aristotle 1976, 91). Practical knowledge is gained by practice, namely by training habits. '[T]he [moral] virtues we do acquire by first exercising them, just as happens in the arts' (Aristotle 1976, 91). Practical knowledge is not so much about general principles (as is theoretical knowledge), but about finding the right moment ('kairos') to do the right thing.

In comparison with the Cartesian view, the Aristotelian approach has the advantage of explaining how we acquire evaluative knowledge in addition to rational, theoretical knowledge. However, the Aristotelian view cannot explain what happens in present-day values education, because it does not reckon with a fundamentally pluralistic situation. According to Aristotle, the state bears responsibility for regulating (by law) how people should be brought up to be good. The legislators who make up the regulations can look, in their turn, to the concept of the human good, which holds for all humankind. So Aristotle does not ask the question of the present-day individual, of how to choose between schools and traditions that hold different conceptions of the good.

This insensitivity for value conflicts in Aristotelian thought also shows in its present-day representatives. In *After Virtue* (MacIntyre 1981), for instance, the importance, for a person to be moral, of belonging to a community is stressed. The question of how to criticize a community of which one is a part, or of how to take position amidst overlapping communities, is not elaborated upon. In the new interest in values education, it is precisely this critical potential of the individual that is sought. Our question now is to clarify anthropologically how this potential can be understood as an element in human development.

Thus, to build our anthropological model of development, we can take from Aristotle the recognition of the importance of training our habits; but this leaves us with the problem that nowadays this training has to take place in a fundamentally open situation, in what is called a supermarket of ideologies. This situation asks of the individual the personal skills to reflect critically on norms and values. It favours a pragmatic approach: when looking for final principles is an unpromising job, we would better ask whether certain norms and values are effective (do they make me and my fellow human beings happier, or healthier, or wiser, or don't they?).

When we have decided to look for effectiveness, however, we do not yet have criteria or principles to decide on the direction of the effectiveness sought for. To find these criteria we have to seek out what orientations we want to follow in living our lives. It should be noted that an orientation is not the same as an ideology: it does not articulate what we think about the world, such that we can order our values and beliefs systematically. It comprises suppositions as well as emotional attachments, and it shows our attitude towards life, in a certain stable practice of life. Reflection on values and norms, therefore, requires not just discussion about and consciousness of ideals; it requires that we also take our practical attitudes and actions into account, *in a practical way*.

More specifically, we have to ask how values education can play a role in the personal digestion of life's experiences, in looking for and holding on to an orientation of life, and in the moulding of our practical relations with our surroundings. In a few years, when we have more experience with this kind of education, it might be interesting to investigate its actual effects on the educational programmes of theology and the sciences. But in advance of that possibility, we should develop a model of personal development, which will (1) enable us to articulate philosophically what the practice of values education is aiming at, and will (2) provide a means to critically assess the developments in this field.

A new anthropological model of development for a pragmatic age

In looking for a new anthropological model of development, we have to reckon with the cultural conditions of a mainly pragmatic spirit, and of pluralism. In these conditions, critical skills are of great importance. Because our model is developed in order to articulate the aims of values education, it has to be founded on an anthropology that offers a profound insight into personal development. We have to outline what aspects there are to this kind of development, in order to understand in what ways values education can contribute to it.

To our benefit some important twentieth-century authors have focused on development in the field of philosophical anthropology. In fact, the view that personal identity is something that is being developed only received real attention in the twentieth century. George Herbert Mead, for instance, has explained the self as a construction one builds in growing up, by internalizing the social structure one lives in. '[O]nly in so far as [the individual] takes the attitudes of the organized social group to which he belongs toward the organized, co-operative social activity or set of such activities in which that group as such is engaged, does he develop a complete self or possess the sort of complete self he has developed' (Mead [1934] 1969, 155). By trying out the roles of different members of the group, the developing individual internalizes the positions possible in his or her social surroundings. This development succeeds, that is, leads to an integrated self, only when the surroundings are internalized as a social *structure*. Mead has articulated this distinctive quality of personal integration in his model of the 'generalized other'.

For our purpose this work provides some important viewpoints, namely the stress on development in becoming a person, and the stress on social interaction in that process of development. Mead's theory, however, falls short with an eye to our purpose, because it fails to take into account (understandably, looking at the time and the society in which it was written) our present-day pluralistic context. His model of personal integration is based on experiences within a stable society, in which clear group identities actually exist. For our present society, with its floating social boundaries, the model should be adapted.

Another shortcoming of Mead's theory is that his behaviourist point of view leads him to ignore the aspects of interpretation and of valuation in an individual's dealing with his or her surroundings. In his model of development the social construction of the self is viewed functionally, that is, from the standpoint of the social scientist, who has placed herself outside the processes she is studying. The hermeneutic questions of how social relationships come to be through meaningful communication, and of how individuals interpret and value each other's messages, are not considered (for a more detailed discussion of Mead, see Roothaan 2001). These questions are, of course, relevant to our goal to build a model through which we can evaluate a kind of education that is directed towards improving individual reflection and (e)valuation.

The aspect of valuation is, however, central in the work of another twentieth-century author: Charles Taylor. Taylor has built an anthropology, which explains the self from the 'hypergoods' one is committed to (Taylor 1982; 1989). Hypergoods are the ideological deep values the individual refers to in weighing his or her everyday goods. Taylor also speaks of 'strong evaluations', which are related to who we want to be in the deepest sense: 'It is those [evaluations] which are closest to what I am as a subject, in the sense that shorn of them I would break down as a person' (Taylor 1982, 124).

In this model, personal development is understood as a further articulation of one's deepest evaluations. Taylor considers this process to include major risks, because in articulating the deep evaluations that underscore my personal identity, not only the evaluations, but also my identity, are at stake. The risks involved comprise falling subject to illusion and losing one's orientation. When articulation, however, succeeds, one's identity is strengthened and one's valuations have gained in 'motivating force'.

Thus, the work of Taylor provides us with another important ingredient for our theory: the hermeneutic insight that one's personal evaluations contribute to one's orientation in life and, thereby, to one's identity. For our purpose, however, we miss in Taylor's theory a real awareness of the practical and pragmatic way in which these evaluations can come to be. In a sense, both Taylor's and Mead's views on personal development do not succeed in answering the problems of the pluralist condition, in stressing reflective and/or structural integration as the goal of personal development, neglecting the importance of the structurally conflicting elements in the individual's identity, as well as in his or her relationships with the world (cf. Roothaan 2001). This shortcoming can be repaired, in my view, by exploring the practical and spiritual aspects of personal development in a way that keeps in view the conflicts of life.

Such an approach can be found in Mary Bateson's *Composing a Life*. In a discussion of the lives of five women, Bateson shows how one can make sense, practically as well as spiritually, of the discontinuities (and even the disappointments) of life, which result from the interdependencies of our lives. As an alternative to the view of development as growth towards reflective integration, or articulation of what we already are in some deep sense, she puts forward a model of growth by acknowledging the multiple alternatives from which we may assemble a life. 'The real challenge comes from the realization of multiple alternatives and the invention of new models. Aspiration ceases to be a one-way street . . . and instead becomes open in all directions . . . The real challenge lies in assembling something new' (Bateson 1989, 62).

Again, we recognize the metaphor of the bricoleur as the person who builds from odds and ends, or even from scrap. The odds and ends for Bateson are multidimensional; they include every aspect of being a human person such as gender, cultural or ethnic identity, professional development, love, being a child of someone, or being a parent, and so on. Thus development in her approach comprises not only the social and evaluative, but also the practical and emotional aspects of being human.

Added to this, it is characteristic for Bateson's view of personal development that she stresses the openness of the individual towards the future, and thereby towards multiple possible directions of development. Speaking on the level of mythology, she puts it in these words: 'Instead of worshipping ancestors or deities conceived of as parents, we must celebrate the mysterious sacredness of that which is still to be born' (Bateson 1989, 240). This openness can be realized by acknowledging the actual multiple commitments present in human lives. By stressing this aspect of personal development, Bateson articulates one of the consequences of adopting a view, which no longer sets a well-defined goal, such as reflective or structural integration, for development. In so doing, she keeps in view the structurally conflicting elements in one's identity.

Adding to the social and evaluative aspects of development, which we took from Mead and Taylor, we can now take from Bateson the stress on the practical and emotional commitments, which also constitute personal development. With these aspects in mind, we will be able to articulate (below) the elements of a model of development, which meets the demands of our pragmatic and pluralistic condition. The model which we will develop *presupposes* the following anthropological insights: (1) the idea that being a person means developing oneself through and in human interdependency,

(2) that it presupposes personal evaluations, and (3) that it is open towards multiple future possibilities.

Building on these presuppositions, the demands of our pluralistic and pragmatic condition can be met by characterizing development in terms of an individual's attitude towards life and of his or her practical relations towards the surrounding world. Someone can express his or her attitude towards some important facts of life, for instance death, or poverty, or sexuality, without relating to persuasions or beliefs. This attitude is expressed in the way in which one *deals* with these facts of life, not only reflectively, but above all practically and spiritually. In this approach the question of meaning is not absent, but it is posed in a pragmatic context. Although people who are developing their personality are concerned with the meaning of what they do or experience, this concern does not have to be ideological in the sense that they (strive to) formulate their persuasions in a consistent manner. The meaning of one's deeds and experiences expresses itself already in the practices of one's life.

The elements of a new anthropological model of personal development can now be articulated. They consist of three different moments (which are not chronologically ordered) in personal development: (1) the growth of experience of life, (2) the development of an orientation in and towards life and (3) the practical realizations of meaning in one's relations with one's surroundings. These moments reflect an anthropology in which the individual is seen as a developing being, building its identity on a combination of hermeneutic activity (interpreting the events of life in the stories which compose one's experience of life) and of practical activity. In what follows I want to look closer into the three moments of personal development in order to provide a model for the articulation and evaluation of what is aimed at in values education.

To begin with experience of life: with this expression I want to indicate that all people are in development, in opposition to the view that personal development reaches its end in adult rationality. Experience is something which can be built up, but which never reaches a final result. It presupposes some kind of reflection, but this does not have to be very sophisticated in an intellectual way. When we say that someone has a lot of experience, we do not mean that he or she just has undergone many impressing events, but rather that this person has interpreted life's events in such a way that a frame of meaning is built, which may help them to interpret or to deal better with future events. Such a frame, of course, also serves to share one's interpreted experience or wisdom with others. (A more extensive treatment is found in Roothaan 2002.)

Although the possibility for composing rich stories about the events and actions in our lives grows with age, the necessity to interpret what we experience and do in life is potentially the same for a child as for an 80-year-old. This means that values education does not have to be restricted to young people. The ability to reflect on professional and personal values can be trained at any moment in life. Values education, then, can start from the general human potentiality to interpret life's events in stories. Because people develop their personality by interpreting their experiences, they can be invited to reconstruct their life-stories in a manner that expresses their values in some field.

The development of an orientation in and towards life is that moment in personal development that consists of a search for direction, in an open (pluralistic) situation. Literally, orientation means finding the east, in order to find one's way on earth in areas where there are no roads yet. In this respect, an orientation differs significantly from a road, which embodies traditionally given norms of direction. Introducing the concept of orientation in anthropology, we therefore reject the idea that there are general roads for personal development.

The concept of orientation implies the recognition of basic insecurity about the way persons should develop. It secures the possibility for discussing the spiritual aspect of personal development, in providing a concept which covers the human attempt to direct oneself towards what one considers to be good and meaningful, but avoids fixing this attempt from a strongly ideological frame of discourse. Thus the concept of orientation does justice to the pluralist condition of our culture and leads us to look for pragmatic criteria of development.

As a third moment in personal development I discerned the practical realizations of meaning in one's relations with one's surroundings. From a rationalist point of view it is not obvious to understand attitudes and actions of persons as aspects of their development. In a rationalist view, the development of a person's mental state is understood to precede his or her good or bad, futile or meaningful behaviour, which, in turn, is seen as an application of the thoughts and ideas that were developed. This view is turned around in our anthropological model, where we say that in relating practically to one's surroundings, a person may realize meaning, and thus develop him- or herself.

Here, my view harmonizes with that of Hans Reinders. In his study on *The Future of the Disabled in Liberal Society*, he proposes the view that the meaning, which we can experience in relationships, does not, in fact, precede our engaging in them. Rather, he states that 'Whatever meaning can be found in sharing one's life with another person, it cannot be known outside that activity itself' (Reinders 2000, 207). This activity of sharing involves opening up to possible joy and fulfilment, but also to the risk of anxiety and grief. Correspondingly I hold that personal development has to be understood as something which has a practical aspect. In this kind of development one may discern an element of reflection and interpretation (in building experience of life), of searching direction (in one's orientation in life), and of relating practically to one's surroundings.

By saying that meaning is realized in practical relations, we have stressed that meaning is not primarily something created in the mind or spirit of a person. This opens the possibility of acknowledging that someone who does not possess many mental capacities is able to realize meaning in his or her relations also (in this respect I move further than Reinders, who discusses the meaning of the life of a disabled person from the point of view of those who take care of him or her). Comparably, a person who has average or high mental capacities will realize meaning by *practically* relating to his or her surroundings as well.

This third moment of development indicates that values education should not just address the intellectual aspect of the person, but rather the person as a whole, in his or her interaction with the world. This interaction also includes our emotional and our bodily involvement in our relationships. Also, the third moment of development provides a theoretical underpinning for a pragmatic approach in education – because it explains the possibility of identifying meaningful relations and practices, without having to identify their meaningfulness according to theoretical or ideological criteria.

We now possess some outline of a new anthropological model of development which will (1) enable us to articulate philosophically what the practice of values education is aiming at, and which will (2) provide a means to critically assess the developments in this field. We can measure them, namely, according to the criteria inherent in our three moments. We can ask if the education stimulates a deeper interpretation of life's events, if it promotes the activity of orientating oneself in life, and if it stimulates the potential to practically realize meaning in life, in relating to one's surroundings. The proposed anthropological approach thus provides a framework for reflection on meanings and values regarding personal development, without asking for final meanings.

Acknowledgements

A first draft of this text was presented at the ninth ESSSAT conference. For many fruitful suggestions to improve the second, elaborated, version, I want to thank Hans Radder from the Free University of Amsterdam. For the suggestion to include Mary Bateson's work in my treatment of the subject matter, I want to thank Alfred Kracher.

References

Aristotle

1976 *The Nicomachean Ethics* (trans. J. A. K. Thomson; London: Penguin Books).

Bateson, Mary Catherine

1989 *Composing a Life* (New York: Grove Press).

Boschhuizen, Rob, and Jan Noordegraaf

2000 'From Facts to Reflection: Choices in Teaching and Studying the History of Linguistics', *Beiträge zur Geschichte der Sprachwissenschaft*, 10: 271–83.

Descartes, René

1985 [1637] *The Philosophical Writings of Descartes*, vol. I (trans. John Cottingham, Robert Stoothoff and Dugald Murdoch; Cambridge/New York/Melbourne: Cambridge University Press).

MacIntyre, Alasdair

1981 *After Virtue: A Study in Moral Theory* (London: Duckworth).

Mead, George Herbert

1969 [1934] *Mind, Self and Society from the Standpoint of a Social Behaviorist* (Chicago/London: University of Chicago Press).

Nussbaum, Martha

1997 *Cultivating Humanity: A Classical Defense of Reform in Liberal Education* (Cambridge/London: Harvard University Press).

Radder, Hans

1996 *In and About the World: Philosophical Studies of Science and Technology* (Albany: State University of New York Press).

Reinders, Hans

2000 *The Future of the Disabled in Liberal Society: An Ethical Analysis* (Notre Dame, IN: University of Notre Dame Press).

Roothaan, Angela

2001 'Levenservaring en levensoriëntatie. Elementen voor een theorie van spirituele identiteit', in G. Groenewoud *et al.* (eds.) *Tegenwoordigheid van Geest. Opstellen over spiritualiteit en mensbeschouwing* (Zoetermeer: Meinema).

2002 'Experience of Nature: A Hermeneutic Approach', in W. Drees (ed.), *Is Nature ever Evil? Religion, Science and Value* (London: Routledge).

Taylor, Charles

1982 'Responsibility for Self', in G. Watson (ed.), *Free Will* (Oxford: Oxford University Press), 111–26.

1989 *Sources of the Self: The Making of the Modern Identity* (Cambridge, MA: Cambridge University Press).

Van Harskamp, Anton
2001 'Naar een postchristelijke religiositeit', *Civis Mundi. Tijdschrift voor politieke filosofie en cultuur* 40 (April): 79–85.

Index